Governing Corporate Tax Management

Chen Zhang · Rajah Rasiah ·
Kee Cheok Cheong

Governing Corporate Tax Management

The Role of State Ownership, Institutions and Markets in China

Chen Zhang
Institute of Belt and Road, Business School
Qingdao University
Qingdao, Shandong, China

Rajah Rasiah
Asia-Europe Institute
University of Malaya
Kuala Lumpur, Malaysia

Kee Cheok Cheong
Institute of China Studies
University of Malaya
Kuala Lumpur, Malaysia

ISBN 978-981-13-9828-5   ISBN 978-981-13-9829-2 (eBook)
https://doi.org/10.1007/978-981-13-9829-2

© The Editor(s) (if applicable) and The Author(s), under exclusive license to Springer Nature Singapore Pte Ltd. 2019
This work is subject to copyright. All rights are solely and exclusively licensed by the Publisher, whether the whole or part of the material is concerned, specifically the rights of translation, reprinting, reuse of illustrations, recitation, broadcasting, reproduction on microfilms or in any other physical way, and transmission or information storage and retrieval, electronic adaptation, computer software, or by similar or dissimilar methodology now known or hereafter developed.
The use of general descriptive names, registered names, trademarks, service marks, etc. in this publication does not imply, even in the absence of a specific statement, that such names are exempt from the relevant protective laws and regulations and therefore free for general use.
The publisher, the authors and the editors are safe to assume that the advice and information in this book are believed to be true and accurate at the date of publication. Neither the publisher nor the authors or the editors give a warranty, expressed or implied, with respect to the material contained herein or for any errors or omissions that may have been made. The publisher remains neutral with regard to jurisdictional claims in published maps and institutional affiliations.

This Palgrave Macmillan imprint is published by the registered company Springer Nature Singapore Pte Ltd.
The registered company address is: 152 Beach Road, #21-01/04 Gateway East, Singapore 189721, Singapore

Preface

Since economic reforms began in 1978, China's enterprises have undergone considerable changes. So too have the taxation system, which has experienced major reforms over the last three decades to closely resemble those of the market economies, which included the introduction of corporate income taxes in the country. Since corporate tax is a significant cost to enterprises, firms have introduced corporate tax management to strengthen financial decision-making. The extant theories on corporate tax management have not always been consistent, which is more so with the empirical evidence from China given its unique transition from a socialist structure to one where the market has gradually increased its role in the economy. Given the complexity of the economy and the paramount role of the state in the economy, there are still loopholes that corporations often exploit to their advantage, which may make tax management in Chinese listed companies inefficient and unpredictable.

The central objective of this study is to analyze the economic consequences of corporate tax management in China. In doing so, the study posits the following three research questions: firstly, what is the impact of corporate tax management on firm performance and how tax management can help maximize firm value?; secondly, what are the market outcomes of corporate tax management and how does government ownership influence these outcomes?; and thirdly, what is the impact of corruption and marketization on corporate tax management, and how do they affect firm performance?

The results show that corporate tax management has a negative direct impact on firms' market value, which supports the agency theory of tax management. Nevertheless, corporate tax management can promote market value through the indirect improvement of firms' profitability and growth, which suggests that tax management can help but they need the deployment of a sound and effective corporate governance mechanism.

Next, the findings show that corporate tax management has the potential to cause adverse future market outcomes so as to cause stock price crashes, which support the bad news hoarding theory. The evidence shows that state ownership cannot alleviate this crash risk. Indeed, municipal listed state-controlled enterprises are more likely to face future crash risks than other enterprises.

Finally, the findings show that corruption affects corporate tax management in a nonlinear way in China. Whereas the evidence lends support for both the "grabbing hand" and "helping hand" theories, the evidence tends to be positive. Furthermore, marketization backed by institutional strengthening tends to mitigate the impact of corruption on corporate tax management at both phases of the inverted U-shaped curve.

Overall, the book shows that corporate tax management is an important financial strategy that can be designed to enhance the wealth of shareholders. However, due to agency problems, the real consequences of tax management have remained uncertain. The solution to address agency problems is to bolster enterprise management with sound internal corporate governance through effective coordination with external markets and institutional development.

We take this opportunity to thank a number of people without whose support the book would not have seen the light of the day. Firstly, we thank the officials of the University of Malaya for awarding Zhang Chen a doctoral scholarship, which enabled her to pursue her doctoral degree, which forms the core of the book. Secondly, we would like to acknowledge the support of Qingdao University. Thirdly, we wish to thank Zhang Chen's parents, Zhang Xincun and Wang Rong. Finally, we would also like to thank her former doctoral thesis supervisor, Dr. Che Hashim Hassan, and friends Zhang Miao and Li Ran.

Qingdao, China	Chen Zhang
Kuala Lumpur, Malaysia	Rajah Rasiah
Kuala Lumpur, Malaysia	Kee Cheok Cheong

Contents

1 Introduction — 1
From Plan to Market — 2
  Ownership Reform — 2
  Institutional Reforms — 3
  Tax Reform — 4
Corporate Taxation and Tax Management — 8
Problematizing Corporate Tax Management — 12
Methodology — 14
Key Questions and Book Outline — 14
References — 16

2 Corporate Tax Management and Chinese Enterprises — 19
Introduction — 19
Theoretical Considerations — 19
  Agency Theory — 20
  Bad News Hoarding Theory — 21
  Helping Hand and Grabbing Hand — 22
Empirical Studies — 24
  Corporate Tax Management — 24
  Consequences of Corporate Tax Management — 25
  Specific Characteristics of China's Enterprises — 27
  State Ownership — 28
  Corruption — 30

	Marketization	31
	Research Gaps	33
	Theoretical Framework	34
	Analytical Framework	37
	References	37
3	**Corporate Governance and Firm Performance**	45
	Introduction	45
	Analytic Framework	46
	Methodology and Data	49
	Measures	49
	Model Specification	52
	Empirical Findings and Analysis	56
	Measurement Model	56
	Structural Model	58
	Summary	61
	References	62
4	**Economic Reforms and Market Outcomes over Time**	69
	Introduction	69
	The China Context	72
	Economic Reforms	72
	Literature Review and Hypotheses Development	74
	Methodology and Data	78
	Sample and Data	78
	Variables Used	81
	Model Specification	82
	Results and Analysis	84
	Descriptive Statistics	84
	Regression Results	87
	Robustness Check for Endogeneity Problems	100
	Chapter Summary	102
	References	104
5	**Corruption, Institutions, and Markets**	109
	Introduction	109
	Literature Review and Hypotheses Development	111

Data and Methodology	115
Sample and Data	115
Variables	116
Model Specification	119
Results and Analysis	122
Descriptive Statistics	122
Corruption and Corporate Tax Management	127
Moderating Effect of Institutional Support	131
Corporate Tax Management, Corruption, and Firm Performance	133
Chapter Summary	136
References	136

6 Conclusions 141
  Introduction 141
  Synthesis of Findings 142
  Implications for Theory 145
  Implications for Policy 146
  Implications for Firms 149
  References 150

Appendix A: Measurement of Firm-Specific Earnings Management (*Discacc*) 153

Appendix B: The Impacts of Three Specific Dimensions of Marketization on the Relationship Between Corruption and Tax Management 155

References 159

Index 177

Symbols and Abbreviations

AGFI	Adjusted goodness of fit index
AVE	Average variance extracted
BTD	Book-tax difference
CFA	Confirmatory factor analysis
CFI	Comparative fit index
CPI	Corruption Perceptions Index
CR	Composite reliability
CSMAR	China Stock Market and Accounting Database
CSRC	China Securities Regulatory Commission
CSRCIC	China Securities Regulatory Commission Industry Classifications
DTAX	Residual book-tax difference measure
DUVOL	Down-to-up volatility
ETR	Corporate effective tax rate
FE	Fixed-effect models
GFI	Good-of-fit index
GMM	Generalized methods of moments
LSOEs	Listed state-owned/controlled enterprises
NCSKEW	Negative conditional return skewness
NFI	Normed fit index
OLS	Ordinary Least Squares
RMR	Root-mean-square residual
RMSEA	Root-mean-square error of approximation
SASAC	State-owned Assets Supervision and Administration Commission of the State Council

SAT   State Administration of Taxation
SEM   Structural equation modeling
SOEs Refer to all state-owned/controlled enterprises
VIF   Variance inflation factor

LIST OF FIGURES

Fig. 1.1	National Tax Revenue from 2005 to 2015 (*Source* National Bureau of Statistics of China)	7
Fig. 2.1	Theoretical framework	36
Fig. 3.1	Conceptual structure of structural equation model (*Source* Plotted by authors)	48
Fig. 3.2	Structural model (*Source* Plotted by authors)	50
Fig. 5.1	Degree of regional corruption by regions, China, 2008–2013 (*Note* The seven-region classification is shown in Table 5.4. *Source* Plotted by authors)	124
Fig. 5.2	NERI index of overall marketization (*Note* The seven-district classification is shown in Table 5.4. *Source* Plotted by authors)	125
Fig. 5.3	The u-shaped effect of corruption on corporate effective tax rate (*Source* Plotted by authors)	130
Fig. 5.4	The u-shaped effect of corruption on industry-adjusted corporate effective tax rate (*Source* Plotted by authors)	130
Fig. B.1	The three specific dimensions of marketization during 2008–2013 (*Note* **Blue line** of *overall* means the overall marketization index in China's 31 provinces; **Red line** of *non-state* means the index of the development of the non-state sector in China's 31 provinces. The index reflects the ownership structure of the economy and the transition from public ownership to private ownership; **Grey line** of *legal* means the index of market intermediaries and the	

legal environment development. The index captures the establishment of intermediate institutions such as law offices, accounting and auditing firms, and the institutional environment ensuring enforcement of contracts and protecting property rights; **Yellow line** of *government* means the index of Government and market relationship. The index refers to the size of government interventions in local markets. *Source* Marketization Index of China's Provinces: NERI Report 2016; Plotted by authors)   156

LIST OF TABLES

Table 1.1	National Tax Revenue, China, 2005–2015 (Yuan)	7
Table 1.2	Enterprise reform measures, China, 1978–2008	8
Table 3.1	Variable, relationships, and definition	51
Table 3.2	Sample selection steps	54
Table 3.3	Correlation	55
Table 3.4	Summary of model fit indices for CFA model	56
Table 3.5	Confirmatory factor model	57
Table 3.6	Discriminant validity matrix	57
Table 3.7	Structural equation model indices	58
Table 3.8	Mediation effect of corporate tax management on market performance through profitability and growth performance	59
Table 3.9	Hypotheses' standardized regression paths	60
Table 4.1	Definition of variables	79
Table 4.2	Descriptive statistics of main variables	83
Table 4.3	Correlation between dependent variables and explanatory variables	85
Table 4.4	Correlation between independent and control variables	86
Table 4.5	Corporate tax management and stock price crash risk	88
Table 4.6	Impact of central government ownership on relationship between tax management and future stock price crash risk	90
Table 4.7	Impact of provincial government ownership on relationship between tax management and future stock price crash risk	95
Table 4.8	Impact of municipal government ownership on relationship between tax management and future stock price crash risk	98
Table 4.9	Impact of tax management on stock price crash risk using system GMM	101

Table 5.1	Variables and descriptions	118
Table 5.2	Distribution of *ETR* by industry	122
Table 5.3	Summary statistics of all corporate financial variables	123
Table 5.4	Descriptive statistics of corruption and marketization	123
Table 5.5	Correlations between variables	126
Table 5.6	Linear relationship between corruption and corporate tax management	128
Table 5.7	Relationship between corruption and corporate tax management	129
Table 5.8	Impact of marketization on the relationship between tax management and corruption	132
Table 5.9	Impact of corporate tax management on firm performance	134
Table 5.10	Moderating effect of corruption on relationship between tax management and firm performance	135
Table B.1	The impact of three specific dimensions of marketization on the relationship between corruption and tax management	157

CHAPTER 1

Introduction

China's experience with economic transition from central planning to a more market-oriented economy is unique, Vietnam being the only other country that most closely resembles China's experience almost a decade later. Because of the gradualist approach adopted—Deng Xiaoping's famous characterization of "feeling the stones to cross the river"—parts of the economy had remained unreformed at any time. This juxtaposition of reformed and unreformed parts of China would have created problems and incurred costs that may not have existed in a market economy that is equipped with strong institutions. At the same time, China was spared the pain that countries that subscribed to the "big bang approach" to use Vaclav Havel's caption, "you cannot cross a chasm in more than one leap" that was principally undertaken by Russia (Bramall, 1995; Chang & Nolan, 1995). Indeed, China's growth spurt stood in sharp contrast to Russia's economic collapse when both countries liberalized (Ellman & Kontorovich, 1998).

The purpose of this book is neither to compare the experiences attendant upon these contrasting approaches nor to assess the merits of the Chinese approach to corporate tax management. Rather, the objective is to examine economic reforms that contributed to marketization and corporate tax management in China. To do so requires appreciation of economic reforms that have been undertaken since 1978 but especially from 1994. This is what the next section sets out to explain.

From Plan to Market

The story of China's successful liberalization began by Deng Xiaoping in 1978 has been told many times. While this story began with the opening-up of the agricultural sector, much of the subsequent liberalization has been targeted at enterprises that saw the rise of the corporate sector. Economic reforms proceeded on several separate but interrelated tracks.

Ownership Reform

The first track is ownership reform that saw first greater autonomy given to state enterprises that dominated all production. Before 1978, the state controlled the whole economy; all enterprises were owned and managed by the state, with planned pricing instead of market pricing. Under this system, there was little incentive to perform. The earliest reforms were in corporate governance, but the limited success achieved by these partial reforms forced the government to introduce broader ownership reforms in 1993. That year saw the consolidation of the state enterprise sector, with many unprofitable state enterprises sold to private investors and large numbers of workers retrenched. In 1996, a policy of "grasping the large, letting go the small" was announced to reduce the size of the state sector, with the state retaining ownership and control of the largest state enterprises. Some state enterprises were also corporatized through the sale of equity to private interests in the Shanghai and Shenzhen stock exchanges set up in 1991–1992.

However, shares in listed enterprises were separated into tradable shares and non-tradable shares, with the state and "legal persons" (e.g., the state, statutory bodies, and corporations) holding the latter, effectively giving the government unchallenged control over listed enterprises despite dilution of state ownership. In contrast, tradable shares were open for trading in the Shanghai and Shenzhen Stock Exchanges owned by institutional and individual shareholders. However, this system was open to abuse in that the state in listed state enterprises could ignore the interests of tradable shareholders. To address this, another ownership restructuring occurred under the "split-share reform" in 2005 whereby non-tradable shares held by the state were converted to tradable shares the public can purchase in the stock markets. As the state reduced its ownership of enterprises, it retained control of what it considered to be the most important ones. This consolidation process also saw the size of state enterprises increase. Nevertheless, the non-state sector, consisting of local government collectives, private enterprises, and foreign companies, grew.

Institutional Reforms

The second track is associated with institutional reform. Institutions were defined by (North, 2005) as the "rules of the game", and firms and organizations as the players who act by these rules. Like Coase (1937) and Williamson (1985), North (2005) considered markets to be the superior institution that left spaces for other institutions (both formal and informal) to correct market failure. However, following Rasiah (2011), in this book we accept markets, which refers to relative prices, as a critical institution but consider other institutions to not only play key roles at times, but also collectively solve coordination problems. Just as we need institutions to solve government failures, we also need institutions to check market failures (see also Zhang & Rasiah, 2015).

Given the early dominance of state enterprises, institutional reforms naturally began with these enterprises. In as early as the Third Plenary Session of the Eleventh National Congress in December 1978, it was announced that the management autonomy of state enterprises would be expanded by linking managers' performance to their rewards. The year 1984 saw the dissociation of state enterprises from the government and the separation of ownership rights and control rights. In January 1987, the contract responsibility system allowed managers to share part of the profits. In November 1993, the Third Plenum Session of the Fourteenth National Congress of the Communist Party of China (CPC) set the target that enterprises would be legal entities in a modern enterprise system. Together with the corporatization of state enterprises, a corporate governance structure was adopted (see Qian & Wu, 2003). In that year, Chinese listed firms were to have a main board of directors and a supervisory board, the latter responsible for monitoring firm behavior (Dahya, Karbhari, & Xiao, 2002). However, unlike the German–Japanese model, a supervisory board in China had no right to appoint and evaluate managers. It was not until after amendment of the Chinese company law in 2006 that the monitoring role of the supervisory board was expanded to include this role.

The system of tradable and non-tradable shares did indeed lead to abuses. Diversion of enterprise assets and profits by holders of non-tradable shares resulted not only in losses to tradable shareholders, but also affected investor confidence in China's capital markets (Jiang & Habib, 2012). To deal with the split-share issue, the so-called "split share reform" was undertaken from 2005 to convert a large proportion of non-tradable shares to tradable shares to allow them to be traded in the stock market in the same way as shares held by private shareholders, which became more sensitive to share price movements.

The split-share reform complemented the Code of Corporate Governance for Listed Companies in 2002 to protect investors' rights, and to set rules and moral standards for directors, supervisors, and other senior managers of listed companies (CSRC, 2002).[1] As part of this Code, independent directors were to be appointed to boards of directors (Jiao, Dong, Hou, & Lee, 2013). These reforms together were intended to reduce agency problems in listed companies. Also in 2005, the China Securities Regulatory Commission (CSRC) allowed state enterprises listed on China's stock exchanges to set up equity incentive plans under stringent conditions (China Securities Regulatory Commission, 2005).[2] These conditions included precise details of incentives for employees and the total quantum of incentive payments.

Tax Reform

The third track involved fiscal reform within which lies the theme of this book—corporate tax management, more commonly referred to as tax avoidance (legal) as opposed to tax evasion (illegal). Chinese enterprises have started to modernize since economic reforms and opening-up begun in 1978. Tax reforms as a key pillar of overall economic reforms has experienced several significant breakthroughs during the last three decades. The development of China's tax system has also undergone three major stages since the founding of the People's Republic of China in 1949.

The first stage lasted from the establishment of the People's Republic of China in 1949 until the introduction of economic reforms in 1978

---

[1] More information please see "Code of Corporate Governance for Listed Companies" (in Chinese), released in 2002 by CSRC. Retrieved from http://www.csrc.gov.cn/tianjin/tjfzyd/tjjflfg/tjbmgz/201210/t20121015_215801.htm.

[2] More information please see "Measures for the Administration of Equity Incentives of Listed Companies (trial)" (In Chinese), which was first released in 2005 by CSRC, and revised in 2016. Retrieved from http://www.csrc.gov.cn/pub/shenzhen/xxfw/tzzsyd/ssgs/sszl/ssgsxx/201410/t20141024_262284.htm.

when China's tax system experienced a bumpy road due to the political and economic conditions at that time. Especially in the period 1957–1978, because of erroneous policies and the impact of the former Soviet Union's closed economic model and fiscal system on Chinese leadership, the construction of China's tax system suffered a serious disruption. The tax reform that was in place was characterized by unbalanced simplification. As a result, many tax organizations were merged into other organizations, and a large number of tax staff were compelled to change jobs, thereby weakening the role of taxation in the economy and hindering the function of taxation.

The second stage stretched from 1978 to 1993, during which time China focused on the establishment and consolidation of a new tax system. Also in this period, China's financial and tax departments organized tax reforms with a view toward establishing a modern tax system appropriate to the early economic conditions of the Chinese economic system under reform. Specifically, the practice of "substitution of tax payment for profit delivery" (*ligaishui*) on state-owned enterprises was implemented in 1984, which established a strong relationship between the State and the enterprises within the taxation system. Until then, state-owned enterprises turned over all profits to the State.

China started its third stage of tax reforms from 1994 to comprehensively transform the tax system. Specifically, three major corporate tax reforms were implemented in 1994, 2008, and 2018. At the end of 1993, China's State Council enacted the *Regulation on the Implementation of Enterprise Income Tax Law of China*, which became effective on January 1, 1994. The scale and scope of the 1994's tax reform was the largest and most comprehensive since the formation of modern China. The Regulation set the corporate statutory tax rate at 33%, while at the same time providing favorable tax incentives to different regions and for specific industries. At that time, the state introduced the policy of first levying and then rebating taxes (FLTRT) for local governments to attract capital investment. Corporate taxes in China were classified as central revenue and local revenue, which were collected by the National Taxation Bureau (*guoshuiju*) and Local Taxation Bureau (*dishuiju*), respectively. However, this policy generated undue competition between local governments. To prevent this, the central government issued a formal ruling to prohibit local governments from providing tax rebates, which took effect on January 1, 2002, which also required local governments to surrender 50% of income tax revenue collected from local enterprises in 2001.

The proportion of corporate income tax collected by the central government increased from 50% in 2002 to 60% in 2003.[3]

The second major reform of corporate income tax took place in 2008. On March 16, 2007, the fifth Session of the tenth National People's Congress (NPC) approved a new Corporate Income Tax Law, which took effect on January 1, 2008. Its unified statutory tax rate of 25% for both domestic and foreign companies, and changed the current tax holiday, preferential tax treatments and transitional provisions. Under the previous tax law, domestic companies were imposed a tax rate of 33% statutory income, while certain foreign companies enjoyed preferential tax rates of between 24% and 15%. Reforms helped improve and standardize China's tax system, which has resulted in the accumulation significant national tax revenue, which provided a solid foundation for China's subsequent economic growth. Despite criticisms (e.g., Hussain & Zhuang, 2013), corporate income tax has become the second largest source of government tax revenue in China.

The third major tax reform took place in 2018. The General Office of the Communist Party of China Central Committee and the General Office of the State Council released a taxation system reform, which integrates the national and local taxation offices at and below the provincial level to enable the tax system to play better its supportive role in state governance. On July 20, 2018, all the new tax bureaus were listed.

Table 1.1 and Fig. 1.1 show Chinese national tax revenues collected from the top main tax categories between 2005 and 2015. The green line in Fig. 1.1 shows that corporate income tax is the second largest national tax revenue in China, which increased sharply from 1.3 trillion Yuan in 2010 to 2.7 trillion Yuan in 2015.

Table 1.2 summarizes the major reform measures that have impacted on Chinese enterprises, both by state and non-state, since economic reforms were introduced in 1978. It is clear that the major reforms targeted the state enterprise sector. However, the emergence of the non-state sector and its subsequent development also owed much to these reforms.

---

[3] The sharing of corporate income taxes: except for the part belonging to the central government as ruled, 60% and 40% of the rest is shared by the central government and the local government, respectively. See more details from "Tax System of The People's Republic of China" by Liu (2014), and "Income Tax Revenue Sharing Reform Plan" issued by Chinese state Council source from http://www.gov.cn/gongbao/content/2002/content_61880.htm (in Chinese).

1 INTRODUCTION   7

Table 1.1 National Tax Revenue, China, 2005–2015 (Yuan)

	Domestic VAT (100 million)	Business tax (100 million)	State excise tax (100 million)	Tariff (100 million)	Personal income tax (100 million)	Corporate income tax (100 million)
2005	10,792.11	4232.46	1633.81	1066.17	2094.91	5343.92
2006	12,784.81	5128.71	1885.69	1141.78	2453.71	7039.60
2007	15,470.23	6582.17	2206.83	1432.57	3185.58	8779.25
2008	17,996.94	7626.39	2568.27	1769.95	3722.31	11,175.63
2009	18,481.22	9013.98	4761.22	1483.81	3949.35	11,536.84
2010	21,093.48	11,157.91	6071.55	2027.83	4837.27	12,843.54
2011	24,266.63	13,679.00	6936.21	2559.12	6054.11	16,769.64
2012	26,415.51	15,747.64	7875.58	2783.93	5820.28	19,654.53
2013	28,810.13	17,233.02	8231.32	2630.61	6531.53	22,427.20
2014	30,855.36	17,781.73	8907.12	2843.41	7376.61	24,642.19
2015	31,109.47	19,312.84	10,542.16	2560.84	8617.27	27,133.87

Source National Bureau of Statistics of China

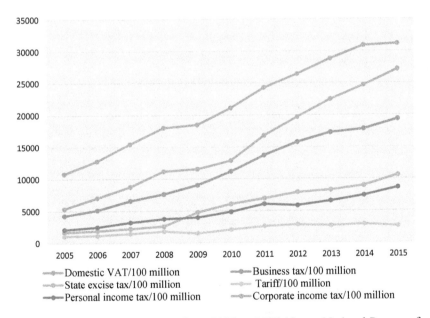

Fig. 1.1 National Tax Revenue from 2005 to 2015 (*Source* National Bureau of Statistics of China)

Table 1.2 Enterprise reform measures, China, 1978–2008

Year	Ownership reform	Governance reform	Fiscal reform
1978–1990		1978 Managerial autonomy of state enterprises expanded 1984 Separation of state ownership and control rights 1987 Contract responsibility system	1984 Taxes replace transfers from state enterprises
1991–2000	1993 Consolidation of state enterprises thro' privatization, closure 1996 "grasping the large, letting go the small"	1993 Corporatization of state enterprises, corporate governance structure established	1994 Tax reform: adopt tax-sharing system, coverage expanded, tax rates set, incentives
2001–	2005 Split-share reform	2002 Code of Corporate Governance 2005 Split-share reform 2005 Incentive schemes for publicly listed state enterprises	2008 New Income Tax Law, unification of tax rates 2018 the reform of the national and local taxation systems: unified tax collection system, the integration of national and local taxation offices

Source Compiled by authors

CORPORATE TAXATION AND TAX MANAGEMENT

Corporate taxation has different roles and consequences for different stakeholders, including governments and enterprises. From the perspective of government, corporate taxation is important to generate fiscal revenue, which is necessary to provide public goods and public utilities. From the perspective of enterprises, corporate tax management can help generate significant cost reduction and to better manage cash flows available to enterprises. Thus, there are incentives for enterprises to manage better taxes, which is why corporate tax management has been introduced by enterprises as a strategy.

Before we proceed further, it is important to understand how tax management came to be a critical issue for enterprises in China. Before the 1980s, China had in place a centrally planned economy controlled by wholly state-owned enterprises, with all profits going directly to the state through transfers instead of taxes. China implemented the "replacement of profit with tax" in 1984 (*ligaishui*) on state-owned enterprises. China was still a command economy at that time, which meant that enterprise income taxes were much different from their counterparts in market economies. Because the government fully controlled wages and prices, there was no motivation to undertake rent-seeking.

However, a series of enterprise reforms with respect to ownership and governance changed the relationship between government and enterprises as the latter's monopoly in purchasing and marketing was eliminated, reducing direct administrative control, and replacing it with "decentralization of power and transfer of profits" (*fangquan rangli*) to state-owned enterprises and their managers. Thus, managers gradually took charge of decision-making authority, while their salaries are tied to enterprise's achievement. These changes have not only been significant in determining the amount of tax revenue generated, but has also opened up opportunities for enterprises to engage in tax management. Thus, the agency phenomenon of moral hazard has emerged in China, while corporate taxes have become an important topic among Chinese enterprises.

Research on and the development of strategies for corporate tax management in China is still in its infancy. From a traditional view of corporate tax management, it represents an activity of transferring wealth from the state or government to shareholders (Desai & Dharmapala, 2009). However, it is too idealistic to assume that such management activities can always increase firm value as there can be agency conflicts between principals and agents inherent in public listed firms. Therefore, corporate tax management can also be deployed to facilitate managerial opportunism (Desai & Dharmapala, 2006, 2009), causing uncertainty in the outcomes of such management activities. Hence, the consequences of tax management have generated widespread attention among stakeholders and researchers.

Moreover, in the setting of modern corporations where there is separation of ownership and control, internal and external factors will influence the ultimate outcomes of tax management, such as corporate governance, institutional environment, and legislative protection (Lee, Dobiyanski, & Minton, 2015; Li, Luo, Wang, & Foo, 2016; Minnick & Noga, 2010). Compared to the developed countries that have a sound and comprehensive legal protection system, the underdeveloped external environment in emerging countries may give rise to more uncertainty with dire corporate tax management outcomes.

In addition, because the establishment and development of China's modern tax system to absorb the role of markets is still relatively new, it is beset by many problems and deficiencies, leaving ample room for opportunist behavior. Corporate tax management provides the tools to encourage such behavior. Because research on corporate tax management in China is relatively new, considerable work needs to be done to better understand the prospects and pitfalls of this practice so that guidelines can be provided to investors, shareholders, and policymakers. In addition, because China is still a developing and transitional country, it may offer helpful lessons for other developing and transition countries, such as the Socialist Republic of Vietnam, the Republic of Kazakhstan, the Lao People's Democratic Republic, and the Kingdom of Cambodia.

Corporate taxes represent one of the most substantial costs to a company resulting in a reduction in its cash flows, so that reducing taxes is a powerful motivational strategy in corporate operations. Consequently, it motivates shareholders to reduce tax burdens through effective management or taxation activities.

Corporate tax management may result in the utilization of either managerial value maximizing strategies or greater agency conflicts between managers and shareholders. Whether positive or negative impacts prevail depends on the robustness of a country's corporate governance. Since corporate opacity could be exploited by opportunistic managers to extract private benefits at shareholders' expenses, investigating the impact of tax management can help investors understand the degree of coupling between tax management and rent extraction (Desai & Dharmapala, 2006).

A fair number of studies have focused on tax management but mostly in advanced market economies. At present, there are few systematic studies on the consequences of corporate tax management in China as existing studies do not provide much guidance for China's transitional economy. Compared with research on developed markets, studies of corporate tax management in emerging markets in general and China in particular are limited. Yet, Chinese enterprises offer a unique difference to existing studies as they tend to show a concentrated ownership structure, limited information disclosure, highly politicized institutional arrangements, and incomplete legislation on investor protection (Svensson, 2005). These leakages and imperfections offer more opportunities for enterprises to engage in different kinds of corporate tax management to reduce their tax burden. However, in the context of widespread abuse of tax management in Chinese enterprises, it may not be accompanied by a simultaneously beneficial consequence to enterprises. Hence, it is important to undertake a systematic analysis to deepen our understanding of the economic consequences of corporate tax management in China.

Moreover, the reforms of state-owned enterprises took place stage by stage through a process of corporatization and privatization targeted at raising funds for expansion and to increase revenue, which have shaped "Chinese-style privatization". In this book, the phased enterprise reform that produced profit-oriented publicly listed state-owned/controlled enterprises is a distinctive set of enterprises unique to China. The enterprise reform has facilitated enterprises to pursue profits, which changed the traditional view of state enterprises that were characterized by lower efficiency when compared to private enterprises. However, partial privatization of wholly state-owned enterprises has evolved its own set of institutional problems. Control rights are transferred to managers, which has offered opportunities to pursue self-interests, such as misappropriating state assets, thereby causing agency costs and increased risks.

Most empirical studies on tax management in China have focused on how firms' internal characteristics, such as firm size, ownership and leverage affect corporate tax management and their outcomes (Adhikari, Derashid, & Zhang, 2006; Badertscher, Katz, & Rego, 2013; Wu, Wang, Luo, & Gillis, 2012), while ignoring the special macro-environmental determinants specific to China. As the world's largest transition economy, China has undergone transition from a centrally planned economy to a market-oriented economy, which makes research on enterprise reforms targeted at incorporating market principles in a socialist structure at the sectoral and national levels useful. Therefore, in attempting to examine the determinants of corporate tax management, we seek to look beyond firm-level determinants to take into account macro-level characteristics.

Before attempting to problematize corporate tax management, a clarification of the concept is necessary. Hanlon and Heitzman (2010, p. 137) state that "if tax avoidance represents a continuum of tax planning strategies where something like municipal bond investments are at one end (lower explicit tax, perfectly legal), then terms, such as 'noncompliance,' 'evasion,' 'aggressiveness,' and 'sheltering' would be closer to the other end of the continuum". Following Hanlon and Heitzman (2010), corporate tax management is defined broadly as any transaction that can reduce a firm's explicit income tax liabilities, resulting in a lower corporate effective income tax rate (ETR). This definition is used here, and covers not only activities that are fully legal, but also those that occupy a grey area, and may also include those that are illegal.[4]

To minimize semantic confusion, the term "tax management" is used throughout the book, while the following terms may also be used interchangeably, for example, "tax avoidance", "tax aggressiveness", and "tax sheltering".

PROBLEMATIZING CORPORATE TAX MANAGEMENT

As mentioned above the traditional view of corporate tax management regards it as an approach toward raising saving by transferring it as profits to shareholders thereby resulting in higher firm value than otherwise. However, with modern corporations (especially listed corporations), one of the most marked characteristics is the separation of ownership and management, which often gives shareholders and managers a different time horizon (Berle & Means, 1967). Managers as direct operators will always know the information earlier and more exhaustively than shareholders, and hence producing information asymmetries. Thus, manager's behavior and decisions can directly influence corporate performance. Therefore, managerial rent extraction can, among other things, include tax management activities (Desai & Dharmapala, 2009; Kim, Li, &

---

[4] There are at least two reasons why no distinction is made between technically legal tax planning and illegal aggressive tax evasion. First, most of the behavior in question surrounds transactions that are often technically legal. Second, the legality of a tax management transaction is normally determined after the fact. Therefore, those avoidance activities may include both certain tax positions and uncertain tax positions that may or may not be challenged and determined illegal.

Zhang, 2011; Zhang, Cheong, & Rajah, 2016), which may compromise the interests of shareholders and governments.

On the plus side, if tax management activities benefit enterprises, then it will be important to examine how the additional resources are used to raise firm value. More cash in the hands of first managers and eventually shareholders does not necessarily translate into benefits for the company. On the negative side, tax management can facilitate rent extraction behavior, increasing the costs of tax management and harming firm wealth. Specifically, managers also face short-term "incentives", such as their employment contract, remuneration, and career concerns, which would motivate them to conceal negative operating performance. The complex and obscure nature of tax management practices provides a mask to help managers hide bad news and financial information from shareholders and the public. The concealing of negative developments would create a huge future moral hazard. When such news reaches breaks out in the open after a prolonged decline or presence of management malaise, its impact on the market often sharply jolts its performance with deleterious consequences, including a stock price crash (Kim, Li, & Zhang, 2011; Li, Luo, Wang, & Foo, 2016). Hence, the outcomes of tax management and how they change over time are well worth exploring.

Modern Chinese listed state-owned enterprises (SOEs) are a product of reform of the former SOEs that started in 1978 (Zhang & Rasiah, 2015), which have been partially privatized, though they remain government controlled. The reforms have transformed them to become profit-oriented with the diffusion of modern corporate governance practices. At the same time, the reforms have also given them more autonomy than before, thereby opening them to conflicts of interests between top executives (bureaucratic agency officials) and shareholders. The autonomy enjoyed by executives motivates them to maximize their personal interests, such as political career or/and compensation, thereby exposing them to increased risks. However, the government as the ultimate controlling shareholder of SOEs also may act to offer them the "helping hand" during times of crises. Hence, it is interesting to explore the role of government ownership when SOEs are struck by crises.

China's economy has recorded dramatic growth since the 1990s following increased marketization. However, China is still a developing country undergoing economic and social transformation, and hence, it is still characterized by imperfect legal regimes coupled with strong government intervention (Chen, 2015; Tu, Lin, & Liu, 2013). That is why several observers have conjectured that corruption in China is widely believed to have risen (Wedeman, 2012). Hence, this study seeks to investigate how marketization has impacted on firms' conduct. In doing so, we also attempt to examine if tax management and corruption are linked since tax reforms were introduced.

Methodology

This book uses a quantitative methodology to investigate the economic consequences of corporate tax management in China's listed firms. All the three research questions use secondary data, which focus on corporate tax management, firm performance, stock price crash risk, China-specific characteristics, and other related firm determinants. For modeling purposes, Structural Equation Modeling (SEM) is deployed to test the relationship between corporate tax management and firm performance in Chapter 3. In Chapter 4, Ordinary Least Square regressions and dynamic systems Generalized Method of Moments regressions are used to answer the second question, which deals with the contemporaneous and future market outcomes of corporate tax management. Chapter 5 uses Ordinary Least Square, Fixed-effect, and Nonlinear regressions to examine the third question, which examines the relationship between macro-level factors, tax management, and firm performance.

Because the sampling size and the specific research models adopted vary by question, the detailed descriptions of the methodology are presented in the analytical Chapters of 3, 4, and 5. These details include research design, models, variables, sample selection, and statistical techniques for hypotheses testing.

Key Questions and Book Outline

Having established the rationale for studying corporate tax management in China since tax reforms were introduced, this book seeks to answer a number of specific questions that cry out for answers. They fall within the broad rubric of analyzing the links between tax management and corporate performance. The first set of questions for which answers are sought in this book are: What is the relationship between corporate tax management and firm performance in China's listed enterprises, and does the after-tax cash arising from tax management raise firms' market value? If so, how? The analysis should provide a broader assessment of tax management in China than most past studies.

The book then seeks to answer the following second set of questions: Does corporate tax management produce extreme market outcomes so as to increase the likelihood of stock price crashes? Can government ownership of enterprises influence these extreme outcomes? In other words, in the sense that tax avoidance during any period may only be a postponement of a burden to another time, that burden must ultimately be felt. Is tax management simply a device for transfer a tax problem to the future? The third and final set of questions the book seeks to examine are: Since corruption and corporate tax management share a common objective, how does corruption and marketization impact corporate tax management in China's listed enterprises? And through these relationships, how does corruption impact firm performance?

Following this introductory chapter, a profound review of the extant theoretical and empirical literature is carried out in Chapter 2. This literature review not only reveals what is the state of research on this topic, but also identifies the research gaps currently confronting past works. Chapter 3 examines quantitatively the relationship between tax management and firm performance using firms' profitability, growth, and market value. It also examines how the additional after-tax cash arising from tax management has impacted firm performance.

Chapter 4 focuses on the extreme market outcomes of corporate tax management. Although Chinese enterprises have experienced a series of reforms, state shares still account for the largest part of shares of listed enterprises in China. This chapter goes on to investigate the moderating role of the different levels of government—central, provincial, and municipal—on the extreme outcomes. Chapter 5 examines how macro determinants of corruption and marketization affect corporate tax management in China's listed enterprises. It then discusses how corruption impacts corporate tax management and the relationship between tax management and firm performance. Since China's enterprises exist in a state of flux, with reforms instituted in each of the three areas described above, answers to these questions need to take into account the outcomes of these reforms. We take account of this by looking at changes in ownership using the distinctions of state and non-state firms in the second set of questions. The findings in these chapters are summed up in Chapter 6, which establish the novelties in the analytical approach used, thereby providing several implications for theory and policy.

References

Adhikari, A., Derashid, C., & Zhang, H. (2006). Public policy, political connections, and effective tax rates: Longitudinal evidence from Malaysia. *Journal of Accounting and Public Policy*, 25(5), 574–595. https://doi.org/10.1016/j.jaccpubpol.2006.07.001.

Badertscher, B. A., Katz, S. P., & Rego, S. O. (2013). The separation of ownership and control and corporate tax avoidance. *Journal of Accounting and Economics*, 56(2–3), 228–250. https://doi.org/10.1016/j.jacceco.2013.08.005.

Berle, A., & Means, G. (1967). *The modern corporation and private property* (2nd ed.). New York: Harcourt.

Bramall, C. (1995). The lessons of history: New economic policy in China and the USSR. In H.-J. Chang & P. Nolan (Eds.), *The transformation of the communist economies: Against the mainstream*. New York: St Martin's Press (Palgrave Macmillan).

Chang, H.-J., & Nolan, P. (1995). *The transformation of the communist economies: Against the mainstream*. New York: St Martin's Press (Palgrave Macmillan).

Chen, T. (2015). Institutions, board structure, and corporate performance: Evidence from Chinese firms. *Journal of Corporate Finance*, 32, 217–237. https://doi.org/10.1016/j.jcorpfin.2014.10.009.

Coase, R. H. (1937). The nature of the firm. *Economica*, 4(16), 386–405. https://doi.org/10.2307/2626876.

Dahya, J., Karbhari, Y., & Xiao, J. Z. (2002). The supervisory board in Chinese listed companies: Problems, causes, consequences and remedies. *Asia Pacific Business Review*, 9(2), 118–137. https://doi.org/10.1080/713999187.

Desai, M. A., & Dharmapala, D. (2006). Corporate tax avoidance and high-powered incentives. *Journal of Financial Economics*, 79(1), 145–179.

Desai, M. A., & Dharmapala, D. (2009). Corporate tax avoidance and firm value. *The Review of Economics and Statistics*, 91(3), 537–546.

Ellman, M., & Kontorovich, V. (1998). *The destruction of the Soviet economic system: An insider's history*. Armonk, NY: M.E. Sharpe.

Hanlon, M., & Heitzman, S. (2010). A review of tax research. *Journal of Accounting and Economics*, 50(2), 127–178. https://doi.org/10.1016/j.jacceco.2010.09.002.

Hussain, A., & Zhuang, J. (2013). Enterprise taxation and transition to a market economy. In D. J. S. Brean (Ed.), *Taxation in modern China* (pp. 43–68). New York, NY: Taylor & Francis.

Jiang, H., & Habib, A. (2012). Split-share reform and earnings management: Evidence from China. *Advances in Accounting*, 28(1), 120–127. https://doi.org/10.1016/j.adiac.2012.04.001.

Jiao, H., Dong, Y., Hou, W., & Lee, E. (2013). Independent directors and corporate performance in China. In *Developing China's capital market: Experiences and challenges* (pp. 176–189). London, UK: Palgrave Macmillan. https://doi.org/10.1057/9781137341570_8.

Kim, J.-B., Li, Y., & Zhang, L. (2011). Corporate tax avoidance and stock price crash risk: Firm-level analysis. *Journal of Financial Economics, 100*(3), 639–662. https://doi.org/10.1016/j.jfineco.2010.07.007.

Lee, B. B., Dobiyanski, A., & Minton, S. (2015). Theories and empirical proxies for corporate tax avoidance. *The Journal of Applied Business and Economics, 17*(3), 21–34.

Li, Y., Luo, Y., Wang, J., & Foo, C.-T. (2016). A theory of managerial tax aggression: Evidence from China, 2008–2013 (9702 observations). *Chinese Management Studies, 10*(1), 12–40. https://doi.org/10.1108/CMS-01-2016-0001.

Liu, Z. (2014). *Tax system of the People's Republic of China* (In Chinese and English Version) (L. Du, Trans., 8th ed.). Beijing, China: China Taxation Publishing House.

Minnick, K., & Noga, T. (2010). Do corporate governance characteristics influence tax management? *Journal of Corporate Finance, 16*(5), 703–718. https://doi.org/10.1016/j.jcorpfin.2010.08.005.

North, D. C. (2005). *Understanding the process of economic change*. Princeton: Princeton University Press.

Qian, Y., & Wu, J. (2003). China's transition to a market economy: How far across the river? In N. C. Hope, D. T. Yang, & M. Y. Li (Eds.), *How far across the river? Chinese policy reform at the millennium* (p. 31). Stanford, CA: Stanford University Press.

Rasiah, R. (2011). The role of institutions and linkages in learning and innovation. *Institutions and Economies, 3*(2), 165–172.

Svensson, J. (2005). Eight questions about corruption. *The Journal of Economic Perspectives, 19*(3), 19–42. https://doi.org/10.1257/089533005774357860.

Tu, G., Lin, B., & Liu, F. (2013). Political connections and privatization: Evidence from China. *Journal of Accounting and Public Policy, 32*(2), 114–135. https://doi.org/10.1016/j.jaccpubpol.2012.10.002.

Wedeman, A. (2012). *Double paradox: Rapid growth and rising corruption in China*. New York, NY: Cornell University Press.

Williamson, O. E. (1985). *The economic institutions of capitalism: Firms markets, relational contracting*. New York: The Free Press.

Wu, L., Wang, Y., Luo, W., & Gillis, P. (2012). State ownership, tax status and size effect of effective tax rate in China. *Accounting and Business Research, 42*(2), 97–114. https://doi.org/10.1080/00014788.2012.628208.

Zhang, C., Cheong, K., & Rasiah, R. (2016). Corporate tax avoidance and performance: Evidence from China's listed companies. *Institutions and Economies*, 8(3), 61–63.

Zhang, M., & Rasiah, R. (2015). *Institutionalization of state policy: Evolving urban housing reforms in China*. Singapore: Springer. https://doi.org/10.1007/978-981-287-570-9.

CHAPTER 2

Corporate Tax Management and Chinese Enterprises

INTRODUCTION

This chapter reviews past works on corporate tax management. Within the broad framework of corporate tax management, the extant theoretical literature addresses three issues that this book examines. Past empirical studies on corporate tax management in modern corporations is dealt with next, with a focus on three specific features of China's market—government ownership, corruption, and marketization. These reviews help identify the research gaps that need to be filled and the accompanying research required to elucidate the China context. The literature review and the knowledge gaps identified pave the way for unraveling the analytical chapters that follow subsequently.

THEORETICAL CONSIDERATIONS

Various theories have evolved to explain the behavior of modern listed enterprises. The agency theory, which is arguably the most relevant to this book, has been widely applied to explain the complex control problems facing modern enterprises as there is generally a separation of control between shareholders and the chief executives that manage the firms. The agency theory deals with the conflict of interest between agents and principals, which is a convenient point to begin discussing the theory. Consistent with agency theory, another theory related to tax management is the bad news hoarding theory, which suggests an undesirable

© The Author(s) 2019
C. Zhang et al., *Governing Corporate Tax Management*,
https://doi.org/10.1007/978-981-13-9829-2_2

market outcome of tax management. Since governments play an important role in China's economic market, two opposite hypotheses related to the role of government—the "helping hand" and the "grabbing hand" will be tested to understand how governments and enterprises interact in a transition economy.

Agency Theory

Although the unbundling of the firm in economic theorization has come a long way (e.g., Penrose, 1959), financial accounts of firms have remained confined to "the firm as a 'black box' operated to meet the relevant marginal conditions with respect to inputs and outputs, thereby maximizing profits, or more accurately, present value" (Jensen & Meckling, 1976, pp. 306–307). Thus, the fundamental principle of the firms is maximizing behavior or more specifically profit maximization. Yet, this theory has ignored conflicts between individual participants. Jensen and Meckling (1976) put forward the agency theory by deploying the metaphor of a contract to describe the agency relationship of the separation between the principal and the agent. Meanwhile, the principal engages the agent to perform tasks on its behalf, and at the same time, delegates authority of corporate decision-making to the agent (Eisenhardt, 1989; Jensen & Meckling, 1976). However, under this conception, individuals are characterized as rational and self-interested in pursuing value-oriented activities (Scott, 2000). If both parties of principal and agent are utility maximizers, a conflict of interest between them will arise. Therefore, it cannot guarantee that the agent will operate in the best interests of the principal, which then may undermine the interests of the principal generating agency costs in the process. Jensen and Meckling (1976) define agency costs as the sum of expenditures of monitoring by the principal and bonding by the agent, and the "residual loss" representing the reduction of principal's interests due to the divergence between the principal and the agent.[1]

The classic work of Allingham and Sandmo (1972) sheds light on the theoretical and empirical analysis of individual tax management. They argue that individuals' motivation with tax management is determined by both extrinsic (the probability of detection and punishment, the penalty

---

[1] See Eisenhardt (1989, p. 59) for an overview of this theory.

structure, and the risk aversion of potential evaders) and intrinsic (civic virtue, and duty) elements. Slemrod (2004) extended this argument to closely held small businesses, including those without well-diversified owners. In this case, the tax situation of the firm and the owners are closely related. But Slemrod (2004) also points out the differences between sole proprietors and large, especially public listed enterprises, stressing the importance of the separation between ownership and control. Chen and Chu (2005) and Crocker and Slemrod (2005) further lend support to the argument that corporate tax management should be analyzed within the framework of principal–agent problems.

From the perspective of the separation of ownership and control, there are two alternative approaches of corporate tax management. On the one hand, corporate tax management can be considered a worthwhile activity, as managers can act on behalf of owners to reduce firms' costs to maximize profits. In this case, managers engaging in corporate tax management to reduce the tax burden are participating in a value enhancement activity, whereby corporate owners offer appropriate incentives to ensure managers make tax-efficient decisions. Efficient corporate tax management generates marginal benefits from tax avoiding transactions that exceed the marginal costs (Hanlon & Heitzman, 2010).

Consequently Phillips (2003) found that compensating business-unit managers on an after-tax basis will reduce corporate effective tax rates (ETRs). In investigating the relationship between tax sheltering and corporate governance, Desai and Dharmapala (2006, 2009) found that the complexity and obfuscation of tax sheltering activities would cause information asymmetry between managers and shareholders, thereby raising the potential for managerial opportunism and resource diversion. Simply put, corporate tax management can be considered as a complement of managerial diversion. Thus, given the potential role of agency costs, the consequences of corporate tax management are inconclusive.

Bad News Hoarding Theory

However, the market in reality, even in advanced countries, always suffers a degree of opaqueness and imperfect protection of property rights. Thus, how the limited information and imperfect protection of investors affect risk bearing between insiders (managers) and outsiders (investors) has drawn wide attention among researchers in recent years. Consistent with the nature of agency problems, Jin and Myers (2006) developed the "bad news hoarding" theory by formulating a theoretical model with country-average data. When firms are in non-transparent markets, outsider investors can obtain market-wide information but limited firm-specific information, while insider managers that manage firms' day-to-day operations, can capture more cash flow and firm-specific information. Because of the conflicting interests between insiders and outsiders, information asymmetry between the two parties can provide the inducement for managers to pursue their self-interests and sacrifice shareholders' interests. Thus, this would facilitate insiders to strenuously conceal firms' bad news to show inflated performance. Prior literature finds that both financial and non-financial incentives motivate managers to withhold bad news. Basu (1997) argued that if managerial compensation is correlated with reported earnings, managers will have high motivation to conceal adverse information. Kothari, Shu, and Wysocki (2009) and Ball (2009) find that the incentive for achieving self-benefits, such as career promotion and empire building, facilitates managers to conceal negative information about the firm to overstate financial performance.

In an environment of information opaqueness, the accumulation of hidden bad news will for a while result in an overvaluation of firms' stock prices. However, attempts to conceal bad news to "protect" the value of the firms can only go on till a certain threshold is reached after which its break out will send stock prices crashing (Hutton, Marcus, & Tehranian, 2009; Jin & Myers, 2006). In this regard, Bleck and Liu (2007) found that managers' attempts to hide firms' poor financial performance hinder shareholders' and investors' ability to distinguish bad projects from good ones at an early stage.

Therefore, Kim, Li, and Zhang (2011) argue that the complex and opaque nature of corporate tax management can be deployed by managers as a tool to mask and manipulate unfavorable performance and other bad news, which may increase the probability of future stock price crashes. Therefore, under the theories of agency cost and bad news hoarding, corporate tax management can lead to potential market risks for enterprises.

Helping Hand and Grabbing Hand

In a country experiencing massive economic transformation, such as China, the government plays an important role intervening in economic activities that affect public goods and public utilities. Hence, civil bureaucrats play an important role in the institutional change that is associated with economic change. There are two alternative hypotheses to explain the interactions between bureaucrats and entrepreneurs in the transition economy. They are the "helping hand" and the "grabbing hand" arguments.

On the one hand, under the "helping hand" perspective (see Frye & Shleifer, 1997), bureaucrats pursue self-interests through promoting local businesses, such as providing help to firms, especially to those with political connections (Cheung, Rau, & Stouraitis, 2008). In this case, the legal system is often compromised. Corruption is a pervasive behavior, but it is relatively limited and organized. Bribe becomes an efficient approach, which amounts to essential transactions costs to help firms gain the helping hand from government. Firms paying a bribe can bypass dysfunctional regulation to obtain preferential treatment. Sometimes it becomes the only route available to firms to effect transactions (Khan, 1989). Prior empirical studies also find that if a firm operates in a less developed governance and weak regulation environment, a bribing mechanism can facilitate economic transactions (Jiang & Nie, 2014; Khan, 1989; Petrou & Thanos, 2014).

On the other hand, under the "grabbing hand" perspective, government bureaucrats pursue their self-interests by intervening unproductively in a disorganized and unpredictable manner so as to expropriate wealth from firms (Frye & Shleifer, 1997; Rasiah, 2018). Under such circumstances the legal system in the country is often compromised (Shleifer & Vishny, 1993). In this case, corruption acts as a "grabbing hand", which creates huge costs for economic activities and distorts resource allocation, and with that long-term economic development (Jiang & Nie, 2014; Mauro, 1995; Petrou & Thanos, 2014; Rasiah, 2018). Consequently, firms have to shoulder high costs and suffer heavy uncertainties.

Frye and Shleifer (1997) argue that the above situations are "ideal types", which may not occur independently. Owing to uneven market development in different regions in China, the extent of institutional change arising from government intervention and marketization may vary considerably across regions, providing an opportunity to explore both views.[2]

---

[2] See Frye and Shleifer (1997, p. 355) for an overview of the "helping hand" and "grabbing hand" theories.

EMPIRICAL STUDIES

Empirical work on corporate tax management spans a wide area. It ranges from the motivations behind tax management, through its techniques to its consequences. However, there is a paucity of such studies on China. We review past works on this topic in this section.

Corporate Tax Management

Corporate tax management is becoming an universal economic phenomenon, arousing broad attention and research into the motivations driving such management activities (Hanlon & Heitzman, 2010). From a traditional perspective, tax management is viewed as a financial strategy targeted at transferring profits from government to shareholders (Desai & Dharmapala, 2009). Thus, the original motivation of firms pursuing tax management is to reduce corporate tax burdens and increase after-tax cash flow (Scholes, Wolfson, Erickson, Hanlon, Maydew, & Shevlin, 2015), which is beneficial to their bottom line by lowering the costs.

However, under the agency cost view of corporate tax management, such obfuscatory tax management activities can shelter managers pursuing various forms of self-interests activities to undertake managerial rent extraction activities, such as earnings manipulation and insider transactions (Desai & Dharmapala, 2006). Managers can disguise and exaggerate tax items to evade transactions under the ostensible objective of reducing firms' tax obligations to conduct managerial opportunism and resource diversion (Desai & Dharmapala, 2006, 2009). Badertscher, Katz, and Rego (2013) support the idea that managers can use tax management to engage in shirking and rent extraction activities to pursue their self-interests. Thus, owing to a conflict of interests between shareholders and managers, corporate tax management becomes an useful instrument of managers to pursue self-interests, which would yield less benefit to or harm the interests of shareholders (Desai & Dharmapala, 2009; Desai, Dyck, & Zingales, 2007).

Furthermore, many studies reveal that due to incomplete and asymmetric information (Fama, 1980; Healy & Palepu, 2001; Scherer, 1988), "corporate myopia" has become a pervasive and severe phenomenon in modern corporations (e.g., Chemmanur & Ravid, 1999; Holden & Lundstrum, 2009; Lundstrum, 2002; Nyman, 2005). On the one hand, managers who control day-to-day operations have more information about their firms, which offers them the space to pursue short-term profits rather than firms' long-term performance (Grant, King, & Polak, 1996). Besides, top executives may set a "tone at the top" stressing short-term cost minimization and profit maximization. On the other hand, shareholders, especially outside investors, often focus on the short time horizon, thereby driving managers toward short-termism conduct (von Thadden, 1995). Graves and Waddock (1990) argue that when institutional ownership dominates firms strategic decision-making tends to be based on limited inside knowledge of firms, which often generates non-neutral decisions and those leaning toward short-term gains. Asker, Farre-Mensa, and Ljungqvist (2014) contend that managers, especially in listed enterprises, tend to prefer short-term profits over long-term performance because of pressure to deliver short-term financial results. Ultimately, managers ultimately succumb to pressure from such short-sighted shareholders to improve short-term performance.

In the "corporate myopia" and "short-termism" perspectives, managers have an incentive to deploy corporate tax management as a tool to engage in short-term actions. In contrast to reducing operating costs, tax savings do not cause directly adverse consequences on a firm's daily operations (Edwards, Schwab, & Shevlin, 2013; Koester, Shevlin, & Wangerin, 2016). Importantly, corporate tax management offers opportunities to managers and short-term investors to manipulate earnings and cover up real corporate performance to boost short-term stock prices.

Consequences of Corporate Tax Management

Taxation as a significant cost affects corporate decision-making conduct and the bottom-line performance. Consequently, reducing corporate taxes has become a powerful motivational force in corporations. While corporate tax management may have various impacts on the interests of stakeholders, the focus here is on its impact on shareholders' wealth effects. Shareholders can encourage managers to reduce corporate tax liabilities to increase their benefits through designing effective compensation incentives (Desai & Dharmapala, 2009). But complex tax avoidance activities could cause internal control system opaqueness, thereby increasing information asymmetry between shareholders and managers (Lee, Dobiyanski, & Minton, 2015).

Information asymmetry can offer opportunities to managers to pursue personal gains, while shareholders are hardly able to observe the real outcomes of tax management. Hence, the consequences of corporate tax management are not entirely clear.

From a theoretical perspective, corporate tax management represents potential value-enhancement activities conducive to achieving shareholders' wealth maximization (Desai & Dharmapala, 2009; Mironov, 2013). However, from the agency theory perspective, the impact of corporate tax management on firm value can be negative and extensive. Although there are obvious gains in after-tax cash flow, Desai and Dharmapala (2006) found that shareholders still may not want managers to work for many tax sheltering activities, because such activities can create managerial rent diversion, which may not necessarily increase shareholders' value.

To confirm the above results, Wilson (2009) examined the stock return performance of tax shelter for the periods before, during, and immediately after sheltering activities. He found that firms with good governance would have significantly higher abnormal returns, which is consistent with corporate tax sheltering activities to increase shareholders' wealth. In addition, Desai and Dharmapala (2009) found a positive but insignificant relationship between tax avoidance and firm value, but a positive relationship among firms with dominant institutional ownership. They argue that tax management should benefit corporate after-tax cash flows, but this impact can potentially offset through poor corporate governance mechanisms. Moreover, the findings of Mironov (2013) support the view that managerial diversion can be concealed in the tax management activities, which can hurt firm performance. Using a sample from China's listed enterprises, Chen, Hu, Wang, and Tang (2014) found that corporate tax avoidance is inversely related to firm value owing to an increase in agency costs, but this relation can be attenuated by information transparency. Thus, if shareholders cannot fully understand the cost-benefit calculus of tax management, it can undermine firm value through a rise in agency costs.

Beyond the unclear firm-level outcomes of corporate tax management, several high-profile corporate accounting scandals, such as Enron and Apple, were revealed with managers accused of using complex tax management conduct to pursue personal interests, causing stock price volatility (Hanlon & Slemrod, 2009; Kim, Li, & Zhang, 2011; Rego & Wilson, 2012). Thus, an increasing number of studies have investigated the market reactions toward corporate tax management activities.

Swenson (1999) found that corporate income taxes as a cost to firms lowers bottom-line profits so that the stock market perceives low-tax paying firms as being better at controlling costs and generating profits. Similarly, Wang, Wang, and Gong (2009) found that there is a positive market reaction in China to companies, which succeeded in reducing tax liabilities. However, Desai and Hines (2002) found that the market does not react positively to ostensible tax-saving moves, and often responds negatively. Hanlon and Slemrod (2009) lend further support to this view that there is a negative reaction in stock markets over aggressive tax avoidance news. They point out that the market can react positively to firms' tax saving activities on the condition that such avoiding activities are not aggressive. Examining the relationship between tax avoidance and future stock price crash risks and using data from the US, Kim, Li, and Zhang (2011) found that the complex and opaque nature of tax avoidance can be used to hide adverse news to mislead investors for an extended period, which may lead to a high likelihood of future stock price crashes. Li, Luo, Wang, and Foo (2016) produced similar results using data from China's listed companies that tax sheltering behavior is positively correlated with future stock price crashes. However, they also argued that this positive relationship can be mitigated by market development and external monitoring mechanisms. External monitoring may be important when information imperfections are serious. Hence, aggressive tax management can be considered as a risk-engendering corporate financial activity.

In sum, prior empirical studies show that the consequences of corporate tax management vary depending on specific circumstances. While some evidences confirm theoretical arguments, others challenge the traditional perspective of tax management, which is a value enhancing activity benefiting corporate shareholders. Under the agency theory perspective of tax management, opportunistic managers can use tax management as a tool to extract rents, which will harm firms' profits and leads to extremely market returns.

Specific Characteristics of China's Enterprises

China is changing from a centrally planned economy to a market-oriented economy, albeit "with Chinese characteristics", and in the process achieving rapid economic growth since the 1980s. Paradoxically, the market shows an obvious characteristic of being relationship-based (*guanxi*) rather than rule-based, with excessive government interventions coupled with a still weak legal system (Chen, 2015). For example, Allen, Qian, and Qian (2005) state that China represents a significant counter-example to the uneven development of law, finance, and economic growth, which is that its economic miracle has largely been achieved under arguably a poor legal protection and financial system. Piotroski and Wong (2012) further find that China's financial market and listed firms operate in an environment of poor information and highly politicized institutional arrangements. The relationship-oriented contracting and social connections attenuate the information quality and protection of property rights. As a result, China is ranked among the least transparent economies, where many loopholes in legislation exist. Hence, it provides numerous opportunities for managers to participate in managerial opportunism.

Given the unique nature of the economic, political, and institutional environment in China, the incentives and consequences of corporate tax management may differ greatly from those in other countries. Thus, to capture the impact of the differences in corporate environment, three distinctive features need to be taken into consideration, *viz.*, government ownership, corruption, and market development.

State Ownership

Given the important role played by state-owned enterprises (SOEs) in China's economy, it is essential to explore the impact of state ownership and control on the consequences of corporate tax management activities. To start with SOE managers mostly are appointed by government (the ultimate controlling shareholder) to act on behalf of the government in corporate decision-making. They shoulder more social and political responsibilities than managers of private firms, such as employments and social security (Jensen & Meckling, 1976; Ross, 1973; Xu, Zhu, & Lin, 2005). Also, compared with managers in private enterprises, SOE managers have more incentives to seek future political advancement. The higher their position in the political hierarchy, the more privileges they will generally enjoy even after they leave their position (Tu, Lin, & Liu, 2013). Since tax is one of the main sources of fiscal revenues, the amount of tax paid by SOEs is deployed as a key factor to evaluate the performance of SOE managers. Hence, SOE managers have strong incentive to pay more taxes than otherwise to achieve social objectives, which may help them to get greater chances of political promotions (Lin, Lu, & Zhang, 2012). Under the above assumption, SOEs would be less likely to avoid taxes, which is sometimes referred to as the bureaucratic incentive effect (Jian, Li, & Zhang, 2013).

However, the reforms of state-owned enterprises have significantly enhanced the efficiency of the managerial labor market, which established performance-based bonus policy to give incentives to SOE managers to perform well in the market. *The Performance Evaluation Guideline for State-Owned Enterprises*, published by the Chinese government in 2002 and 2006, explicitly states that firms' economic performance is one of the key evaluation factors. Therefore, SOE managers have incentives to pursue a self-serving agenda (for political career advancement and higher compensation) as well by using tax management to conceal adverse operating outcomes to mask poor performance.

Jian, Li, and Zhang (2013) claim that SOEs pursue incentives to engage in tax management, because of their direct connection with government officials. Government ownership can help SOEs gain a "helping hand" from the government through tax incentives, while at the same time reducing the likelihood of tax audits, and even avoiding or limiting being punished in the event of being caught for tax evasion (Jian, Li, & Zhang, 2013; Li, Wang, Wu, & Xiao, 2016; Wu, Wang, Luo, & Gillis, 2012). Simply put, managers of SOEs have more opportunities to take advantage of the preferential treatment from government to avoid taxes for personal interests. In addition, Tang and Firth (2011) argue that listed local state-owned/controlled enterprises (including provincial level and municipal level listed SOEs), have more incentives to seek earnings and tax management opportunities. This is because local governments as the largest shareholders are the biggest beneficiaries of high after-tax profits. In addition, the tax-sharing policy in China requires local governments to share the income tax paid by local SOEs with the central government. Hence, local governments have strong incentives to encourage local SOEs to boost earnings.

As the above discussion shows, managers of SOEs have more space and motivation to use their political connections to pursue their self-interests, such as to advance upward their political career, or attract lucrative compensation contracts. But in the meanwhile, such conduct may cause potential risk. Thus, the question arises as to whether governments as ultimate controlling shareholders of SOEs will protect them when they encounter crisis. In addition, whether there exist different impacts among firms controlled by different government administrative ranks is another question to ask.

Corruption

Unlike productive rents (which are extracted from an economy to enable the poor and support those engaged in innovation activities), unproductive rents that dissipate resources undermine economic development (Rasiah, 2018). In this regard, government officials and businessmen are rational people with self-serving characteristics. Generally, officials' bribe-taking or enterprises' bribery will be conducted when they believe that their benefits exceed the costs and penalty in the execution of the process.

China represents a worthy study for the topic on corruption because of its cultural characteristics in social and business behavior and the impact of central planning in the governance of firms. China has undergone dramatic reforms since 1978 with the market playing an important role since but one that is still relationship-oriented (also known as *"guanxi"*) rather than being rule-based as in the western countries (Martinsons, 2005). This has caused the paradoxical phenomenon of rapid economic growth with rising corruption in China (Wedeman, 2012), which is difficult to comprehend especially when the former has been sustained over several decades. Corruption in China is deemed as "normal" conduct (Jain, 2001), or even as *"qianguize"* ("hidden rules of the game"), which exists in social, political, and economic activities (Faure and Fang, 2008). Recent research also demonstrates that corruption in China is "intensified" and "institutionalized" (Jianming and Zhizhou, 2008; Wederman, 2004), which is growing in sophistication and complexity, even as economic interaction increases (Gong, 2002).

Besides the above cultural traditions in China, Oi (1989) attributed corruption to the incompleteness of China's economic reforms. During China's fiscal decentralization reforms, the central government granted more autonomy and authority to local governments, giving local officials more discretionary powers than before. Thus, the increased discretionary power simultaneously provides more opportunities for local officials to seek bribes (Ngo, 2008). Under a high rate of government intervention, Ngo (2008) found that firms are more prone to bribe local government officials for extra preferential policies and economic advantage, including direct subsidies, such as tax benefits, tax breaks or tax reduction, and grants. Manion (1996) examines corruption in Chinese enterprise licensing system, and finds that problematic institutional design, bureaucratic discretion, and ambiguity of government regulations, have enabled officials to offer bribes in the process of licensing.

On corruption, scholars have begun to contest its impact by showing two opposite views. From a traditional view of corruption, it acts as a "grabbing hand", representing a significant cost for economic activities that may distort resource allocation negatively to effect growth and development of economic activities (Jiang & Nie, 2014; Krueger, 1974; Mauro, 1995; Petrou & Thanos, 2014). However, some studies support the view that it could act as the "helping hand" or "greasing the wheels" in countries that suffer from poor governance, ill-functioning institutions, and heavy regulation since a bribing mechanism that entails a transactions cost can help circumvent, such inefficiency and facilitate economic activities (Egger & Winner, 2005; Jiang & Nie, 2014; Khan, 1989; Sharma & Mitra, 2015). In this scenario, the marginal benefits of corruption are higher than its marginal costs. Hence, the effect of corruption on economic activities may be more complicated than it first appears.

In the context of a transition economy, whether corruption is harmful is becoming an interesting and important empirical question. Presently, a large number of studies of the impact of corruption have been done in macro literature, such as economic development and FDI (Barassi & Zhou, 2012; Gunter, 2017; Petrou & Thanos, 2014; Saha & Ben Ali, 2017). However, at the firm level, only few studies have addressed this issue, especially in the case of transition countries. China as the largest transition economy serves as an important case. Because of the incomplete market mechanism in China, we cannot simply put corruption into a black or white box. Moreover, corruption plays a complicated role that would influence the interests of different parties, both at the micro-level and macro-level. Thus, it is crucial to examine the impact of corruption on corporate tax management and through tax management on firm performance.

Marketization

It is generally recognized that institutional variation exists across countries and provinces, thanks to many in-depth cross-country comparative analyses (Chen, Zhai, Wang, & Zhong, 2015; Zhang & Rasiah, 2015).

But some studies assume that institutional environments are similar across different regions within a country. In other words, they assume institutional homogeneity within a country (Acemoglu & Robinson, 2012; Aguilera, 2005). However, recent studies find that institutional environments can be heterogenous across different locations within a country, especially in a large and/or transition economy (Chen, Zhai, Wang, & Zhong, 2015; Hong, Wang, & Kafouros, 2015; Ma, Tong, & Fitza, 2013; Zhang & Rasiah, 2015).

Since China implemented economic reforms and the open-door policy in the last three decades, some notable changes of institutional environment have taken place. More specifically, China is experiencing the changing of structure from a central-planned system to a market-oriented economy, showing a disparity in regional marketization (Hong, Wang, & Kafouros, 2015; Su & Wan, 2014; Wei, Wu, Li, & Chen, 2011). Formal institutional change has also witnessed a transformation from simply central planning to one in which the central government initiates the plans, the provincial government intermediates between the central government and the municipal and county governments, while the last two implement (Zhang & Rasiah, 2015). A survey by Fan, Wang, and Zhu (2007) found that different regional histories, natural environments, regional development patterns, and social cultures provide significant variations of regional institutional environment, which together lead to an uneven pace of regional market development. The market is just one institution among many, and while government policy enlists it as a key instrument for engendering the conditions of economic growth, the orderly transition toward the market requires the strengthening of other institutions, such as law and order.

In a region with a high degree of marketization, the market functions efficiently when the legal protection mechanism is robust, Chen, Zhai, Wang, and Zhong (2015) argue that government interventions and interruptions are fewer, and information asymmetry is reduced. Meanwhile, Hong, Wang, and Kafouros (2015) and Su and Wan (2014) argue that in regions with a lower degree of marketization, government intervention is more extensive, facilitating grabbing behavior by the government, especially among the lower administrative government officials. However, Zhang and Rasiah (2015) provide evidence to argue that effective coordination between government intervention and markets is critical to ensure that institutions evolve to discipline both the market and government positively. Marketization as an inherent external governance mechanism

(Wei, Wu, Li, & Chen, 2011) would impact macroeconomic development and corporate behavior directly and indirectly.

Research Gaps

We identified a number of research gaps from the above review of related theories and past empirical studies, which will guide our study on the different consequences of corporate tax management in China.

Firstly, most prior studies are based on samples from cross-country or developed countries, which often fail to control for the systemic differences among economies at different stages of development. This would have prevented researchers from exploring the outcomes of corporate tax management in developing countries incisively, and to make meaningful inferences. Therefore, in focusing on intra-country information in China's market, this book seeks to overcome the above problem.

Secondly, prior studies that examined the economic consequences of tax management have shown mixed results. From one perspective, corporate tax management is viewed as a corporate financial strategy that is potentially value-enhancing. However, how such tax management results in value enhancement has remained largely unexplored. From another perspective, corporate tax management is viewed as a tool for managers to pursue self-interests, which expose firms to different and uncertain risks, such as reducing firm value and causing extreme market outcomes. Unfortunately, too, most recent studies have focused on the developed countries, leaving considerable room to explore the linkages in emerging countries like China each with their unique characteristics.

Thirdly, most previous studies argue that SOEs are inefficient, but are able to borrow based on preferential treatment from government. However, China's reforms have transformed SOEs to function like modern enterprises, giving greater autonomy and decision-making power to their executives. Executives, then, have incentives to use their political connections to pursue their self-interest agenda, such as a political career and compensation contracts, all of which may cause hidden dangers for SOEs. Most extant studies have concentrated on the impact of government ownership on firm decision-making or firm performance. The empirical research on whether government ownership influences the probability of extreme outcomes is scarce. In addition, the question of whether there are different impacts among firms controlled by different levels of government is again lacking.

Fourthly, there is an extensive theoretical and empirical literature on the impact of corruption at the macro and mezzo economic levels, such as GDP growth, FDI, and industry development. Until recently, however, there have been relatively few studies on the effects of corruption at the micro firm-level. Despite the conventional wisdom about the harmful effect of corruption, in the context of Chinese relationship-based society, the impact of corruption is relatively unclear. Specifically, the causal pathways linking political corruption and corporate tax management are little known. Therefore, this study will investigate the impact of corruption on corporate tax management. The results will provide a more rigorous understanding of how corruption impacts firm-level financial activities in China or other emerging countries that are characterized by imperfect markets.

Finally, compared with developed countries with well-developed legal and social systems, the impact of external institutional development is much more important in transition economies (Chen, Lee, & Li, 2008; Zhang & Rasiah, 2015). In the context of China, because of differences in the history, natural, social, and even cultural environments between regions, large regional institutional gaps, including the uneven process of marketization exist. Most empirical research examines the impacts of firm-level governance characteristics on corporate tax management, but have overlooked the macro-institutional characteristics. Hence, China represents a worthwhile research laboratory to explore the impact of institutional development on corporate tax management.

Theoretical Framework

Since achieving shareholders' wealth maximization is the main goal of a firm, corporate tax as a major cost item impacts corporate performance. Managerial actions designed to minimize corporate tax obligations are increasingly becoming important as taxation plays an ever more important role in fiscal mobilization. Consequently, corporate tax management has seen increasing impact on countries' fiscal revenue, and economic growth. In traditional theory, tax management activities are costless to investors, the avoidance activities result simply in the transfer of value from the state to shareholders. However, the above view overlooks an important feature of modern corporations that is the separation of ownership and control. According to rational choice theory, an individual is referred to as *homo economicus*, who is characterized as rational, and hence, would pursue his or her self-interests. Shareholders (principals) are the owners of enterprises, while managers (agents) are the persons in charge of the enterprises. If the managers are also the owners of enterprises, the principals and agents have a common interest, which is maximization of profits. However, if the agents are not the owners of enterprise resources or only have an employment relationship with principals, they only sign a contract that specifies what the agents do with the resource, and how the returns are divided between the agents and the principals. From this point of view, the managers can use their control rights to pursue self-serving maximization activity rather than maximizing shareholders' wealth, which causes interest conflicts between principals and agents. In the context of information asymmetry and information opaqueness between principals and agents, agents as the party having more information are open to engage in managerial opportunism. Thus, the deviation from the principals' interests caused by the agents results in agency costs. As an example, Desai, Dyck, and Zingales (2007) propose a situation in which self-interested managers structure the firm in a complex manner in order to facilitate transactions that reduce corporate taxes and divert corporate resources for private use. Therefore, under the agency theory framework, the consequences of tax management are not entirely clear.

Furthermore, bad news hoarding theory reinforces the agency cost view of corporate tax management, which points out that managers have incentives to conceal negative corporate news for their personal interests. When the managers' ability to conceal bad news reaches a tipping point, all of the undisclosed negative information will be suddenly released into the stock market, often resulting in a stock price crash for the affected firm. Complex and opaque tax management activities can be used as an effective means by managers to manipulate earnings and hide bad news for an extended period, which can cause a high likelihood of future crashes. Thus, manipulative and complex forms of corporate tax management can lead to future extreme outcomes in the financial market.

To extend and contribute to the literature on corporate tax management in China and other transition economies, macro-level characteristics should be taken into consideration. Due to economic reforms and fiscal decentralization, China's regional economic development has occurred at different speeds, concurrently with rising corruption. Hence, the helping hand and grabbing hand theories have been introduced to explain how macro environment influences corporate tax behavior and its consequences. In the "helping hand" view, firms can make profits by paying a bribe premium, such as managers bribing local officials to achieve corporate tax saving. The bribe acts as a certain transactions cost to "grease" the wheels of government administration. In the "grabbing hand" view, if firms operate in an environment with widespread and rampant corruption, which means governments are unable to control bureaucrats from fearlessly engaging in unproductive rent-seeking activities. In this case, the bribing system acts as a "grabbing hand", where the firms' net losses/costs via bribing are higher than their net gains. As a result, it may affect negatively the enthusiasm of firms for avoiding tax or obtaining tax-related benefits via bribery. Therefore, the impact of corruption on economic activities may not be linear in that both theoretical arguments can coexist at different levels of corruption.

The overall theoretical framework is shown in Fig. 2.1. The three questions to be dealt with in the succeeding chapters are also shown.

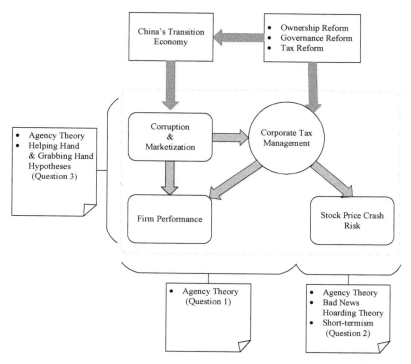

Fig. 2.1 Theoretical framework

ANALYTICAL FRAMEWORK

Following the above review, this study investigates the economic consequences of corporate tax management in China in the analytical Chapters 3–5. Firstly, under the perspective of agency theory, corporate tax management can provide tools and masks to managers to achieve their self-serving objectives, as a result harming firm value (Chen Chen, Cheng, & Shevlin, 2010; Desai & Dharmapala, 2009).

Chapter 3 tests the relationship between tax management and firm value to provide a preliminary understanding of the firm-level consequence of corporate tax management in China's listed enterprises. Then, the chapter investigates as to how firms through corporate tax management increase firms' market value.

In Chapter 4, the study is motivated by both agency theory and bad news hoarding theory to investigate the extreme market outcomes of corporate tax management. In China, political promotion is an effective incentive mechanism for SOEs' managers (Cao, Lemmon, Tian, & Pan, 2009), which facilitates them to conceal adverse operating outcomes. In addition, this further evaluates the effect of different levels of government ownership on the relationship between tax management and stock price crash risk.

Chapter 5 examines how macro-level characteristics of corruption and marketization impact to assess the relationship between corporate tax management and its economic consequences, Firstly, the chapter examines the direct impact of regional corruption on corporate tax management. The results will be used to explain whether corruption acts as a "helping hand" or as a "grabbing hand". It then explores the effect of market reforms by examining how marketization moderates the impact of corruption on corporate tax management. At the end, the chapter evaluates how does corruption influences the consequences of corporate tax management.

REFERENCES

Acemoglu, D., & Robinson, J. (2012). *Why nations fail: The origins of power, prosperity, and poverty.* New York: Crown Business.

Aguilera, R. V. (2005). Corporate governance and director accountability: An institutional comparative perspective. *British Journal of Management, 16,* S39–S53. https://doi.org/10.1111/j.1467-8551.2005.00446.x.

Allen, F., Qian, J., & Qian, M. (2005). Law, finance, and economic growth in China. *Journal of Financial Economics, 77*(1), 57–116. https://doi.org/10.1016/j.jfineco.2004.06.010.

Allingham, M. G., & Sandmo, A. (1972). Income tax evasion: A theoretical analysis. *Journal of Public Economics, 1*(3–4), 323–338. https://doi.org/10.1016/0047-2727(72)90010-2.

Asker, J., Farre-Mensa, J., & Ljungqvist, A. (2014). Corporate investment and stock market listing: A puzzle? *The Review of Financial Studies, 28*(2), 342–390. https://doi.org/10.1093/rfs/hhu077.

Badertscher, B. A., Katz, S. P., & Rego, S. O. (2013). The separation of ownership and control and corporate tax avoidance. *Journal of Accounting and Economics, 56*(2–3), 228–250. https://doi.org/10.1016/j.jacceco.2013.08.005.

Ball, R. (2009). Market and political/regulatory perspectives on the recent accounting scandals. *Journal of Accounting Research, 47*(2), 277–323. https://doi.org/10.1111/j.1475-679X.2009.00325.x.

Barassi, M. R., & Zhou, Y. (2012). The effect of corruption on FDI: A parametric and non-parametric analysis. *European Journal of Political Economy, 28*(3), 302–312. https://doi.org/10.1016/j.ejpoleco.2012.01.001.

Basu, S. (1997). The conservatism principle and the asymmetric timeliness of earnings. *Journal of Accounting and Economics, 24*(1), 3–37. https://doi.org/10.1016/S0165-4101(97)00014-1.

Bleck, A., & Liu, X. (2007). Market transparency and the accounting regime. *Journal of Accounting Research, 45*(2), 229–256. https://doi.org/10.1111/j.1475-679X.2007.00231.x.

Cao, X. J., Lemmon, M., Tian, G., & Pan, X. (2009). *Political promotion, CEO compensation, and their effect on firm performance*. Research Collection Lee Kong Chian School of Business.

Chemmanur, T. J., & Ravid, S. A. (1999). Asymmetric information, corporate myopia, and capital gains tax rates: An analysis of policy prescriptions. *Journal of Financial Intermediation, 8*(3), 205–231. https://doi.org/10.1006/jfin.1999.0262.

Chen, K.-P., & Chu, C. Y. C. (2005). Internal control versus external manipulation: A model of corporate income tax evasion. *The RAND Journal of Economics, 36*(1), 151–164.

Chen, S., Chen, X., Cheng, Q., & Shevlin, T. (2010). Are family firms more tax aggressive than non-family firms? *Journal of Financial Economics, 95*(1), 41–61. https://doi.org/10.1016/j.jfineco.2009.02.003.

Chen, T. (2015). Institutions, board structure, and corporate performance: Evidence from Chinese firms. *Journal of Corporate Finance, 32*, 217–237. https://doi.org/10.1016/j.jcorpfin.2014.10.009.

Chen, X., Hu, N., Wang, X., & Tang, X. (2014). Tax avoidance and firm value: Evidence from China. *Nankai Business Review International, 5*(1), 25–42. https://doi.org/10.1108/NBRI-10-2013-0037.

Chen, X., Lee, C.-W. J., & Li, J. (2008). Government assisted earnings management in China. *Journal of Accounting and Public Policy, 27*(3), 262–274. https://doi.org/10.1016/j.jaccpubpol.2008.02.005.

Chen, Y., Zhai, R.-R., Wang, C., & Zhong, C. (2015). Home institutions, internationalization and firm performance: Evidence from listed Chinese firms. *Management Decision*, *53*(1), 160–178. https://doi.org/10.1108/MD-05-2014-0311.

Cheung, Y.-L., Rau, P. R., & Stouraitis, A. (2008, April). *The helping hand, the lazy hand, or the grabbing hand? Central vs. local government shareholders in publicly listed firms in China* (Center for Economic Institutions Working Paper Series).

Crocker, K. J., & Slemrod, J. (2005). Corporate tax evasion with agency costs. *Journal of Public Economics*, *89*(9), 1593–1610. https://doi.org/10.1016/j.jpubeco.2004.08.003.

Desai, M. A., & Dharmapala, D. (2006). Corporate tax avoidance and high-powered incentives. *Journal of Financial Economics*, *79*(1), 145–179.

Desai, M. A., & Dharmapala, D. (2009). Earnings management, corporate tax shelters, and book-tax alignment. *National Tax Journal*, *62*(1), 169–186.

Desai, M. A., Dyck, A., & Zingales, L. (2007). Theft and taxes. *Journal of Financial Economics*, *84*(3), 591–623. https://doi.org/10.1016/j.jfineco.2006.05.005.

Desai, M. A., & Hines, J. R. J. (2002). Expectations and expatriations: Tracing the causes and consequences of corporate inversions. *National Tax Journal*, *55*(3), 409–440. https://doi.org/10.17310/ntj.2002.3.03.

Edwards, A., Schwab, C. M., & Shevlin, T. J. (2013). *Financial constraints and the incentive for tax planning*. Paper presented at the 2013 American Taxation Association Midyear Meeting: New Faculty/Doctoral Student Session. https://ssrn.com/abstract=2216875.

Egger, P., & Winner, H. (2005). Evidence on corruption as an incentive for foreign direct investment. *European Journal of Political Economy*, *21*(4), 932–952. https://doi.org/10.1016/j.ejpoleco.2005.01.002.

Eisenhardt, K. M. (1989). Agency theory: An assessment and review. *Academy of Management Review*, *14*(1), 57–74. https://doi.org/10.5465/AMR.1989.4279003.

Fama, E. F. (1980). Agency problems and the theory of the firm. *Journal of Political Economy*, *88*(2), 288–307.

Fan, G., Wang, X., & Zhu, H. (2007). *NERI index of marketization of China's provinces: 2006 report (in Chinese)*. Beijing: Economic Science Press.

Faure, G. O., & Fang, T. (2008). Changing Chinese values: Keeping up with paradoxes. *International Business Review*, *17*(2), 194–207. https://doi.org/10.1016/j.ibusrev.2008.02.011.

Frye, T., & Shleifer, A. (1997). The invisible hand and the grabbing hand. *The American Economic Review*, *87*(2), 354–358.

Gong, T. (2002). Dangerous collusion: Corruption as a collective venture in contemporary China. *Communist and Post-Communist Studies, 35*(1), 85–103. https://doi.org/10.1016/S0967-067X(01)00026-5.

Grant, S., King, S., & Polak, B. (1996). Information externalities, share-price based incentives and managerial behaviour. *Journal of Economic Surveys, 10*(1), 1–21. https://doi.org/10.1111/j.1467-6419.1996.tb00001.x.

Graves, S. B., & Waddock, S. A. (1990). Institutional ownership and control: Implications for long-term corporate strategy. *The Executive, 4*(1), 75–83. https://doi.org/10.5465/AME.1990.4274714.

Gunter, F. R. (2017). Corruption, costs, and family: Chinese capital flight, 1984–2014. *China Economic Review, 43*, 105–117. https://doi.org/10.1016/j.chieco.2017.01.010.

Hanlon, M., & Heitzman, S. (2010). A review of tax research. *Journal of Accounting and Economics, 50*(2), 127–178. https://doi.org/10.1016/j.jacceco.2010.09.002.

Hanlon, M., & Slemrod, J. (2009). What does tax aggressiveness signal? Evidence from stock price reactions to news about tax shelter involvement. *Journal of Public Economics, 93*(1–2), 126–141. https://doi.org/10.1016/j.jpubeco.2008.09.004.

Healy, P. M., & Palepu, K. G. (2001). Information asymmetry, corporate disclosure, and the capital markets: A review of the empirical disclosure literature. *Journal of Accounting and Economics, 31*(1–3), 405–440. https://doi.org/10.1016/S0165-4101(01)00018-0.

Holden, C. W., & Lundstrum, L. L. (2009). Costly trade, managerial myopia, and long-term investment. *Journal of Empirical Finance, 16*(1), 126–135. https://doi.org/10.1016/j.jempfin.2008.05.001.

Hong, J., Wang, C., & Kafouros, M. (2015). The role of the state in explaining the internationalization of emerging market enterprises. *British Journal of Management, 26*(1), 45–62. https://doi.org/10.1111/1467-8551.12059.

Hutton, A. P., Marcus, A. J., & Tehranian, H. (2009). Opaque financial reports, R2, and crash risk. *Journal of Financial Economics, 94*(1), 67–86. https://doi.org/10.1016/j.jfineco.2008.10.003.

Jain, A. K. (2001). Corruption: A review. *Journal of Economic Surveys, 15*(1), 71–121. https://doi.org/10.1111/1467-6419.00133.

Jensen, M. C., & Meckling, W. H. (1976). Theory of the firm: Managerial behavior, agency costs and ownership structure. *Journal of Financial Economics, 3*(4), 305–360. https://doi.org/10.1016/0304-405X(76)90026-X.

Jian, M., Li, W., & Zhang, H. (2013). *How does state ownership affect tax avoidance? Evidence from China* (Working Paper). Nanyang Technological University and Fuzhou University.

Jiang, T., & Nie, H. (2014). The stained China miracle: Corruption, regulation, and firm performance. *Economics Letters, 123*(3), 366–369. https://doi.org/10.1016/j.econlet.2014.03.026.

Jianming, R., & Zhizhou, D. (2008). Institutionalized corruption: Power over-concentration of the first-in-command in China. *Crime, Law and Social Change, 49*(1), 45–59. https://doi.org/10.1007/s10611-007-9090-4.

Jin, L., & Myers, S. C. (2006). R2 around the world: New theory and new tests. *Journal of Financial Economics, 79*(2), 257–292. https://doi.org/10.1016/j.jfineco.2004.11.003.

Khan, M. H. (1989). *Clientelism, corruption and capitalist development: An analysis of state intervention with special reference to Bangladesh* (PhD thesis). Cambridge University, Cambridge.

Kim, J.-B., Li, Y., & Zhang, L. (2011). Corporate tax avoidance and stock price crash risk: Firm-level analysis. *Journal of Financial Economics, 100*(3), 639–662. https://doi.org/10.1016/j.jfineco.2010.07.007.

Koester, A., Shevlin, T., & Wangerin, D. (2016). The role of managerial ability in corporate tax avoidance. *Management Science.* https://doi.org/10.1287/mnsc.2016.2510.

Kothari, S. P., Shu, S., & Wysocki, P. D. (2009). Do managers withhold bad news? *Journal of Accounting Research, 47*(1), 241–276. https://doi.org/10.1111/j.1475-679X.2008.00318.x.

Krueger, A. O. (1974). The political economy of the rent-seeking society. *American Economic Review, 64*(3), 291.

Lee, B. B., Dobiyanski, A., & Minton, S. (2015). Theories and empirical proxies for corporate tax avoidance. *The Journal of Applied Business and Economics, 17*(3), 21–34.

Li, C., Wang, Y., Wu, L., & Xiao, J. Z. (2016). Political connections and tax-induced earnings management: Evidence from China. *The European Journal of Finance, 22*(4–6), 413–431. https://doi.org/10.1080/1351847X.2012.753465.

Li, Y., Luo, Y., Wang, J., & Foo, C.-T. (2016). A theory of managerial tax aggression: Evidence from china, 2008–2013 (9702 observations). *Chinese Management Studies, 10*(1), 12–40. https://doi.org/10.1108/CMS-01-2016-0001.

Lin, B., Lu, R., & Zhang, T. (2012). Tax-induced earnings management in emerging markets: Evidence from China. *The Journal of the American Taxation Association, 34*(2), 19–44. https://doi.org/10.2308/atax-10236.

Lundstrum, L. L. (2002). Corporate investment myopia: A horserace of the theories. *Journal of Corporate Finance, 8*(4), 353–371. https://doi.org/10.1016/S0929-1199(01)00050-5.

Ma, X., Tong, T. W., & Fitza, M. (2013). How much does subnational region matter to foreign subsidiary performance? Evidence from Fortune Global 500 corporations' investment in China. *Journal of International Business Studies, 44*(1), 66–87. https://doi.org/10.1057/jibs.2012.32.

Manion, M. (1996). Corruption by design: Bribery in Chinese enterprise licensing. *The Journal of Law, Economics, and Organization, 12*(1), 167–195. https://doi.org/10.1093/oxfordjournals.jleo.a023356.

Martinsons, M. G. (2005). Online success in a relationship-based economy—Profiles of e-commerce in China. In R. M. Davison, R. W. Harris, S. Qureshi, D. R. Vogel, & G.-J. de Vreede (Eds.), *Information systems in developing countries: Theory and practice* (pp. 173–191). Hong Kong: City University of Hong Kong Press.

Mauro, P. (1995). Corruption and growth. *The Quarterly Journal of Economics, 110*(3), 681–712. https://doi.org/10.2307/2946696.

Mironov, M. (2013). Taxes, theft, and firm performance. *The Journal of Finance, 68*(4), 1441–1472. https://doi.org/10.1111/jofi.12026.

Ngo, T.-W. (2008). Rent-seeking and economic governance in the structural nexus of corruption in China. *Crime, Law and Social Change, 49*(1), 27–44. https://doi.org/10.1007/s10611-007-9089-x.

Nyman, I. (2005). Stock market speculation and managerial myopia. *Review of Financial Economics, 14*(1), 61–79. https://doi.org/10.1016/j.rfe.2004.06.002.

Oi, J. C. (1989). *State and peasant in contemporary China: The political economy of village government*. Berkeley: University of California Press.

Penrose, E. (1959). *The theory of the growth of the firm*. Oxford: Oxford University Press.

Petrou, A. P., & Thanos, I. C. (2014). The "grabbing hand" or the "helping hand" view of corruption: Evidence from bank foreign market entries. *Journal of World Business, 49*(3), 444–454. https://doi.org/10.1016/j.jwb.2013.10.004.

Phillips, J. D. (2003). Corporate tax-planning effectiveness: The role of compensation-based incentives. *The Accounting Review, 78*(3), 847–874. https://doi.org/10.2308/accr.2003.78.3.847.

Piotroski, J. D., & Wong, T. J. (2012). Institutions and information environment of Chinese listed firms. In J. P. H. Fan & R. Morck (Eds.), *Capitalizing China* (pp. 201–242). Chicago and London: University of Chicago Press.

Rasiah, R. (2018). *Developmental states: Land schemes, parastatals and poverty alleviation in Malaysia*. Bangi: Universiti Kebangsaan Malaysia Press.

Rego, S. O., & Wilson, R. (2012). Equity risk incentives and corporate tax aggressiveness. *Journal of Accounting Research, 50*(3), 775–810. https://doi.org/10.1111/j.1475-679X.2012.00438.x.

Ross, S. A. (1973). The economic theory of agency: The principal's problem. *The American Economic Review, 63*(2), 134–139.

Saha, S., & Ben Ali, M. S. (2017). Corruption and economic development: New evidence from the Middle Eastern and North African countries. *Economic Analysis and Policy, 54,* 83–95. https://doi.org/10.1016/j.eap.2017.02.001.

Scherer, F. M. (1988). Corporate takeovers: The efficiency arguments. *The Journal of Economic Perspectives, 2*(1), 69–82.

Scholes, M. S., Wolfson, M. A., Erickson, M., Hanlon, M., Maydew, E. L., & Shevlin, T. (2015). *Taxes and business strategy: A planning approach* (5th ed.). London, UK: Pearson Education.

Scott, J. (2000). Rational choice theory. In G. Browning, A. Halcli, & F. Webster (Eds.), *Understanding contemporary society: Theories of the present*. Thousand Oaks, CA: Sage.
Sharma, C., & Mitra, A. (2015). Corruption, governance and firm performance: Evidence from Indian enterprises. *Journal of Policy Modeling, 37*(5), 835–851. https://doi.org/10.1016/j.jpolmod.2015.05.001.
Shleifer, A., & Vishny, R. W. (1993). Corruption. *The Quarterly Journal of Economics, 108*(3), 599–617. https://doi.org/10.2307/2118402.
Slemrod, J. (2004). The economics of corporate tax selfishness. *National Tax Journal, 57*(4), 877–899. https://doi.org/10.17310/ntj.2004.4.06.
Su, K., & Wan, R. (2014). State control, marketization, and firm value: Evidence from China. *Journal of Applied Business Research, 30*(6), 1577–1586. https://doi.org/10.19030/jabr.v30i6.8875.
Swenson, C. (1999). Increasing stock market value by reducing effective tax rates. *Tax Notes, 83*, 1503–1505.
Tang, T., & Firth, M. (2011). Can book-tax differences capture earnings management and tax management? Empirical evidence from China. *The International Journal of Accounting, 46*(2), 175–204. https://doi.org/10.1016/j.intacc.2011.04.005.
Tu, G., Lin, B., & Liu, F. (2013). Political connections and privatization: Evidence from China. *Journal of Accounting and Public Policy, 32*(2), 114–135. https://doi.org/10.1016/j.jaccpubpol.2012.10.002.
von Thadden, E.-L. (1995). Long-term contracts, short-term investment and monitoring. *The Review of Economic Studies, 62*(4), 557–575. https://doi.org/10.2307/2298077.
Wang, Y., Wang, L., & Gong, C. (2009). Reform of enterprise income tax, earnings management and its economic consequences. *Journal of Economic Research Journal, 3*, 10.
Wedeman, A. (2012). *Double paradox: Rapid growth and rising corruption in China*. New York, NY: Cornell University Press.
Wederman, A. (2004). The intensification of corruption in China. *The China Quarterly, 180*, 895–921. https://doi.org/10.1017/S0305741004000670.
Wei, Z., Wu, S., Li, C., & Chen, W. (2011). Family control, institutional environment and cash dividend policy: Evidence from China. *China Journal of Accounting Research, 4*(1–2), 29–46. https://doi.org/10.1016/j.cjar.2011.04.001.
Wilson, R. J. (2009). An examination of corporate tax shelter participants. *The Accounting Review, 84*(3), 969–999. https://doi.org/10.2308/accr.2009.84.3.969.
Wu, L., Wang, Y., Luo, W., & Gillis, P. (2012). State ownership, tax status and size effect of effective tax rate in China. *Accounting and Business Research, 42*(2), 97–114. https://doi.org/10.1080/00014788.2012.628208.

Xu, L. C., Zhu, T., & Lin, Y.-M. (2005). Politician control, agency problems and ownership reform. *Economics of Transition*, *13*(1), 1–24. https://doi.org/10.1111/j.1468-0351.2005.00205.x.

Zhang, M., & Rasiah, R. (2015). *Institutionalization of state policy: Evolving urban housing reforms in China*. Singapore: Springer. https://doi.org/10.1007/978-981-287-570-9.

CHAPTER 3

Corporate Governance and Firm Performance

INTRODUCTION

To the extent that taxation impacts firms' bottom line, the textbook argument that tax imposes a burden on firms has been subject to extensive research. However, compared with research on developed markets, especially the US, studies of tax management on the emerging markets, including China, are limited. Also, much of the research on this topic has been directed at linking taxation to firm characteristics, such as firm size, ownership, and leverage (Adhikari, Derashid, & Zhang, 2006; Badertscher, Katz, & Rego, 2013; Wu, Wang, Luo, & Gillis, 2012). Little work has broached the dynamic aspect of this topic, which is to see how corporate tax management can be deployed as a useful method to promote firm performance. After all it is not the purpose of governments to raise revenue at the expense of transferring what is legally the right of firms to retain.

If successfully deployed, a tax management strategy would transfer wealth from the state back to firms (Desai & Dharmapala, 2009a, b). In short, it should result in relatively lower taxes incurred, which would result in higher after-tax cash flows that could influence positively stock prices if it gives the impression to shareholders that it demonstrates firms' competency at accounting for costs (see Swenson, 1999). This may not always be true though, as the empirical evidence from China shows otherwise. There is evidence from modern corporations of how conflicts of interest between managers and shareholders create opportunities for managerial diversions, which ultimately discount the value of firms (Chen & Chu, 2005; Crocker & Slemrod, 2005; Desai & Dharmapala, 2006, 2009a, b).

Further, even if shareholders' wealth is maximized, tax management can still produce both adverse firm- and macro-level effects (Hanlon & Heitzman, 2010; Hanlon & Slemrod, 2009; Robinson, Sikes, & Weaver, 2010). At the firm level, tax management diminishes firms' discharge of their social irresponsibility (Erle, 2008). At the macro-level, reducing taxes represents a loss of resources to the government, which would then diminish the resources at its disposal to finance the provision of public goods and public utilities (Sikka, 2010).

Thus, there is a powerful case to examine further the impact of corporate tax management targeted at reducing taxes on firm performance. In this chapter, we examine the evidence from China. Specifically, this chapter seeks to answer the first objective of the book, viz. what is the impact of corporate tax management on firm performance, and how does this take place? This question can be divided into three sub-questions: one, is there a link between tax management and firm value in China and what is the magnitude and nature of this link?; two, have China's transition and corporate reforms moved China's enterprise environment closer to the norm of the developed countries? three, are there gaps in China's reform experience?

ANALYTIC FRAMEWORK

Corporate tax management is traditionally viewed as a tax-reducing device that transfers back financial resources from the government to firms to maximize shareholders' value, although an expanding body of work on agency theory emphasizes that tax management is closely related to corporate governance because of its implications for agency costs. In practice, the complexity and ambiguity of tax management can encourage managers to engage in various forms of managerial rent extraction, such as earnings manipulation and insider transactions, which would reduce after-tax cash flows (Desai & Dharmapala, 2009a, b; Desai, Dyck, & Zingales, 2007). The Enron case is a striking example. In the 1990s, Enron made use of structured financing transactions to evade taxes, leading to government prosecution, and eventually, its collapse. In addition, firms also need to shoulder the combined tax avoidance costs, which include direct tax planning, compliance, and non-tax costs. Lee,

Dobiyanski, and Minton (2015) suggest that if shareholders cannot fully understand the cost-benefit calculus, tax management activities could become counter-productive and in that sense reduce firm value.

Empirical research on the impact of corporate tax management on firm value has produced mixed findings. For example, Desai and Dharmapala (2009a, b) found no significant relationship between tax avoidance and firm value, but a positive relationship in firms that show dominant institutional ownership. They consider that shareholders' ability to control managers can add value to tax avoidance. Hanlon and Slemrod (2009) examination of market reaction to news about firms' application for tax shelters to dampen stock prices. Furthermore, Chen, Hu, Wang, and Tang (2014) showed that tax avoidance is also inversely related to firm value, but this can be mitigated by increasing information transparency.

In contrast to works from the developed countries, Claessens and Fan (2002) argued that agency problems in Asian countries are compounded by a lack of corporate transparency to check rent-seeking and insider transactions. China represents a special case because of central planning still being a key instrument of government. Piotroski, Wong, and Zhang (2015) argued that China's financial market and listed firms are operating in an environment of poor information. In addition, China's taxation system only started to open up over the last three decades, and thus, is still evolving with many loopholes. These factors provide unwarranted space for managers to engage in managerial opportunism, and to optimize their self-serving interests. Given the above, corporate tax management may not necessarily increase firm value, and hence, we first *hypothesize in this chapter that corporate tax management has a direct negative relationship with firms' market value.*

There is extensive empirical evidence that shows that firms with good profitability and growth performance are generally associated with strong shareholder value. For example, Varaiya, Kerin, and Weeks (1987) found that firms' profitability and growth significantly impact shareholders' value. Naceur and Goaied (2002) found that future value creation is significantly and positively related to a firm's profitability in Tunisia. Furthermore, Fama and French (1998) argued that firms with a good record of profitability showed a positive relationship between taxation of dividends and firm value. For these reasons, high profitability and growth performance should be important factors in firm value maximization.

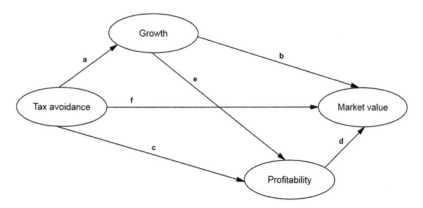

Fig. 3.1 Conceptual structure of structural equation model (*Source* Plotted by authors)

The extant literature also shows that corporate governance has a significant positive association with profitability and growth. For example, Durnev and Kim (2005) found firms with better corporate governance practices to grow faster and to be more profitable. In addition, Peni and Vähämaa (2012) found that large publicly traded US banks with stronger corporate governance mechanisms have higher profitability than otherwise. Moreover, Harford, Mansi, and Maxwell (2012) showed that firms with lower shareholder rights spend cash more quickly than those with stronger rights. Besides, Yen (2005) found that firms with management-friendly board structures would choose projects with promising growth prospects. These results call for the use of mediators[1] in the relationship between corporate tax management and firm value. The above evidence led us to two additional but related hypotheses: one, *profitability performance mediates the relationship between tax management and market value* (path *cd* in Fig. 3.1); and two, *growth performance mediates the relationship between tax management and market value* (path *ab* in Fig. 3.1).

---

[1] From a theoretical perspective, the most common application of mediation is to explain why a relationship between two constructs exists. When exogenous constructs are viewed as "inputs" to a model explaining some final "outcomes" that is represented by an endogenous construct, then, any construct acting between them shall involve some mediation (Black, Babin, & Anderson, 2009, pp. 766–770).

Firms' profitability and performance is a function of firms' history of generating returns (Miller, Washburn, & Glick, 2013), with growth performance representing firms' past ability to grow in size (Whetten, 1987). Firm size is positively associated with economies of scale and market power, both of which result in higher future profitability. Moreover, the market value of firms is normally based on their expected performance, which should be correlated with firms' profitability and growth performance (Santos & Brito, 2012). Hence, we hypothesize that *corporate tax management is positively but indirectly (through growth and profitability) associated with market value* (path aed in Fig. 3.1).

METHODOLOGY AND DATA

We discuss in this section the methodology and data used in the chapter. We start with the measures used followed by the specification of the models. Subsequently we describe the sampling procedure used and data collected. The section finishes with the analytical techniques used.

Measures

Four constructs are used in the model to examine the relationships between corporate tax management, growth, profitability, and market performance, which are discussed below. Figure 3.2 shows the relationship between the observed and latent variables.

Corporate Tax Management

Past research has considered corporate effective tax rate (ETR) as a proxy for corporate tax burden (Gupta & Newberry, 1997; Richardson, Wang, & Zhang, 2016; Wu, Wang, Luo, & Gillis, 2012), which is also simultaneously used as an index to measure the effectiveness of tax management. Following Badertscher, Katz, and Rego (2013), this chapter adopts two corporate effective tax rates (ETRs) to represent tax management (risky and non-risky strategies). The first measure is the *ETR1*, which is defined and measured under Generally Accepted Accounting Principles (GAAP) as total corporate income tax expenses divided by pre-tax income. The second measure is *ETR2*, which is defined and measured on a cash basis as corporate income tax expenses minus deferred tax expenses divided using pre-tax income. Lower effective tax rates represent a lower corporate tax burden, which refers to firms with a higher

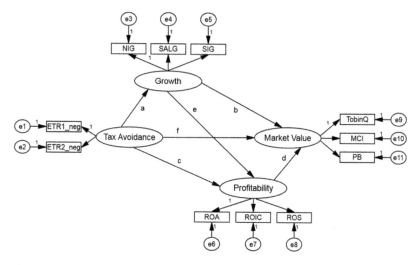

Fig. 3.2 Structural model (*Source* Plotted by authors)

level of corporate tax management. To provide a direct and intuitive understanding of the relationship between corporate tax management and firm performance, in the model process, the chapter uses the opposite number of the two ETRs, denoted by *ETR1_neg* and *ETR2_neg* (see Table 3.1).

All ETR measures are well understood by financial statement users. Specifically, GAAP ETR is affected by changes in tax reserves and the valuation allowance, while Cash ETR is influenced by the timing of tax payments, settlements with tax authorities, and some type of earnings management (Hanlon & Heitzman, 2010). However, while focusing on ETRs as proxy for tax management and its link with firm value, this chapter does not investigate the differences between the two measures.

Profitability Performance

Profitability is one of the major performance dimensions of concern in this chapter. It is defined as the firm's earnings net of costs and is commonly measured by return on assets (*ROA*), return on invested capital (*ROIC*), and return on sales (*ROS*). The *ROA* is the most commonly used accounting measure of performance in financial research (Cable & Mueller, 2008), and it has been shown to represent firms' performance

Table 3.1 Variable, relationships, and definition

Constructs	Causes–effects	Definition
A. Tax management	**Causes**	
	ETR1_neg	Opposite number of Effective tax rate 1 (ETR1)
		ETR1_neg = − Tax expenses/pre-tax income
	ETR2_neg	Opposite number of Effective tax rate 2 (ETR2)
		ETR2_neg = − (Tax expenses-deferred tax expense)/pre-tax income
B. Firm performance	**Effects**	
1. Profitability	ROA	Return on total asset
		Net income/total assets
	ROIC	Return on invested capital
		Net operating profit after taxes/invested capital
	ROS	Net profit margin
		Net income/revenues
2. Growth	SIG	Sales income growth rate
		(Sales income$_{i,t}$ − Sales income$_{i,t-1}$)/Sales income$_{i,t-1}$
	SALG	Sales growth rate;
		(Sales$_{i,t}$ − Sales$_{i,t-1}$)/Sales$_{i,t-1}$
	NIG	Net income growth rate
		(Net income$_{i,t}$ − Net income$_{i,t-1}$)/Net income$_{i,t-1}$
3. Market value	TobinQ	Tobin's Q*
	PB	Price-to-book ratio
	MCI	Market capitalization improvement

In China, due to the special split-share structure, some shares are not tradable in the stock market. Tobin's Q was measured as: market price per share number of tradable shares + book value of the equity per share * number of non-tradable shares + book value of total debt)/book value of total assets
Source Prepared by authors

well (Peng & Luo, 2000; Rowe & Morrow, 1999), which demonstrates the ability of firms to use their assets to generate profit. The *ROS* is also used by many researchers (Delen, Kuzey, & Uyar, 2013; Jang & Park, 2011), because it can reflect profits from a company's sales in the short-term. The *ROIC* measures the return earned on the invested capital. Damodaran (2007) notes that *ROIC* is a key input in both corporate finance and valuation. This chapter deploys all the three measures to make up the latent variable of profitability (see Table 3.1).

Growth Performance

Firms' growth performance in this chapter is measured using growth rates of sales revenue (*SALG*), sales income (*SIG*), and net income (*NIG*). Sales growth has been used to measure firms' growth rates in many studies (e.g., Anthony & Ramesh, 1992; Brush, Bromiley, & Hendrickx, 2000; Jang & Park, 2011; Serrasqueiro, 2009). Wang and You (2012) believe that growth rate of sales income would yield more reliable estimation results than other measures in the case of China. Moreover, net income growth represents the rate at which firms have grown profits, and there are often doubts over whether firms would provide this information accurately (Rasiah & Thangiah, 2017). Stocks that experience faster net income growth are generally favored over those with slower net income growth (Delen, Kuzey, & Uyar, 2013). Therefore, this chapter deploys growth rate of net income (see Table 3.1).

Market Performance

This chapter measures firms' market performance using three market-based measures of return, viz., Price-to-book (*PB*) ratio, Tobin's Q (*TobinQ*), and Market capitalization improvement (*MCI*). The *PB* ratio takes the ratio of stock price to book value per share (Brealey & Myers, 2000; Montgomery, Thomas, & Kamath, 1984). The Tobin's Q is the ratio of the market value of a firm's debt and equity to the ending total value of assets (Desai & Dharmapala, 2009a, b; Yu, 2013). It is widely used because it takes account of the book and market values of equity and the value of debt (Desai & Dharmapala, 2009a, b; Firth, Gong, & Shan, 2013). Market capitalization denotes the stock market's valuation of a firm (Abdolmohammadi, 2005) and is defined in this chapter as the improvement of the total market value of the shares outstanding (see Table 3.1).

Model Specification

Figure 3.2 shows the structural model which underpins the causal relationships among the four latent constructs, viz., corporate tax management, growth, profitability, and market value. The direct relationship between corporate tax management and firms' market value (Hypothesis 3.1) is first examined using China's listed enterprises (Fig. 3.2, Path *f*). Given existing evidence on profitability, growth and corporate governance relationships and the impact of their relationships on firms' market performance, this chapter investigates the mediating roles of profitability and growth in the relationship between corporate tax management and market value. Paths *ab*, *cd*, and *aed* (Fig. 3.2) represent three different but specific indirect relationships between corporate tax management and firms' market value.

Data and Sampling
Annual time series data covering the period 2004–2012 is used in this chapter. For *ETR1*, deferred tax expenses were calculated based on the previous year's data, which means that the period of analysis begins from 2005. All data were obtained from the China Stock Market and Accounting Research (CSMAR) database.[2] However, data used for estimation exclude the following: (1) financial industry firms which, according to the China Securities Regulatory Commission Industry Classifications (CSRCIC), are heavily regulated and their tax incentives differ from firms in other industries; (2) firms enjoying "Special Treatment" (ST) stocks[3]; (3) firms where both of the *ETR1* and *ETR2* show negative values or values larger than one (e.g., Adhikari, Derashid, & Zhang, 2006; Dyreng, Hanlon, & Maydew, 2008; Gupta & Newberry, 1997; Wu, Wu, Zhou, & Wu, 2012)[4]; and (4) observations with missing values. Finally, a sample of 7651 firm-year observations is employed over the period 2005–2012. The sample selection process is shown in Table 3.2.

Because the bootstrap method is sensitive to extreme values (Ette & Onyiah, 2002), this chapter winsorizes data at the 2.5% level to reduce the effect of outliers (Zhang, Farrell, & Brown, 2008). All estimations were done using the AMOS Version 21. Table 3.3 shows the correlation coefficients between variables.

[2] The CSMAR database is developed by Shenzhen GTA Information Technology Corporation Limited. Co., Ltd., and designed by the China Accounting and Finance Research Centre of the Hong Kong Polytechnic University.

[3] All stocks labeled ST have seen their business in the red for two consecutive years representing the firms with financial problem or other abnormal conditions, which are technically on the brink of delisting. ST or Special Treatment shares and the original idea behind this classification is that it would act as a warning to investors.

[4] To make the ETRs more interpretable, the study winsorized the ETRs at 0 and 1. Specifically, the study excluded the firms with negative corporate income tax expenses or with so high corporate income tax expenses exceed pre-tax income, because they would lead to non-meaningful ETR and confounding effects.

Table 3.2 Sample selection steps

Non-financial China's A-share listed companies	Total sample
Initial observations	19,184
Less: observations with ETRs[a] less than 0 or more than 1	17,330
Less: ETRs with missing value	10,183
Less: MV[b] variables with missing value	8556
Less: GP[c] variables with missing value	7653
Less: PP[d] variables with missing value	7651
Number of observations in the final analysis	7651

[a]ETRs include ETR1 and ETR2
[b]MV, latent variable of Market value performance, including P/B ratio, Tobin's Q and MCI
[c]GP, latent variable of Growth performance, including sales growth, net income growth, and sales income growth
[d]PP, latent variable of Profitability performance, including ROA, ROS, ROIC
Source Prepared by authors

Statistical Modeling

Structural equation modeling (SEM) is used in this chapter for hypothesis testing for three reasons. Firstly, SEM is suited to examine causal relationships between corporate tax management and firm performance by looking at three aspects of firm financial performance. Secondly, the chapter uses 14 observed variables in which are embedded four latent variables that traditional multivariate techniques are not good in handling (Byrne, 2009). Thirdly, SEM is the best statistical technique available to test for mediation effects (Anderson & Gerbing, 1992; Baron & Kenny, 1986).

The SEM consists of the measurement model and the structural model. Firstly, tests of the measurement model are undertaken first so that it is not affected by possible interactions between the models. Confirmatory factor analysis (CFA) are then conducted on the full measurement model to examine model fit. The structural model is then used to estimate the causal relationships among the four latent constructs.

Where the data was found to follow a multivariate non-normal distribution, the bootstrap (Preacher & Hayes, 2008) and Mackinnon PRODCLIN2 methods (MacKinnon, Fritz, Williams, & Lockwood, 2007) were used in the estimation and analyses. The chi-square (χ^2) is used as the first model fit index. Where χ^2 is found to be heavily influenced by sample size, other goodness-of-fit indices were used (Byrne, 2009; Black, Babin, & Anderson, 2009; MacCallum & Austin, 2000). This chapter also deploys

Table 3.3 Correlation

	ETR1_neg	ETR2_neg	NIG	SALG	SIG	ROA	ROIC	ROS	TobinQ	MCI	PB
ETR1_neg	1										
ETR2_neg	0.773***	1									
NIG	0.102***	0.092***	1								
SALG	0.044***	0.024**	0.394***	1							
SIG	0.046***	0.062***	0.823***	0.405***	1						
ROA	0.277***	0.297***	0.238***	0.196***	0.192***	1					
ROIC	0.162***	0.173***	0.163***	0.172***	0.122***	0.709***	1				
ROS	0.231***	0.244***	0.147***	0.064***	0.109***	0.627***	0.498***	1			
TobinQ	0.127***	0.119***	0.135***	0.052***	0.132***	0.420***	0.334***	0.231***	1		
MCI	0.027**	0.018	0.307***	0.211***	0.303***	0.174***	0.114***	0.100***	0.481***	1	
PB	0.058***	0.041***	0.213***	0.170***	0.203***	0.364***	0.317***	0.178***	0.772***	0.579***	1

Note *, **, and *** indicate statistical significance at the 10, 5, and 1% levels, respectively
All variables are defined in Table 3.1
Source Computed by authors

several other model fit indices, which include the root mean square error of approximation (RMSEA), root mean square residual (RMR), goodness of fit index (GFI), adjusted goodness of fit index (AGFI), comparative fit index (CFI), and, normed fit index (NFI). In a model with good fit, the GFI, CFI, AGFI, and NFI should be above 0.9 (Byrne, 2009; Black, Babin, & Anderson, 2009). The RMSEA and RMR should be less than 0.08 for it to be acceptable (Hu & Bentler, 1998).

Empirical Findings and Analysis

This section shows the goodness-of-fit for both the models, that is, the measurement model and structural model. In addition, we analyze the results of the hypothesized relationships between latent constructs.

Measurement Model

Table 3.4 shows model fit indices for the overall measurement model, which indicate that the model is acceptable since all of them have statistically significant relationships with their factors (Black, Babin, & Anderson, 2009).

Composite reliability (CR) and average variance extracted (AVE) measures were used to measure reliability. As shown in Table 3.5, the indicators are internally consistent because the composite reliability scores for all the constructs exceeded the recommended value of 0.70 (O'Rourke & Hatcher, 2013). Reliability is further confirmed with the AVE results of the constructs, which exceeded the desired 0.5 (Fornell & Larcker, 1981). To assess construct validity, convergent validity is assessed by determining whether each indicator's estimated pattern coefficient on its posited underlying construct factor in the measurement

Table 3.4 Summary of model fit indices for CFA model

Model	χ^2	df	GFI	AGFI	CFI	NFI	RMSEA	RMR
CFA	1790	38	0.961	0.933	0.957	0.956	0.078	0.024

Note 5000 bootstrap samples (Dechow, Sloan, and Sweeney 1995)
RMSEA—Root-mean-square error of approximation; RMR—Root-mean-square residual; GFI—Good-of-fit index; AGFI—Adjusted goodness of fit index; NFI—Normed fit index; CFI—Comparative fit index
Source Computed by authors

Table 3.5 Confirmatory factor model

Constructs and variables	Factor loadings	Composite reliability (C.R)[a]	Average variance extracted (AVE)[b]
Tax avoidance		0.873	0.776
ETR1 (ETR1_neg)	0.85		
ETR2 (ETR2_neg)	0.92		
Market value performance		0.840	0.643
Market capitalization improvement (MCI)	0.61		
Price to book ratio (PB)	0.94		
Tobin's Q (TobinQ)	0.83		
Profitability performance		0.834	0.632
ROA	0.96		
ROIC	0.74		
ROS	0.65		
Growth performance		0.814	0.613
Sales revenue growth (SALG)	0.44		
Net income growth (NIG)	0.91		
Sales income growth (SIG)	0.90		

Note 5000 bootstrap samples
[a]$CR = (\Sigma Standardized\ loadings)^2 / [(\Sigma Standardized\ loadings)^2 + \Sigma \varepsilon_j]$
[b]$AVE = \Sigma(Standardized\ loadings^2) / [\Sigma(Standardized\ loadings^2) + \Sigma \varepsilon_j]$, where ε_j is the measurement error
Source Computed by authors

Table 3.6 Discriminant validity matrix

	Tax avoidance	Growth	Profitability	Market value
Tax avoidance	**0.776**	0.009	0.112	0.006
Growth		**0.613**	0.062	0.064
Profitability			**0.632**	0.179
Market value				**0.643**

Note The AVE for the respective constructs are shown in bold
Source Computed by authors

model is significant (Anderson & Gerbing, 1988; Marsh & Grayson, 1995). Table 3.5 shows that convergent validity is assured since all factor loadings for the items are greater than 0.4 and are statistically significant ($p < 0.001$) (see Cabrera-Nguyen, 2010). Also, for discriminant validity, the average variance extracted for each construct must be greater than the squared correlations between the construct and other constructs in the model (Nusair & Hua, 2010). Table 3.6 shows that the squared correlations are lower than their corresponding AVE for the latent variables. Overall, therefore, the measurement model is shown to be valid and acceptable.

Structural Model

The overall structural model fit indices are shown in Table 3.7. All the indices show acceptable fits (Black, Babin, & Anderson, 2009), indicating that the model fits the data well. Since both models are shown to be valid and reliable, the path relationships among the constructs can now be analyzed.

Table 3.7 Structural equation model indices

Model	χ^2	GFI	AGFI	CFI	NFI	RMSEA	RMR
CFA	1790	0.961	0.933	0.957	0.956	0.078	0.024

Note 5000 bootstrap samples
RMSEA—Root-mean-square error of approximation; RMR—Root-mean-square residual; GFI—good-of-fit index; AGFI—Adjusted goodness of fit index; NFI—Normed fit index; CFI—Comparative fit index
Source Computed by authors

In the multiple-step multiple mediator model (Hayes, 2009), the sampling distributions of ab, cd, aed (Fig. 3.2) tend to be asymmetric, with nonzero skewness and kurtosis (Bollen & Stine, 1990; Hayes, 2009; Stone & Sobel, 1990). Using the bootstrapping method and Mackinnon PRODCLIN2, this chapter found the structural model's total, specific mediation, and direct effects to be statistically significant (Hayes, 2009; MacKinnon, Fritz, Williams, & Lockwood, 2007; Preacher & Hayes, 2008), which shows that partial mediation effects exists (see Table 3.8).[5]

The results in Table 3.8 show that the specific indirect effects of tax avoidance on firm value through profitability and growth are significantly

---

[5] For bootstrapping percentile and bias-corrected methods, and Mackinnon PRODCLIN2, if zero is not between the lower and upper bound, then the effect is nonzero with 95% confidence (Hayes, 2009). Percentile and bias-corrected methods were used to identify the existence of indirect effects. Then, Mackinnon PRODCLIN2 was used to identify and distinguish the specific indirect effects.

Table 3.8 Mediation effect of corporate tax management on market performance through profitability and growth performance

Variables	Point estimate	Product of coefficients		Bootstrapping						Mackinnon Prodclin2. 95% CI	
				Bias-corrected 95% CI		Percentile 95% CI					
		SE	Z	Lower	Upper	Lower	Upper			Lower	Upper
Total effect	0.567	0.096	5.906	0.380	0.757	0.375	0.752			0.252	0.606
Total direct effect	−0.520	0.094	−5.536	−0.709	−0.340	−0.709	−0.341			−0.697	−0.344
Total indirect effect	1.088	0.061	17.849	0.970	1.211	0.970	1.211				
Specific indirect effects											
ab	0.108									0.076	0.143
cd	0.918									0.824	1.017
ae	0.061	0.001	61.018	0.005	0.010	0.005	0.010			0.005	0.010
ed		0.006	0.000	0.059	0.081	0.059	0.081			0.059	0.079

Note 5000 bootstrap sample
The results based on unstandardized parameter estimates. CI—Confidence Interval
Source Calculated by authors

Table 3.9 Hypotheses' standardized regression paths

Hypotheses	Regression paths coefficients	Standard path	Results
H3.1	Tax avoidance → Market value	−0.073	Support
H3.2a	Tax avoidance → Growth → Market value	0.015	Support
H3.2b	Tax avoidance → Profitability → Market value	0.128	Support
H3.3	Tax avoidance → Growth → Profitability → Market value	0.009	Support

Note All regression parts are significant at 1% level
Source Computed by authors

different from zero.[6] Thus, all three mediation hypotheses (H3.2a, H3.2b, and H3.3) are supported. Specifically, the total indirect effect through the three specific mediation paths of *ab*, *cd*, and *aed* (shown in Table 3.8), has a point estimate (total effect minus direct effect) of 1.088 with a nonzero value between lower and upper bound in 95% BC and Percentile bootstrap CI. In addition, the specific indirect effect through profitability (point estimate = 0.918, viz, path *cd* in Table 3.8, tax management → profitability → market value) is larger than that through growth (point estimate = 0.108, viz, path *ab* in Table 3.8, tax management → growth → market value) and growth * profitability (point estimate = 0.061, viz., path *aed* in Table 3.8, tax management → growth → profitability → market value). Thus, it is clear that profitability and growth are mediators for tax avoidance's impact on firm value.

Overall, the results of the SEM model are summarized in Table 3.9, which indicate that firms that avoid taxes affect their market value both directly and indirectly, the latter through increasing firm's profitability and growth. The indirect relationship between tax avoidance and market value through growth and then profitability (*aed*) (see Fig. 3.1) is positive, which indicates that good growth performance can raise market power to enhance profits and cash generation. The evidence from China shows that corporate tax management has not produced the undesired consequence of negatively impacting on growth and profitability.

---

[6] In Table 3.8, because zero is not contained in the interval between lower and upper bound, the specific indirect effects can be distinguished in terms of magnitude.

SUMMARY

Tax reforms have been a major pillar of overall economic reforms in most countries, which seek to balancing the budget. China is no exception. This chapter analyzed the impact of corporate tax management on firm performance in China. Using data on A-share (main market) public-listed companies, it analyzed how corporate tax management impacts market value both directly and through the mediators of profitability and growth. An assessment of corporate tax management is critical also because, if it is unscrupulously pursued, will deny government's revenue that will be necessary to finance government expenditure. Nevertheless, the results offer three important findings that offer important implications for tax governance in China specifically, and the rest of the world generally.

Firstly, the results reveal that corporate behavior in China differs from those found in most countries. Besides, existing studies show no direct impact of corporate tax management on firm value (Desai & Dharmapala, 2009a, b). In contrast, our results show a significant and positive relationship that is made up of direct (negative) and indirect (positive) effects. Secondly, the similarities between China and market economies suggest that China's corporate reforms have moved the Chinese corporate environment closer to that of frontier of market economies.

Thirdly, the results also show the specific circumstances facing China's. The significant negative direct relationship between tax management and market value in China's listed firms may also suggest the workings of the agency cost theory of tax avoidance and its consequences on managerial rent extraction. We did not examine whether increased profitability and growth were bereft of managerial rents. China's still evolving market reforms show that there are imperfections that require addressing through legal and other provisions to prevent unproductive managerial rent extraction. Nonetheless, the positive indirect relationships between tax management and market value through the mediating role of firm profitability and growth performance suggest that tax management could be continued but they need to be bolstered by legal regulations to reduce the possible negative consequences from managerial rent-seeking.

The above results were obtained using the SEM approach, which offers a more robust set of results than past studies that were based on traditional regression equations. Also, past studies have not investigated the impact of after-tax cash from corporate tax management activities on firm value. Hence, this chapter provides direct evidence on how tax trimming can help maximize firm performance.

What implications can we draw from the findings? Firstly, China's corporate reforms applied to enterprises differ from, though it is converging toward the structure of market economies. The question arises as to how urgent and whether it is necessary for China's corporate tax system to be transformed to the latter, as has been repeatedly advised. Secondly, and more specifically, these findings leave open the question of the relevance of fully market-oriented corporate tax management practices when state-ownership, as well as state governance structures are an important element of corporate operations in China. In China, state ownership is an important firm characteristic that impacts on firms' financial decisions, which requires further research to track the consequences of enterprise reforms. Thirdly, what types of policies related to critical aspects, such as governance, tax, and regulatory that can be considered to limit the abuses that can follow corporate tax management. Given that tax avoidance affects directly as well as indirectly firm value, it is not sufficient to put in place policies that only directly address tax avoidance issues.

REFERENCES

Abdolmohammadi, M. J. (2005). Intellectual capital disclosure and market capitalization. *Journal of Intellectual Capital, 6*(3), 397–416. https://doi.org/10.1108/14691930510611139.

Adhikari, A., Derashid, C., & Zhang, H. (2006). Public policy, political connections, and effective tax rates: Longitudinal evidence from Malaysia. *Journal of Accounting and Public Policy, 25*(5), 574–595. https://doi.org/10.1016/j.jaccpubpol.2006.07.001.

Anderson, J. C., & Gerbing, D. W. (1988). Structural equation modeling in practice: A review and recommended two-step approach. *Psychological Bulletin, 103*(3), 411–423. https://doi.org/10.1037/0033-2909.103.3.411.

Anderson, J. C., & Gerbing, D. W. (1992). Assumptions and comparative strengths of the two-step approach. *Sociological Methods and Research, 20*(3), 321–333.

Anthony, J. H., & Ramesh, K. (1992). Association between accounting performance measures and stock prices. *Journal of Accounting and Economics, 15*(2), 203–227. https://doi.org/10.1016/0165-4101(92)90018-W.

Badertscher, B. A., Katz, S. P., & Rego, S. O. (2013). The separation of ownership and control and corporate tax avoidance. *Journal of Accounting*

and *Economics*, *56*(2–3), 228–250. https://doi.org/10.1016/j.jacceco.
2013.08.005.
Baron, R. M., & Kenny, D. A. (1986). The moderator-mediator variable distinction in social psychological research: Conceptual, strategic, and statistical considerations. *Journal of Personality and Social Psychology*, *51*(6), 1173–1182. https://doi.org/10.1037/0022-3514.51.6.1173.
Bollen, K. A., & Stine, R. (1990). Direct and indirect effects: Classical and bootstrap estimates of variability. *Sociological Methodology*, *20*, 115–140. https://doi.org/10.2307/271084.
Brealey, R. A., & Myers, S. C. (2000). *Principles of corporate finance* (6th ed.). Boston: McGraw-Hill.
Brush, T. H., Bromiley, P., & Hendrickx, M. (2000). The free cash flow hypothesis for sales growth and firm performance. *Strategic Management Journal*, *21*(4), 455–472. https://doi.org/10.1002/(SICI)1097-0266(200004)21: 4<455:AID-SMJ83>3.0.CO;2-P.
Byrne, B. M. (2009). *Structural equation modeling with AMOS: Basic concepts, applications, and programming* (2nd ed.). New York and London: Routledge.
Cable, J. R., & Mueller, D. C. (2008). Testing for persistence of profits' differences across firms. *International Journal of the Economics of Business*, *15*(2), 201–228. https://doi.org/10.1080/13571510802134353.
Cabrera-Nguyen, P. (2010). Author guidelines for reporting scale development and validation results in the Journal of the Society for Social Work and Research. *Journal of the Society for Social Work and Research*, *1*(2), 99–103.
Chen, K.-P., & Chu, C. Y. C. (2005). Internal control versus external manipulation: A model of corporate income tax evasion. *The RAND Journal of Economics*, *36*(1), 151–164.
Chen, X., Hu, N., Wang, X., & Tang, X. (2014). Tax avoidance and firm value: Evidence from China. *Nankai Business Review International*, *5*(1), 25–42. https://doi.org/10.1108/NBRI-10-2013-0037.
Claessens, S., & Fan, J. P. H. (2002). Corporate governance in Asia: A survey. *International Review of Finance*, *3*(2), 71–103. https://doi.org/10.1111/1468-2443.00034.
Crocker, K. J., & Slemrod, J. (2005). Corporate tax evasion with agency costs. *Journal of Public Economics*, *89*(9), 1593–1610. https://doi.org/10.1016/j.jpubeco.2004.08.003.
Damodaran, A. (2007). *Return on Capital (ROC), Return on Invested Capital (ROIC) and Return on Equity (ROE): Measurement and implications* (Working Paper). New York: University-Stern School of Business. http://ssrn.com/abstract=1105499.
Dechow, P. M., Sloan, R. G., & Sweeney, A. P. (1995). Detecting earnings management. *The Accounting Review*, *70*(2), 193–225.

Delen, D., Kuzey, C., & Uyar, A. (2013). Measuring firm performance using financial ratios: A decision tree approach. *Expert Systems with Applications*, *40*(10), 3970–3983. https://doi.org/10.1016/j.eswa.2013.01.012.

Desai, M. A., & Dharmapala, D. (2006). Corporate tax avoidance and high-powered incentives. *Journal of Financial Economics*, *79*(1), 145–179.

Desai, M. A., & Dharmapala, D. (2009a). Corporate tax avoidance and firm value. *The Review of Economics and Statistics*, *91*(3), 537–546.

Desai, M. A., & Dharmapala, D. (2009b). Earnings management, corporate tax shelters, and book-tax alignment. *National Tax Journal*, *62*(1), 169–186.

Desai, M. A., Dyck, A., & Zingales, L. (2007). Theft and taxes. *Journal of Financial Economics*, *84*(3), 591–623. https://doi.org/10.1016/j.jfineco.2006.05.005.

Durnev, A., & Kim, E. H. (2005). To steal or not to steal: Firm attributes, legal environment, and valuation. *The Journal of Finance*, *60*(3), 1461–1493. https://doi.org/10.1111/j.1540-6261.2005.00767.x.

Dyreng, S. D., Hanlon, M., & Maydew, E. L. (2008). Long-run corporate tax avoidance. *Accounting Review*, *83*(1), 61–82. https://doi.org/10.2308/accr.2008.83.1.61.

Erle, B. (2008). Tax risk management and board responsibility. In W. Schön (Ed.), *Tax and corporate governance* (pp. 205–220). Berlin and Heidelberg: Springer. https://doi.org/10.1007/978-3-540-77276-7_15.

Ette, E. I., & Onyiah, L. C. (2002). Estimating inestimable standard errors in population pharmacokinetic studies: The bootstrap with winsorization. *European Journal of Drug Metabolism and Pharmacokinetics*, *27*(3), 213–224. https://doi.org/10.1007/BF03190460.

Fama, E. F., & French, K. R. (1998). Taxes, financing decisions, and firm value. *The Journal of Finance*, *53*(3), 819–843. https://doi.org/10.1111/0022-1082.00036.

Firth, M., Gong, S. X., & Shan, L. (2013). Cost of government and firm value. *Journal of Corporate Finance*, *21*, 136–152. https://doi.org/10.1016/j.jcorpfin.2013.01.008.

Fornell, C., & Larcker, D. F. (1981). Evaluating structural equation models with unobservable variables and measurement error. *Journal of Marketing Research*, *18*(1), 39–50. https://doi.org/10.2307/3151312.

Gupta, S., & Newberry, K. (1997). Determinants of the variability in corporate effective tax rates: Evidence from longitudinal data. *Journal of Accounting and Public Policy*, *16*(1), 1–34. https://doi.org/10.1016/S0278-4254(96)00055-5.

Hair, J. F., Jr., Black, W. C., Babin, B. J., & Anderson, R. E. (2009). *Multivariate data analysis* (7th ed.). London: Pearson.

Hanlon, M., & Heitzman, S. (2010). A review of tax research. *Journal of Accounting and Economics*, *50*(2), 127–178. https://doi.org/10.1016/j.jacceco.2010.09.002.

Hanlon, M., & Slemrod, J. (2009). What does tax aggressiveness signal? Evidence from stock price reactions to news about tax shelter involvement. *Journal of Public Economics, 93*(1–2), 126–141. https://doi.org/10.1016/j.jpubeco.2008.09.004.

Harford, J., Mansi, S. A., & Maxwell, W. F. (2012). Corporate governance and firm cash holdings in the U.S. In S. Boubaker, B. D. Nguyen, & D. K. Nguyen (Eds.), *Corporate governance: Recent developments and new trends* (pp. 107–138). Berlin and Heidelberg: Springer. https://doi.org/10.1007/978-3-642-31579-4_5.

Hayes, A. F. (2009). Beyond Baron and Kenny: Statistical mediation analysis in the new millennium. *Communication Monographs, 76*(4), 408–420. https://doi.org/10.1080/03637750903310360.

Hu, L.-T., & Bentler, P. M. (1998). Fit indices in covariance structure modeling: Sensitivity to underparameterized model misspecification. *Psychological Methods, 3*(4), 424–453. https://doi.org/10.1037/1082-989X.3.4.424.

Jang, S., & Park, K. (2011). Inter-relationship between firm growth and profitability. *International Journal of Hospitality Management, 30*(4), 1027–1035. https://doi.org/10.1016/j.ijhm.2011.03.009.

Lee, B. B., Dobiyanski, A., & Minton, S. (2015). Theories and empirical proxies for corporate tax avoidance. *The Journal of Applied Business and Economics, 17*(3), 21–34.

MacCallum, R. C., & Austin, J. T. (2000). Applications of structural equation modeling in psychological research. *Annual Review of Psychology, 51*(1), 201–226.

MacKinnon, D. P., Fritz, M. S., Williams, J., & Lockwood, C. M. (2007). Distribution of the product confidence limits for the indirect effect: Program PRODCLIN. *Behavior Research Methods, 39*(3), 384–389. https://doi.org/10.3758/bf03193007.

Marsh, H. W., & Grayson, D. (1995). Latent variable models of multitrait-multimethod data. In R. H. Hoyle (Ed.), *Structural equation modeling: Concepts, issues, and applications* (pp. 177–198). Thousand Oaks, CA: Sage.

Miller, C. C., Washburn, N. T., & Glick, W. H. (2013). Perspective—The myth of firm performance. *Organization Science, 24*(3), 948–964. https://doi.org/10.1287/orsc.1120.0762.

Montgomery, C. A., Thomas, A. R., & Kamath, R. (1984). Divestiture, market valuation, and strategy. *Academy of Management Journal, 27*(4), 830–840. https://doi.org/10.2307/255881.

Naceur, S. B., & Goaied, M. (2002). The relationship between dividend policy, financial structure, profitability and firm value. *Applied Financial Economics, 12*(12), 843–849. https://doi.org/10.1080/09603100110049457.

Nusair, K., & Hua, N. (2010). Comparative assessment of structural equation modeling and multiple regression research methodologies: E-commerce context. *Tourism Management, 31*(3), 314–324. https://doi.org/10.1016/j.tourman.2009.03.010.

O'Rourke, N., & Hatcher, L. (2013). *A step-by-step approach to using SAS for factor analysis and structural equation modeling* (2nd ed.). Cary, NC: SAS Institute.

Peng, M. W., & Luo, Y. (2000). Managerial ties and firm performance in a transition economy: The nature of a micro-macro link. *Academy of Management Journal*, 43(3), 486–501. https://doi.org/10.2307/1556406.

Peni, E., & Vähämaa, S. (2012). Did good corporate governance improve bank performance during the financial crisis? *Journal of Financial Services Research*, 41(1), 19–35. https://doi.org/10.1007/s10693-011-0108-9.

Piotroski, J. D., Wong, T. J., & Zhang, T. (2015). Political incentives to suppress negative information: Evidence from Chinese listed firms. *Journal of Accounting Research*, 53(2), 405–459. https://doi.org/10.1111/1475-679X.12071.

Preacher, K. J., & Hayes, A. F. (2008). Asymptotic and resampling strategies for assessing and comparing indirect effects in multiple mediator models. *Behavior Research Methods*, 40(3), 879–891. https://doi.org/10.3758/brm.40.3.879.

Rasiah, R., & Thangiah, G. (2017). Government policies, regional trading agreements and the economic performance of local electronics component producing SMEs in Malaysia. *Journal of Southeast Asian Economies*, 34(2), 302–321.

Richardson, G., Wang, B., & Zhang, X. (2016). Ownership structure and corporate tax avoidance: Evidence from publicly listed private firms in China. *Journal of Contemporary Accounting & Economics*, 12(2), 141–158. https://doi.org/10.1016/j.jcae.2016.06.003.

Robinson, J. R., Sikes, S. A., & Weaver, C. D. (2010). Performance measurement of corporate tax departments. *The Accounting Review*, 85(3), 1035–1064. https://doi.org/10.2308/accr.2010.85.3.1035.

Rowe, W. G., & Morrow, J. L. (1999). A note on the dimensionality of the firm financial performance construct using accounting, market, and subjective measures. *Canadian Journal of Administrative Sciences*, 16(1), 58–71. https://doi.org/10.1111/j.1936-4490.1999.tb00188.x.

Santos, J. B., & Brito, L. A. L. (2012). Toward a subjective measurement model for firm performance. *BAR-Brazilian Administration Review*, 9(SPE), 95–117. http://dx.doi.org/10.1590/S1807-76922012000500007.

Serrasqueiro, Z. (2009). Growth and profitability in Portuguese companies: A dynamic panel data approach. *Amfiteatru Economic*, 11(26), 565–573.

Sikka, P. (2010). Smoke and mirrors: Corporate social responsibility and tax avoidance. *Accounting Forum*, 34(3–4), 153–168. https://doi.org/10.1016/j.accfor.2010.05.002.

Stone, C. A., & Sobel, M. E. (1990). The robustness of estimates of total indirect effects in covariance structure models estimated by maximum. *Psychometrika*, 55(2), 337–352. https://doi.org/10.1007/BF02295291.

Swenson, C. (1999). Increasing stock market value by reducing effective tax rates. *Tax Notes, 83,* 1503–1505.

Varaiya, N., Kerin, R. A., & Weeks, D. (1987). The relationship between growth, profitability, and firm value. *Strategic Management Journal, 8*(5), 487–497. https://doi.org/10.1002/smj.4250080507.

Wang, Y., & You, J. (2012). Corruption and firm growth: Evidence from China. *China Economic Review, 23*(2), 415–433. https://doi.org/10.1016/j.chieco.2012.03.003.

Whetten, D. A. (1987). Organizational growth and decline processes. *Annual Review of Sociology, 13,* 335–358. https://doi.org/10.1146/annurev.so.13.080187.002003.

Wu, L., Wang, Y., Luo, W., & Gillis, P. (2012a). State ownership, tax status and size effect of effective tax rate in China. *Accounting and Business Research, 42*(2), 97–114. https://doi.org/10.1080/00014788.2012.628208.

Wu, W., Wu, C., Zhou, C., & Wu, J. (2012b). Political connections, tax benefits and firm performance: Evidence from China. *Journal of Accounting and Public Policy, 31*(3), 277–300. https://doi.org/10.1016/j.jaccpubpol.2011.10.005.

Yen, S.-W. (2005). Growth opportunities and governance structure choices. Available at SSRN. http://dx.doi.org/10.2139/ssrn.687003.

Yu, M. (2013). State ownership and firm performance: Empirical evidence from Chinese listed companies. *China Journal of Accounting Research, 6*(2), 75–87. https://doi.org/10.1016/j.cjar.2013.03.003.

Zhang, Y., Farrell, K. A., & Brown, T. A. (2008). Ex-dividend day price and volume: The case of 2003 dividend tax cut. *National Tax Journal, 61*(1), 105–127.

CHAPTER 4

Economic Reforms and Market Outcomes over Time

INTRODUCTION

Taxation is a significant cost borne by firms, which affects firms' decision-making behavior regarding the available choices on the magnitude and structure of output, disposal of net profit, direction of capital investment, among many other things. Thus, reducing the corporate tax burden has become a powerful motivational force in corporate conduct. Indeed, corporate tax management has emerged as an important financial strategy desired by shareholders to improve firm value. Expert accountants are hired by corporations for this purpose. However, following a series of high-profile corporate accounting scandals, such as Enron, Amazon, and Apple, where managers were accused of using complex tax management as a mask to seek unproductive rentier interests at the expense of the interests of shareholders in addition to causing immense loss of tax revenue to the government. Hence, the extreme consequences of manipulative tax management have aroused much attention by investors, governments, and researchers. Shareholders and governments in particular have consequently raised the bar for good corporate governance practices.

In a traditional theoretical framework, the main purpose of doing corporate business is to achieve the maximization of shareholders' value over the long term. Managers, who are employed to act on behalf of shareholders, are required to have a long-term horizon that requires a strong focus on planning. However, in reality this norm is sometimes compromised owing to both information asymmetry and greed. Firstly, because of the effective separation between managers who run the firms, and shareholders who own the firms' asymmetric information between the two leaves the space for the former to exploit the situation. Managers responsible for corporate shareholders are always better and earlier informed than shareholders who meet at most a few times a year. Also, between the two groups, managers are the ones exposed to the actual running of the firms compared to the shareholders. At the same time, managers face many powerful short-term incentives and pressures, such as employment contracts and remuneration that attract a focus on short-term profitability and stock prices. Hence, managers may conceal firms' negative outcomes to realize their personal interests. For example, the bonuses and employment contracts of managers are generally more tied to firms' current performance rather than long-term performance, and even if the managers choose projects that yield little at present but high returns in future, they may not only not be rewarded in profit-sharing schemes but actually penalized for failure to produce immediate returns.

Besides, managers are often subject to contract termination, which often drives even the clean-headed managers to seek short-term benefits. Thus, instead of seeking long-term returns, short-term goals have become the focus of attention of most managers. Second, recent research reveals that because of incomplete information and fierce competition, shareholders of modern public listed enterprises are more like share traders shifting their focus from long toward a short time horizon, such as quarterly, half yearly, or annual profit. And top executives may set a "tone at the top" stressing short-term cost minimization and profit maximization. Hence, managerial myopia is becoming a pervasive and dominant concern of modern corporations. Unlike reducing operating costs, tax saving does not cause direct adverse consequences on a firm's daily operation. More importantly, the complex and opaque nature of tax management also offers opportunities to managers and short-sighted investors for earnings manipulation and cover up corporate real operating performance to boost short-term stock price, which may cause corporate shares to be mispriced. The resulting mispricing would further facilitate corporate over-investment and maintain previous inefficient projects that will discount corporate future outcomes and raise future unsustainable. Once the true situations are exposed to the stock market some time in future, however, the firm's stock price will crash.

China's case makes for even more challenges. In contrast to developed countries with a robust tax system, China's situation differs from that of most other countries in that reforms are still taking place after years of state control, the tax system is still in a state of transition. Despite this, the coverage of the present system is still not comprehensive and has many loopholes thereby offering opportunities to corporations to exploit. In addition, the opaque nature of the Chinese stock market (Piotroski, Wong, & Zhang, 2015) provides further space for managers to utilize tax management as a medium for earnings manipulation and resource diversion. Many manipulative tax management activities in China have since the turn of the millennium aroused scrutiny at home and abroad, for example, *Gujing* Distillery Company (*gujing gongjiu*).

China represents a case worthy of study also because its development model of state-led growth is different from that of South Korea and Taiwan as it has many state-owned/controlled enterprises (SOEs) in business (Amsden, 1989; Wade, 1990). In addition, central planning still sets the direction for political governance in the country (Zhang & Rasiah, 2015). As instruments of the government, SOEs have long been criticized by Western scholars to have been extractive, and that would stunt further growth in the country (see, for example, Acemoglu & Robinson, 2012). At the same time, there is also evidence of state enterprise efficiency and profitability (Li & Cheong, 2019). In the context of this study, China's SOEs executives may be motivated to take advantage of preferential treatment from the government to avoid taxes and pursue self-interests, such as political career advancement and cash compensations.

Government ownership of SOEs in China is categorized by several government tiers, which are central, provincial, and municipal (includes prefectural city- and county-level) SOEs (Zhang & Rasiah, 2015). Central SOEs (*yangqi*) are generally large and complex organizations in "pillar" (key or strategic) industries with support from well-resourced central administration and are subject to strict auditing. SOEs are ultimately controlled by the central government and their top executives normally have high administrative ranks, which could motivate executives to conceal adverse corporate outcomes to protect their political careers. Provincial SOEs are second-tier SOEs controlled by provincial governments,[1] where both the SOEs' executives and government officials

---

[1] There are 31 provinces in the mainland China, which includes 22 provinces, 5 autonomous regions (Tibet autonomous Region, Xinjiang Uygur Autonomous Region, Guangxi Zhuang autonomous region, Inner Mongolia autonomous region, Ningxia Hui Autonomous Region), and 4 directly administered municipalities (Beijing, Tianjin, Shanghai, and Chongqing).

have strong political incentives because of opportunities that could be appropriated to leapfrog political ranks from local to central positions. In contrast, municipal SOEs are mostly far away from central government control, and the executives generally have low or even no political rank, as well as earn low salaries, thus providing the temptation for these executives to use their political connection and/or to collude with local government officials to maximize their self-interests through tax management activities.

Considering the above, this chapter attempts to answer the second research question of this book, that is, what is the likelihood of extreme market outcomes resulting from corporate tax management among China's listed enterprises, and how does government ownership affect these extreme outcomes? Extreme outcomes refer to stock market price crashes. Accordingly, we seek answers for the following three sub-questions: First, can corporate tax management be associated with lower crash risks in the current year and higher crash risks in the future? Second, do different levels of state ownership affect the relationship between corporate tax management and stock price crash differently? And third, can investing in listed state-owned/controlled enterprises be considered for investors who are risk averse?

THE CHINA CONTEXT

The context that is important here relates to the nature of state enterprises that has resulted from rounds of enterprise reform. As with non-state enterprises, these reforms have also given impetus to proactive tax management.

Economic Reforms

State-owned enterprises (SOEs) were launched in China initially as ideological organizations established as work units (*gongzuo danwei*) to support social and political rather than economic objectives (Leung & Cheng, 2013). Managers appointed by the government as SOEs' staff were seen as owning an "iron rice bowl" (*tiefanwan*) with cradle-to-grave benefits (Hua, Miesing, & Li, 2006). Hence, SOEs were viewed as highly inefficient. At the same time, there was virtually no incentive to engage in any form of tax management.

However, following the introduction of economic reforms in 1978, as with China in general, SOEs have undergone considerable changes (Zhang & Rasiah, 2015). Enterprise reform in China took place step by step since 1978, revealing a process of corporatization and privatization with a view to raise funds for expansion and to increase revenue for the government. During the first two stages, non-state firms were allowed to operate, and their dynamic growth increased competitive pressure on the SOEs and the government bureaucrats managing them. This led to the managers of SOEs being granted with more autonomy and incentives to improve their performance (Kang & Kim, 2012). Meanwhile, the government replaced the old command structure of government revenue transfer with a market-oriented system of taxation.

Company Law was promulgated in December 1993 to provide the legal framework for transforming and corporatizing traditional wholly SOEs into modern corporations with properly defined property rights. To focus on strategic enterprises, the SOE reform strategy turned to "Keeping the large and letting go the small approach" (*zhuadafangxiao*). Under this policy, one thousand large state enterprises were selected for the government to maintain controlling rights to shape the core of China's modern enterprise system from when these enterprises started to introduce a modern corporate structure and adopt professional management practices. The remaining 300 thousand small and medium SOEs were privatized or closed through leases, mergers, sales, and liquidation. The State-owned Assets Supervision and Administration Commission of the State Council (SASAC) was then established in June 2003 to oversee all SOEs. Corresponding changes in employee management policies have taken place. A labor contract system[2] was introduced, while managers'

---

[2] In 2003, "Interim Regulations on Supervision and Management of State-owned Assets of Enterprises" are promulgated by the China State Council Article and states that "the state-owned assets supervision and administration authority shall establish a system for evaluating the performance of the responsible persons of enterprises, sign performance contracts with the responsible persons of enterprises appointed by it, and conduct annual and office-term evaluation of the responsible persons according to the performance contract". And in 2009, the government issued the regulations on top managers' pay of state enterprises. The cash compensation of a top manager in an SOE includes three parts: a bases salary, a performance-based bonus, and an incentive income, while the performance-based bonus is flexible and varying based on the firm performance.

wages and salaries were tied to enterprises' profitability, depending on the extent to which the SOEs achieved their key performance targets like sales and profit targets. Reforms allowed SOEs to retain a large part of firm profits and much more autonomy than before. While SOEs have since been expected to be more profitable and efficient, it also opened the gates for the emergence of conflict of interests in the top executives and shareholders.

The evolving marketization of the SOEs also experienced the potential for executives to pursue their personal interests, which has raised problems on several occasions. For example, the Accounting Information Quality Inspection Announcement (No. 21) of China's Ministry of Finance (2009) revealed that some state-owned enterprises have different degrees of problems associated with tax payment practices and performance evaluation standards, and access to bank loans. The report alleged that the *Changling* branch of Sinopec's asset management firm in Jilin Province offered its employees a total of 50.1 million yuan as bonus without approval. In addition, Sinopec also falsely stated 52.1 million yuan as income recorded in its books and 4.1 million yuan owner's equity, and other accounting irregularities, which resulted in failure to pay 11.8 million yuan in taxes in 2009. The report of the National Audit Office published of 15 central SOEs in 2011 stated that they falsified income and profit to the tune of 3.8 billion and 5.9 billion yuan respectively, while seven of them failed to pay 471.0 million yuan in taxes.

Literature Review and Hypotheses Development

Owing to the potential for abuse, serious concerns have remained about corporate tax management (Hanlon & Heitzman, 2010). Traditionally, efficient corporate tax management would be seen as a firm value-maximizing activity, but one that transfers the benefits from government back to enterprises (Hanlon & Heitzman, 2010). Modern corporate management emerged first to incorporate accountants to screen professionally the preparation of tax filings so that individuals (personal income tax) and corporations (corporate income tax) do not unnecessarily pay additional taxes.

It has since evolved to attract to two alternative views. On the one hand, tax management has evolved to incorporate more dimensions, thereby making more complex agency conflict between owners and managers than before. Managers can disguise complex tax avoiding transactions under the ostensible objective of alleviating firms' tax burden to take advantage of managerial opportunism and resource diversion (Desai & Dharmapala, 2006, 2009a, b). For example, Badertscher et al. (2013) find that managers can use tax management to engage in shirking and rent-extraction activities to pursue their self-interests against that of shareholders'.

On the other hand, especially involving modern listed enterprises, there is a clear gap between theory and practice. In theory, shareholders as the owners of enterprises should be concerned with enterprises' long-term interests and development. However, because of the information asymmetries and the prevalence of random events, investors cannot effectively predict long-term performance, which often turns them to engage in short-termism behavior, such as higher dividend payouts and share price (Kim, Kim, Mantecon, & Song, 2019; Pogach, 2018). Even managers are subject to unpredictable random events. Therefore, the performance of managers may be tied by shareholders through the board of directors to short-term performance targets, such as profits and share prices. Hence, the motivation is high for managers to seek incentives for short-term rather than long-term growth, which would cause serious consequences.

Extreme market outcomes resulting in stock price crashes has become a hot topic (Krugman, 2009; Stiglitz, 2010). Jin and Myers (2006) developed the "bad news hoarding" theory using empirical evidence to show that enterprises in an information opaque market are more likely to have a high risk of the stock price crash than otherwise. Specifically, the lack of information transparency gives managers a variety of "motivations" to strategically conceal firms' bad news for their short-term personal interests, such as to secure salary increments, career promotions. When these incentives disappear or the accumulated negative information breaches a certain threshold, the undisclosed negative information will suddenly breakout into the stock market, thereby causing a bearish run. Hutton, Marcus, and Tehranian (2009) and Kim, Li, and Li (2014) found a positive relationship between opaqueness of financial reports and future crash risk.

The complex and opaque characteristics of tax management offer tools and opportunities for managers to conceal firms' negative information for a certain period, which leads to the high probability of future stock price crash. Using US firm-level data, Kim, Li, and Zhang (2011) examined the effect of corporate tax avoidance on future crash risk. Their results show that tax avoidance is positively correlated with future crash risk, but this relationship can be avoided for firms with a strong external monitoring mechanism.

Whereas Abdul Wahab and Holland (2012), Badertscher, Katz, and Rego (2013), and Desai and Dharmapala (2009a, b) focused their research on the developed countries, Claessens and Fan (2002) documentation of corporate governance conditions in Asian countries where agency problems seem to be worse as they are characterized by low corporate transparency, strong rent-seeking conduct, relation-based transactions, and complex ownership and risky financial structures. In addition to concentrated ownership structures, weak legal protection, highly politicized institutional arrangements, rent-seeking behavior, and corruption, Piotroski and Wong (2012) found that China suffers from an opaque information environment and weak corporate transparency. Using Chinese data, Piotroski, Wong, and Zhang (2011) found that China's stock market has a significantly higher negative skewness in daily excess returns than the global average. The concealing of bad news may cause a greater frequency of stock market crashes in the future China than the rest of the world owing to the low information transparency levels. Hence, we test for the following two hypotheses: one, *corporate tax management is negatively associated with contemporaneous stock price crash risk* (H4.1), and two, *corporate tax management is positively associated with future stock price crash risk* (H4.2).

Most past studies claim that governments as custodians of state-owned and controlled enterprises appoint bureaucrats on their behalf to serve their social and political interests, such as employment and social security (Jensen & Meckling, 1976; Ross, 1973; Xu, Zhu, & Lin, 2005). However, this view not only overlooks the responsibility of SOEs to serve the people, as well as the nature and structure of incentives facing individual bureaucrats and managers in modern China. There are two strands of literature related to listed state-owned/controlled enterprises that are relevant for this chapter. The first strand shows that managers of listed SOEs (LSOEs) are mostly bureaucrats appointed by the government to represent them (ultimate controlling shareholders) in firms' decision-making. Compared with managers in private enterprises, managers in LSOEs have more incentives to seek future political advancement. Advancement to higher levels of the political hierarchy will offer them more privileges even after they leave their position in the LSOEs (Tu, Lin, & Liu, 2013). Hence it is natural that managers in LSOEs try to put up outstanding firm performance to the government, which then will motivate them to conceal adverse operating outcomes. The second strand shows that reforms have gradually improved the efficiency of the managerial labor market for SOEs, especially for LSOEs, and the performance-based bonus policy gives their managers further incentives to conceal negative information and inflate performance achievements.

Furthermore, China's economic reform has transformed the country's fiscal system from a centralized to a decentralized one into different levels of government viz., national, provincial, and municipal governments (including cities, prefectures, and counties). Accordingly, government ownership is affiliated with different administrative levels of government control. Bureaucrats heading different levels of SOEs have different motivations for undertaking tax management. Hence, when analyzing the agency problems of China's SOEs, the different levels of government ownership should be taken into consideration.

Since central SOEs play a strategically important role in the national economy, the top executives are given a higher administrative rank at the vice-ministerial level (*fubuji*) or departmental-level (*zhengtingji*), which come with important political privileges (Leutert, 2016). Therefore, the political benefits are the main incentive of central SOEs' executives that motivates them to conceal their firms' bad news. However, because of the important role of central SOEs in China's economy, when they are faced financial problems, the government generally bails them out to contain social unrest (Wang, Wong, & Xia, 2008). Consequently, central SOEs are offered a large security margin to stave off bankruptcy.

Local SOEs generally lack strict and independent accounting auditing and property evaluation, which leads to a high probability of moral hazard so that agents can take advantage of information asymmetry to pursue self-interests (Mi & Wang, 2000; Piotroski & Wong, 2012; Yang, 2016). Mi and Wang (2000) and Chen, Lee, and Li (2008) find that there is high collusion between Chinese local government and SOEs' managers, which results in abnormally high agency costs and inefficiency. Specifically, as an agent of the controlling shareholder, local government officials can directly interfere in the running of their SOEs (Fan, Wong, & Zhang, 2007), such as hiring acquiescent auditors to seek private gains (Shleifer, 1998). Wang, Wong, and Xia (2008) find that Chinese local SOEs tend to hire small local auditors from the same region that is conducive to conceal bad accounting information. Moreover, local governments are deemed as privatization-friendly leaders, keen to privatize their SOEs to increase local fiscal revenue and more importantly to seek personal benefits from the privatized firms (Liu, Sun, & Woo, 2006). Existing research also finds that local governments are big players behind a series of privatization exercises, especially at the municipal and county levels (Garnaut, Song, Tenev, & Yao, 2005; Tenev, Zhang, & Brefort, 2002).

Under China's modern corporate tax management system, SOE executives have strong motivation to pursue a self-serving agenda (for political career advancement and higher compensation) by using tax management to conceal bad news and exaggerate their performance. Compared with other enterprises, municipal-SOEs may face a comparatively higher risk of closure when experience downturns and financial scandals. Because of the weaker protection from government, underperforming municipal SOEs are easily abandoned or privatized by municipal governments. Thus, we frame the following three hypotheses for testing, viz., one, *firms controlled by the central government will show a weaker correlation between tax management and future risk of stock price crashing* (H4.3a); two, *firms controlled by provincial governments will show weaker correlation between tax management and future risk of stock price crashing* (H4.3b); and three, *firms controlled by municipal government will show a stronger correlation between tax management and future risk of stock price crashing* (H4.3c).

METHODOLOGY AND DATA

Having set up the hypotheses for the chapter, we discuss the data and methodology that were to be used. The section describes the sample and data, followed by the variables formulated. It finishes with the framing of the analytical model used.

Sample and Data

This chapter uses data for all China's A-share (main market) listed enterprises in the Shanghai and Shenzhen Stock Exchanges, excluding enterprises in the finance industry over the period from 2008[3] to 2013. All data are from the China Stock Market and Accounting Research (CSMAR) database. In addition, to get more complete and accurate

---

[3] During the fifth Session of the tenth National People's Congress (NPC) on March 16, 2007, the new Corporate Income Tax Law was approved and became effective on January 1, 2008. The new tax law set a unified tax rate of 25% for both domestic companies and foreign invested companies, and changed the current tax holiday, preferential tax treatments, and transitional provisions. Under the previous tax law, domestic companies had been assessed at a 33% statutory income tax rate; while certain foreign companies enjoyed preferential tax rates of 24% or 15%. To mitigate the effect of new Corporate Income Tax Law, the sampling in this chapter began in 2008.

Table 4.1 Definition of variables

Dependent variables (stock price crash risk)

NCSKEW	The negative coefficient of skewness, calculated by taking the negative of the third moment of firm-specific weekly returns for each sample year and dividing it by the standard deviation of firm-specific weekly returns raised to the third power. See Eq. (4.2) for details
DUVOL	It captures asymmetric volatilities between negative and positive firm-specific weekly returns. Firstly, all the weeks with firm-specific weekly returns have been separated into down weeks and up weeks. In the down weeks, the firm-specific weekly returns are below the annual mean, while, in the up weeks, the firm-specific weekly returns are above the annual mean. The standard deviations for the two subsamples are computed separately and then the log of the ratio of the standard deviation of the down weeks to that of the up weeks is calculated. See Eq. (4.3) for details

Independent variables (corporate tax management)

ETR	ETR is corporate current effective income tax rate, calculated as (income tax expenses-deferred tax expense)/pre-tax income. ETR is set to missing when the denominator is zero or negative. This chapter truncates ETR to the range [0, 1]
LETR	LETR is three years' average ETR. LETR is set to missing when the denominator is zero or negative. This chapter truncates LETR to the range [0, 1]
BTD	BTD is the total book-tax difference, which equals book income less taxable income scaled by lagged assets. Book income is pre-tax income. Taxable income is calculated by current tax expenses divided by the statutory tax rate
DTAX	The residual book-tax difference (Desai & Dharmapala, 2006), which equals the residual from the following firm fixed effects regression, $BTD_{i,t} = \beta_1 TACC_{i,t} + \mu_i + \varepsilon_{i,t}$, where BTD is the total book-tax difference and TACC is total accruals

State ownership (OWNER)

Central	A dummy variable, 1 if central government is the corporate ultimate controller, and 0 otherwise
Provincial	A dummy variable, 1 if provincial government is the corporate ultimate controller, which includes 22 provinces, 5 autonomous regions, and 4 directly administered municipalities (Beijing, Tianjin, Shanghai, and Chongqing), 0 is otherwise
Muni	A dummy variable, 1 if municipal government is the corporate ultimate controller, and 0 otherwise. Where municipal government in this chapter refers to prefectural-level cities in China, which are administrative level below provincial governments but higher than township

(continued)

Table 4.1 (continued)

OWNER*TAX	An interaction variable equals OWNER times four different measures of corporate tax management, which are $Central*ETR_{i,t-1}$, $Central*LETR_{i,t-1}$, $Central*BTD_{i,t-1}$, and $Central*DTAX_{i,t-1}$; $Provincial*ETR_{i,t-1}$, $Provincial*LETR_{i,t-1}$, $Provincial*BTD_{i,t-1}$, and $Provincial*DTAX_{i,t-1}$; $Muni*ETR_{i,t-1}$, $Muni*LETR_{i,t-1}$, $Muni*BTD_{i,t-1}$, and $Muni*DTAX_{i,t-1}$
Control variables	
DTURN	DTURN is the average monthly share turnover for the current fiscal year minus the average monthly share turnover for the previous fiscal year. The monthly stock turnover is calculated as monthly trading volume divided by the total number of circulating shares outstanding during the month
SIGMA	SIGMA is the standard deviation of firm-specific weekly returns over the fiscal year
RET	RET is the mean of firm-specific weekly returns over the fiscal year
SIZE	SIZE is the natural logarithm of firm's total assets
MB	MB is the market-to-book ratio
LEV	LEV is the firm financial leverage, calculated as total liabilities scaled by the book value of assets
ROA	ROA is firm profitability, calculated as net income divided by total assets
Discacc	It is the absolute value of discretionary accruals, where discretionary accruals are estimated from the modified Jones model (Dechow, Sloan, & Sweeney, 1995). See Appendix A

ownership data, part of the state ownership data was collected from corporate annual reports.

Following Wang, Wong, and Xia (2008), Wu, Wang, Luo, and Gillis (2012), and Bradshaw, Liao, and Ma (2012), listed state-owned/controlled enterprises are defined as those of which their ultimate controller is the central, provincial, or municipal government. If there were two or more types of owners controlling a listed firm, the chapter classified the firm's ownership type based on the largest shareholder.

In addition, firms whose firm-year observations are fewer than 26 weeks of stock return and have non-positive book values and total assets were excluded from the data used. Also excluded were firms with corporate effective income tax rates (ETRs) with negative values or values larger than one. With these exclusions, the sample of panel data consisted of 6706 firm-year observations. Table 4.1 provides the definition of the list of variables used in this chapter. To eliminate the effect of outliers, the chapter winsorizes variables by excluding values at the top and bottom 1%.

Variables Used

Four measures of corporate tax management were used to capture the different aspects of corporate tax management activities. Corporate effective tax rates can reflect all tax management transactions, even aggressive tax avoidance through permanent book-tax differences (Chen, Chen, Cheng, & Shevlin, 2010). The first measure is corporate current effective income tax rate (*ETR*). It is defined as tax expenses minus deferred tax expenses over pre-tax income. In addition, a three-year ETR (*LETR*) to produce a better matching between taxes paid and the income related to these taxes (Dyreng, Hanlon, & Maydew, 2008) is also used. Two additional measures complement the *ETR*, *viz.*, book-tax difference measures, that is, book-tax difference (*BTD*) and residual book-tax difference (*DTAX*). The residual book-tax difference captures more risky tax avoidance associated with tax shelter transactions (Hanlon & Heitzman, 2010). Table 4.2 provides the detailed definitions of these four variables.

Following Xu, Li, Yuan, and Chan (2014), Kim, Li, and Li (2014), and Xu, Jiang, Chan, and Yi (2013), two measures of stock price crash risk were constructed using firm-specific weekly returns. The first estimated firm-specific weekly returns, which is symbolized as $W_{i,t}$.

$$R_{i,t} = \alpha_i + \beta_1 R_{m,t-2} + \beta_2 R_{m,t-1} + \beta_3 R_{m,t} + \beta_4 R_{m,t+1} + \beta_5 R_{m,t+2} + \varepsilon_{i,t} \quad (4.1)$$

where $R_{i,t}$ is the return on stock i in week t and $R_{m,t}$ is the value-weighed A-share market return in week t. The firm-specific weekly return for firm i in week t is measured by $W_{i,t} = \ln(1+\varepsilon_{i,t})$, where $\varepsilon_{i,t}$ is the residual in Eq. (4.1).

Following Chen, Hong, and Stein (2001) and Kim, Li, and Zhang (2011), the first measure of crash risk used is the negative conditional return skewness, denoted by *NCSKEW*, calculated by taking the negative of the third moment of firm-specific weekly returns for each year and dividing it by the standard deviation of firm-specific weekly returns raised to the third power. A higher value of *NCKEW* corresponds to more left-skewed distributions, indicating higher crash risk. Equation (4.2) shows the *NCSKEW* for each firm i in year t.

$$NCSKEW_{i,t} = -\left[n(n-1)^{3/2} \sum W_{i,t}^3\right] / \left[(n-1)(n-2)\left(\sum W_{i,t}^2\right)^{3/2}\right] \quad (4.2)$$

The second measure of crash risk is down-to-up volatility (*DUVOL*), which captures asymmetric volatilities between negative and positive firm-specific weekly returns. Specifically, the analysis first separates all the weeks with firm-specific weekly returns into down weeks and up weeks. The down weeks means that firm-specific weekly returns are lower than the annual mean, and the up weeks are the firm-specific weekly returns that are higher than the annual mean. The standard deviations for the two subsamples are computed separately, which are used to calculate the $DUVOL$ for firm i in year t are as follows:

$$DUVOL_{i,t} = \ln\left\{\left[(n_u - 1)\sum\nolimits_{down} W_{i,t}^2\right] \Big/ \left[(n_d - 1)\sum\nolimits_{up} W_{i,t}^2\right]\right\} \quad (4.3)$$

A higher value for $NCSKEW$ and $DUVOL$ is consistent with a greater likelihood of the stock price crash risk, and vice versa.

Model Specification

To test H4.1 and H4.2, the following regression model, Eq. (4.4), is estimated. In the model, there are two alternative measures of *Crash Risk*, which are $NCSKEW$ and $DUVOL$. Four measures of tax management (*Tax*) are deployed: ETR, $LETR$, $DTAX$, and BTD, and standard errors are two-way clustered by year and firm.

$$\begin{aligned}
Crash\,Risk_{i,t} =\ & \alpha_0 + \beta_1 Tax_{i,t} + \beta_2 Tax_{i,t-1} + \beta_3 NCSKEW_{i,t-1} + \beta_4 DTURN_{i,t-1} \\
& + \beta_5 RET_{i,t-1} + \beta_6 SIGMA_{i,t-1} + \beta_7 ROA_{i,t-1} \\
& + \beta_8 MB_{i,t-1} + \beta_9 SIZE_{i,t-1} + \beta_{10} LEV_{i,t-1} \\
& + \beta_{11} Discacc_{i,t-1} + Industry\,Dummies \\
& + Year\,Dummies + \varepsilon_{i,t} \quad\quad\quad\quad\quad\quad\quad\quad\quad\quad (4.4)
\end{aligned}$$

Equation (4.5) estimates the moderating effect of government ownership on the relationship between tax management and future stock price crash. A dummy variable of state ownership $OWNER$, and an interaction term between state ownership and tax management $OWNER*TAX$ were set up for that. $OWNER$ represents the enterprises' ultimate controller, which is the central, provincial, and municipal governments: *Central, Provincial*, and *Muni*. Table 4.2 shows the detailed definitions.

$$\begin{aligned}
Crash\,Risk_{i,t} =\ & \alpha_0 + \beta_1 Tax_{i,t} + \beta_2 Tax_{i,t-1} + \beta_3 OWNER*TAX_{i,t-1} \\
& + \beta_4 OWNER_{i,t-1} + \beta_5 NCSKEW_{i,t-1} + \beta_6 DTURN_{i,t-1} \\
& + \beta_7 RET_{i,t-1} + \beta_8 SIGMA_{i,t-1} + \beta_9 ROA_{i,t-1} \\
& + \beta_{10} MB_{i,t-1} + \beta_{11} SIZE_{i,t-1} + \beta_{12} LEV_{i,t-1} \\
& + \beta_{13} Discacc_{i,t-1} + Industry\,Dummies \\
& + Year\,Dummies + \varepsilon_{i,t} \quad\quad\quad\quad\quad\quad\quad\quad\quad\quad (4.5)
\end{aligned}$$

Table 4.2 Descriptive statistics of main variables

Variables	N	Mean	Std. dev.	Min	P25	Median	P75	Max
Crash risk measures								
$NCSKEW_{i,t}$	6706	−0.558	0.880	−3.062	−1.104	−0.570	0.024	1.601
$DUVOL_{i,t}$	6706	−0.100	0.347	−0.909	−0.343	−0.106	0.147	0.697
Tax management measures								
$ETR_{i,t}$	6706	0.220	0.140	0.000	0.141	0.197	0.274	0.994
$LETR_{i,t}$	6706	0.212	0.123	0.000	0.144	0.194	0.266	0.991
$TS_{i,t}$	6706	−0.010	0.197	−0.864	−0.076	−0.004	0.060	0.829
$BTD_{i,t}$	6706	0.091	0.099	−0.058	0.031	0.063	0.115	0.609
$ETR_{i,t−1}$	4464	0.215	0.129	0.000	0.141	0.196	0.272	0.985
$LETR_{i,t−1}$	4464	0.210	0.118	0.000	0.142	0.194	0.265	0.985
$TS_{i,t−1}$	4464	0.000	0.195	−0.864	−0.066	0.002	0.066	0.829
$BTD_{i,t−1}$	4464	0.099	0.103	−0.058	0.036	0.070	0.126	0.609
Control variables								
$NCSKEW_{i,t−1}$	4464	−0.505	0.885	−3.062	−1.079	−0.522	0.108	1.601
$DTURN_{i,t−1}$	4464	0.309	0.209	0.034	0.151	0.253	0.416	0.988
$LEV_{i,t−1}$	4464	0.493	0.194	0.063	0.353	0.499	0.640	0.940
$MB_{i,t−1}$	4464	0.206	0.237	0.001	0.003	0.093	0.393	0.800
$ROA_{i,t−1}$	4464	0.054	0.045	−0.058	0.023	0.042	0.073	0.223
$SIZE_{i,t−1}$	4464	9.568	0.536	8.287	9.200	9.502	9.887	11.191
$SIGMA_{i,t−1}$	4464	0.064	0.021	0.028	0.049	0.061	0.076	0.124
$RET_{i,t−1}$	4464	0.002	0.012	−0.023	−0.007	0.000	0.008	0.031
$Discacc_{i,t−1}$	4464	0.151	0.140	0.002	0.055	0.117	0.210	0.853

The sample contains from 2008 to 2013 with non-missing values. P25 refers to percentile 25, and P75 refers to percentile 75
Source Computed by authors

Several control variables as potential predictors of crash risk were included. $DTURN_{i,t-1}$ is the detrended average monthly stock turnover, which is a proxy for investor heterogeneity or for differences of opinion among investors. $NCSKEW_{i,t-1}$ is the lagged negative skewness of firm-specific stock returns. Kim, Li, and Zhang (2011) show that the last year return skewness is likely to influence the return skewness in the current year. The variable $SIGMA_{i,t-1}$ is the standard deviation firm-specific stock returns of last year, and $RET_{i,t-1}$ is the average firm-specific weekly return in the last year. In addition, several standard corporate control variables were included, viz., $SIZE_{i,t-1}$ (the firm's natural log of total assets), $MB_{i,t-1}$ (the ratio of the market value of equity to the book value of equity), $LEV_{i,t-1}$ (the ratio of the book value of total liabilities scaled by total assets), and $ROA_{i,t-1}$ (net income divided by total assets). The variable $Discacc_{i,t-1}$ refers to absolute discretionary accruals, which measures accrual manipulation and is estimated from the modified Jones model (Dechow, Sloan, & Sweeney, 1995). Moreover, industry and year dummies are also included to control for the effects of industry and time, respectively.

Results and Analysis

We present and analyze the results in this section. The first sub-section deals with descriptive statistics followed by the multi-variate regressions.

Descriptive Statistics

Table 4.2 presents a summary of descriptive statistics of the variables used in this chapter. The average and median of $ETR_{i,t}$ and $LETR_{i,t}$ respectively, were 22.0 and 21.2%, and 19.7 and 19.4%, respectively, which are below the statutory corporate income tax rate of 25.0%. This suggests that more than half of the sample firms have a lower corporate effective tax rate than the statutory rate suggesting that corporate tax management is a significant strategy used by China's listed enterprises.

Table 4.3 shows the correlation coefficients between the dependent variables and the explanatory variables. The results show that the two dependent variables of NCSKEW and DUVOL are mostly significant and highly correlated with the four measures of tax management both in year t and $t-1$. Table 4.4 reports the correlation matrix of the independent variables and the control variables. The table shows that

Table 4.3 Correlation between dependent variables and explanatory variables

	ETR_t	ETR_{t-1}	$LETR_t$	$LETR_{t-1}$	$DTAX_t$	$DTAX_{t-1}$	BTD_t	BTD_{t-1}	$NCSKEW_{t-1}$
$NCSKEW_t$	0.01	−0.057***	−0.024*	−0.040***	0.037***	0.057***	0.035***	0.131***	−0.083***
$DUVOL_t$	0.046***	−0.043***	0.009	−0.030**	0.044***	0.063***	−0.030**	0.101***	−0.104***

	$DTURN_{t-1}$	LEV_{t-1}	MB_{t-1}	ROA_{t-1}	$SIZE_{t-1}$	$SIGMA_{t-1}$	RET_{t-1}	$Discacc_{t-1}$
$NCSKEW_t$	0.102***	−0.015	0.008	0.131***	0.044***	0.013	0.241***	0.021
$DUVOL_t$	0.104***	0	−0.088***	0.101***	0.092***	−0.182***	0.307***	−0.009

Note *, **, *** indicate significance at 10, 5, and 1%, respectively
Source Computed by authors

Table 4.4 Correlation between independent and control variables

	ETR_t	ETR_{t-1}	$LETR_t$	$LETR_{t-1}$	$DTAX_t$	$DTAX_{t-1}$	BTD_t	BTD_{t-1}	$NCSKEW_{t-1}$	$DTURN_{t-1}$	LEV_{t-1}	MB_{t-1}
ETR_t	0.500***											
$LETR_t$	0.748***	0.778***										
$LETR_{t-1}$	0.441***	0.770***	0.812***									
$DTAX_t$	−0.046***	−0.050***	−0.001	0.000								
$DTAX_{t-1}$	0.015	−0.039***	−0.003	0.007	0.095***							
BTD_t	−0.147***	−0.121***	−0.110***	−0.103***	0.351***	−0.013						
BTD_{t-1}	−0.092***	−0.126***	−0.097***	−0.096***	−0.001	0.385***	0.560***					
$NCSKEW_{t-1}$	−0.022	−0.008	−0.038**	−0.038**	−0.089***	0.062***	−0.028*	0.039***				
$DTURN_{t-1}$	0.005	−0.018	−0.008	0.008	0.122***	−0.001	−0.092***	−0.164***	−0.226***			
LEV_{t-1}	0.204***	0.210***	0.259***	0.229***	−0.02	−0.037**	−0.230***	−0.222***	−0.059***	0.019		
MB_{t-1}	−0.034***	−0.012	−0.011	−0.001	−0.122***	−0.001	0.071***	0.188***	0.074***	−0.156***	−0.011	
ROA_{t-1}	−0.173***	−0.227***	−0.206***	−0.190***	0.020	0.233***	0.593***	0.792***	0.048**	−0.137***	−0.415***	0.055***
$SIZE_{t-1}$	0.154***	0.142***	0.193***	0.157***	−0.033**	0.071***	−0.067***	0.081***	−0.025*	−0.340***	0.386***	−0.006
$SIGMA_{t-1}$	−0.036**	−0.006	−0.004	0.030**	0.009	−0.003	0.031**	0.007	−0.081***	0.371***	0.065***	0.280***
RET_{t-1}	−0.024	−0.064***	−0.026*	−0.023	0.164***	−0.061***	0.164***	0.076***	−0.537***	0.436***	0.024	−0.069***
$Disacc_{t-1}$	0.027*	0.027*	0.043***	0.041***	−0.023	0.140***	0.026*	0.245***	0.005	−0.031**	0.194***	0.175***

	ROA_{t-1}	$SIZE_{t-1}$	$SIGMA_{t-1}$	RET_{t-1}
$SIZE_{t-1}$	−0.027*			
$SIGMA_{t-1}$	−0.044***	−0.221***		
RET_{t-1}	0.075***	−0.034**	0.000	
$Disacc_{t-1}$	−0.051***	0.135***	0.074***	0.008

Note *, **, *** indicate significance at 10, 5, and 1%, respectively
Source Computed by authors

almost all the correlations between variables are less than 0.6. The correlations between ETR_t and $LETR_t$, ETR_{t-1} and $LETR_t$, and ETR_{t-1} and $LETR_{t-1}$ are above 0.7. Since they are used as independent variables in separate models, these do not cause problems of collinearity. Nevertheless, we undertook a further check on multicollinearity using the variance inflation factor (VIF) statistics. The results show that the VIF values of all variables are less than 5, which indicate that multicollinearity was not an issue in the regression results.

Regression Results

Table 4.5 shows the empirical results of the ordinary least squares (OLS) regressions with $NCSKEW_{i,t}$ and $DUVOL_{i,t}$ as the dependent variables of crash risk, respectively. The independent variable of tax management is proxied by ETR, $LETR$, $DTAX$, and BTD in year t and $t-1$, respectively. Regressions also include the following control variables: $NCSKEW_{i,t-1}$, $DTURN_{i,t-1}$, $RET_{i,t-1}$, $SIGMA_{i,t-1}$, $SIZE_{i,t-1}$, $MB_{i,t-1}$, $LEV_{i,t-1}$, $ROA_{i,t-1}$, $Discacc_{i,t-1}$, with industry fixed effects and year fixed effects. Standard errors in parentheses are heteroskedasticity-robust and clustered at both firm level and year level.

Panel A of Table 4.5 shows the results of $NCSKEW$ as the dependent variable of crash risk. In column (1) of Panel A, the coefficient of $ETR_{i,t-1}$ is highly significant with a negative sign (-0.330 with $t=-3.495$), while the coefficient of $ETR_{i,t}$ is also highly significant with a positive sign (0.325 with $t=3.300$). Because a lower ETR represents a higher level of tax management, the results indicate that tax management in year t is negatively correlated with crash risk in year t, but tax management in year $t-1$ is positively correlated with crash risk in year t. The coefficients associated with $DTAX$ and BTD in year t under both models [columns (3) and (4) in Table 4.6] are negative and highly significant at 1% level (-0.190 with $t=-13.424$, and -0.976 with $t=-5.533$, respectively), while the coefficients of the two proxies in year $t-1$ are positive and highly significant (0.113 with $t=2.139$, and 0.592 with $t=7.232$, respectively). Since the higher BTD and $DTAX$ represent higher-level tax management, the results in columns (3) and (4) of Table 4.6 are consistent with the results shown in column (1). Therefore, the results in Panel A of Table 4.6 support our hypotheses, which means that corporate tax management is negatively associated with

Table 4.5 Corporate tax management and stock price crash risk

	(1) ETR	(2) LETR	(3) DTAX	(4) BTD
Panel A: Dependent variable: NCSKEW$_{i,t}$				
ETR$_{i,t}$	0.325***			
	(3.300)			
ETR$_{i,t-1}$	−0.330***			
	(−3.495)			
LETR$_{i,t}$		0.076		
		(0.676)		
LETR$_{i,t-1}$		−0.241**		
		(−2.454)		
DTAX$_{i,t}$			−0.190***	
			(−13.424)	
DTAX$_{i,t-1}$			0.113**	
			(2.139)	
BTD$_{i,t}$				−0.976***
				(−5.533)
BTD$_{i,t-1}$				0.592***
				(7.232)
NCSKEW$_{i,t-1}$	0.056*	0.055*	0.055*	0.056*
	(1.836)	(1.805)	(1.880)	(1.778)
DTURN$_{i,t-1}$	−0.170	−0.160	−0.177	−0.223*
	(−1.391)	(−1.333)	(−1.393)	(−1.840)
RET$_{i,t-1}$	16.827***	16.711***	17.507***	18.605***
	(2.833)	(2.783)	(2.961)	(3.150)
SIGMA$_{i,t-1}$	1.381	1.422	1.401	1.373
	(0.794)	(0.826)	(0.829)	(0.767)
SIZE$_{i,t-1}$	0.105*	0.109**	0.102*	0.082
	(1.941)	(2.058)	(1.795)	(1.527)
MB$_{i,t-1}$	−0.019	−0.020	−0.037	−0.050
	(−0.414)	(−0.457)	(−0.855)	(−1.016)
LEV$_{i,t-1}$	−0.039	−0.028	−0.036	−0.030
	(−0.487)	(−0.369)	(−0.412)	(−0.313)
ROA$_{i,t-1}$	1.634***	1.638***	1.555***	1.727***
	(5.083)	(5.067)	(4.923)	(3.698)
Discacc$_{i,t-1}$	0.062	0.063	0.038	−0.020
	(0.821)	(0.826)	(0.498)	(−0.309)
Industry effect	Yes	Yes	Yes	Yes
Year effect	Yes	Yes	Yes	Yes
Constant	−2.005***	−2.058***	−1.970***	−1.713**
	(−2.785)	(−2.877)	(−2.617)	(−2.365)
N	4464	4464	4464	4464
Adjusted R^2	0.223	0.221	0.222	0.227

	(1) ETR	(2) LETR	(3) DTAX	(4) BTD
Panel B: Dependent variable: $DUVOL_{i,t}$				
$ETR_{i,t}$	0.169***			
	(4.633)			
$ETR_{i,t-1}$	−0.139***			
	(−3.880)			
$LETR_{i,t}$		0.101**		
		(2.034)		
$LETR_{i,t-1}$		−0.115**		
		(−2.511)		
$DTAX_{i,t}$			−0.067***	
			(−3.454)	
$DTAX_{i,t-1}$			0.051*	
			(1.924)	
$BTD_{i,t}$				−0.534***
				(−8.323)
$BTD_{i,t-1}$				0.234***
				(4.918)
$NCSKEW_{i,t-1}$	0.015	0.014	0.015	0.015
	(1.419)	(1.412)	(1.491)	(1.397)
$DTURN_{i,t-1}$	−0.062	−0.058	−0.063	−0.092
	(−1.010)	(−0.953)	(−0.999)	(−1.472)
$RET_{i,t-1}$	5.720***	5.656**	5.941***	6.783***
	(2.633)	(2.574)	(2.710)	(3.100)
$SIGMA_{i,t-1}$	0.737	0.763	0.753	0.750
	(1.504)	(1.561)	(1.574)	(1.444)
$SIZE_{i,t-1}$	0.053**	0.054**	0.052*	0.042
	(2.026)	(2.100)	(1.899)	(1.601)
$MB_{i,t-1}$	−0.017	−0.018	−0.024	−0.030*
	(−1.132)	(−1.201)	(−1.499)	(−1.762)
$LEV_{i,t-1}$	−0.042	−0.038	−0.039	−0.035
	(−1.523)	(−1.488)	(−1.349)	(−1.068)
$ROA_{i,t-1}$	0.335***	0.341***	0.289**	0.533**
	(2.890)	(3.110)	(2.374)	(2.445)
$Discacc_{i,t-1}$	−0.032	−0.031	−0.043	−0.059**
	(−1.170)	(−1.145)	(−1.416)	(−2.058)
Industry effect	Yes	Yes	Yes	Yes
Year effect	Yes	Yes	Yes	Yes
Constant	−0.993***	−1.013***	−0.984***	−0.849***
	(−3.134)	(−3.206)	(−2.953)	(−2.597)
N	4464	4464	4464	4464
Adjusted R^2	0.341	0.338	0.339	0.351

Note ***, **, and * are significance at 1, 5, and 10% levels, respectively
Source Computed by authors

Table 4.6 Impact of central government ownership on relationship between tax management and future stock price crash risk

	(1) ETR	(2) LETR	(3) DTAX	(4) BTD
Panel A: Dependent variable: NCSKEW$_{i,t}$				
ETR$_{i,t}$	0.325***			
	(3.292)			
ETR$_{i,t-1}$	−0.309***			
	(−3.033)			
Central*ETR$_{i,t-1}$	−0.096			
	(−0.635)			
LETR$_{i,t}$		0.076		
		(0.647)		
LETR$_{i,t-1}$		−0.284**		
		(−2.560)		
Central*LETR$_{i,t-1}$		0.269		
		(1.150)		
DTAX$_{i,t}$			−0.190***	
			(−15.210)	
DTAX$_{i,t-1}$			0.075	
			(1.035)	
Central*DTAX$_{i,t-1}$			0.269	
			(1.269)	
BTD$_{i,t}$				−0.966***
				(−5.383)
BTD$_{i,t-1}$				0.585***
				(6.283)
Central*BTD$_{i,t-1}$				0.131
				(0.261)
Central$_{i,t-1}$	0.059	−0.016	0.039	0.024
	(0.965)	(−0.215)	(1.163)	(0.353)
NCSKEW$_{i,t-1}$	0.056*	0.055*	0.055*	0.056*
	(1.816)	(1.790)	(1.873)	(1.781)
DTURN$_{i,t-1}$	−0.166	−0.162	−0.175	−0.221*
	(−1.377)	(−1.396)	(−1.402)	(−1.842)
RET$_{i,t-1}$	16.837***	16.826***	17.509***	18.588***
	(2.838)	(2.802)	(2.969)	(3.169)
SIGMA$_{i,t-1}$	1.300	1.356	1.331	1.307
	(0.727)	(0.761)	(0.781)	(0.709)
SIZE$_{i,t-1}$	0.100*	0.103*	0.097	0.078
	(1.779)	(1.866)	(1.636)	(1.363)
MB$_{i,t-1}$	−0.016	−0.020	−0.036	−0.048
	(−0.345)	(−0.436)	(−0.845)	(−0.980)
LEV$_{i,t-1}$	−0.037	−0.021	−0.037	−0.027
	(−0.462)	(−0.272)	(−0.422)	(−0.288)
ROA$_{i,t-1}$	1.668***	1.668***	1.592***	1.728***

4 ECONOMIC REFORMS AND MARKET OUTCOMES OVER TIME 91

	(1) ETR	(2) LETR	(3) DTAX	(4) BTD
	(5.062)	(5.024)	(4.893)	(3.648)
$Discacc_{i,t-1}$	0.066	0.066	0.050	−0.018
	(0.871)	(0.868)	(0.623)	(−0.284)
Industry effect	Yes	Yes	Yes	Yes
Year effect	Yes	Yes	Yes	Yes
Constant	−1.966***	−1.996***	−1.926**	−1.675**
	(−2.665)	(−2.745)	(−2.496)	(−2.236)
N	4464	4464	4464	4464
Adjusted R^2	0.223	0.221	0.223	0.227
Panel B: Dependent variable: $DUVOL_{i,t}$				
$ETR_{i,t}$	0.169***			
	(4.628)			
$ETR_{i,t-1}$	−0.133***			
	(−3.513)			
$Central^*ETR_{i,t-1}$	−0.030			
	(−0.799)			
$LETR_{i,t}$		0.101**		
		(1.998)		
$LETR_{i,t-1}$		−0.129**		
		(−2.268)		
$Central^*LETR_{i,t-1}$		0.084		
		(1.424)		
$DTAX_{i,t}$			−0.067***	
			(−3.438)	
$DTAX_{i,t-1}$			0.040	
			(1.123)	
$Central^*DTAX_{i,t-1}$			0.070	
			(0.829)	
$BTD_{i,t}$				−0.531***
				(−8.254)
$BTD_{i,t-1}$				0.230***
				(4.135)
$Central^*BTD_{i,t-1}$				0.053
				(0.380)
$Central_{i,t-1}$	0.021	−0.003	0.015*	0.007
	(1.446)	(−0.125)	(1.755)	(0.415)
$NCSKEW_{i,t-1}$	0.015	0.014	0.014	0.015
	(1.408)	(1.413)	(1.488)	(1.397)
$DTURN_{i,t-1}$	−0.060	−0.058	−0.062	−0.091
	(−0.995)	(−0.973)	(−0.997)	(−1.476)
$RET_{i,t-1}$	5.725***	5.694***	5.945***	6.777***
	(2.638)	(2.599)	(2.722)	(3.110)
$SIGMA_{i,t-1}$	0.707	0.737	0.726	0.728

(continued)

Table 4.6 (continued)

	(1) ETR	(2) LETR	(3) DTAX	(4) BTD
	(1.434)	(1.484)	(1.533)	(1.385)
$SIZE_{i,t-1}$	0.051*	0.052**	0.050*	0.040
	(1.933)	(1.985)	(1.809)	(1.507)
$MB_{i,t-1}$	−0.016	−0.018	−0.023	−0.029*
	(−1.076)	(−1.167)	(−1.473)	(−1.762)
$LEV_{i,t-1}$	−0.041	−0.035	−0.039	−0.034
	(−1.481)	(−1.400)	(−1.298)	(−1.046)
$ROA_{i,t-1}$	0.347***	0.353***	0.302**	0.533**
	(3.077)	(3.260)	(2.546)	(2.471)
$Discacc_{i,t-1}$	−0.031	−0.030	−0.039	−0.059**
	(−1.136)	(−1.107)	(−1.223)	(−2.018)
Industry effect	Yes	Yes	Yes	Yes
Year effect	Yes	Yes	Yes	Yes
Constant	−0.978***	−0.991***	−0.967***	−0.836**
	(−3.056)	(−3.110)	(−2.876)	(−2.515)
N	4464	4464	4464	4464
Adjusted R^2	0.341	0.338	0.339	0.351

Note ***, **, and * are significance at 1, 5, and 10% levels, respectively
Source Computed by authors

contemporaneous stock price crash risk (H4.1), but positively associated with future stock price crashes (H4.2).

Panel B of Table 4.5 reports the results of $DUVOL_{i,t}$ as an alternative measure of the dependent variable of *crash risk*, which is used to test the robustness of the results. The results show that $DUVOL_{i,t}$ is significant and positively correlated with $ETR_{i,t}$ and $LETR_{i,t}$, but negatively correlated with $ETR_{i,t-1}$ and $LETR_{i,t-1}$ [columns (1) and (2) of Panel B]. In addition, in columns (3) and (4) of Panel B, $DUVOL_{i,t}$ has significantly negative relationships with $DTAX_{i,t}$ and $BTD_{i,t}$, and significantly positive relationships with $DTAX_{i,t-1}$ and $BTD_{i,t-1}$. Therefore, the results of $DUVOL$ as the dependent variable are in line with the results reported in Panel A of Table 4.5, suggesting that the results are robust. Thus, the findings support our hypotheses (H4.1 and H4.2), indicating that firms with more tax management activities is less prone to crash in the current year but more prone to crash in the future.

According to the results presented in Table 4.5, corporate tax management would raise the likelihood of future crash risk. Consequently, we assess the impact of state ownership on the relationship between tax management and future stock price crashes by including in Eq. 4.5, state ownership ($OWNER_{i,t-1}$) and the interaction term of $OWNER*TAX_{i,t-1}$. To increase the power of the test, three dummy variables, that is, *central, province,* and *muni*, to represent Central SoEs, Provincial SoEs, and Municipal SoEs, were used.

Table 4.6 reports the results of the impact of central government ownership on the relationship between tax management and future crash risk. The dependent variables are *NCSKEW* and *DUVOL*, respectively in Panels A and B. The independent variables of tax management are proxied by *ETR, LETR, DTAX,* and *BTD*, respectively. The interaction terms, $Central*ETR_{i,t-1}$, $Central*LETR_{i,t-1}$, $Central*BTD_{i,t-1}$, and $Central*DTAX_{i,t-1}$ were deployed, while the moderator is central government ownership, denoted by $Central_{i,t-1}$. The estimated regressions include the following control variables: $NCSKEW_{i,t-1}$, $DTURN_{i,t-1}$, $RET_{i,t-1}$, $SIGMA_{i,t-1}$, $SIZE_{i,t-1}$, $MB_{i,t-1}$, $LEV_{i,t-1}$, $ROA_{i,t-1}$, $Discacc_{i,t-1}$, with industry fixed effects and year fixed effects. Standard errors in parentheses are heteroskedasticity-robust and clustered at both firm and year levels.

As shown in Panel A of Table 4.6, with $NCSKEW_{i,t}$ as the dependent variable, after interaction terms have been included, tax management in year t is still negatively associated with crash risk in year t. Specifically, $ETR_{i,t}$ has a significantly positive coefficient, while $DTAX_{i,t}$ and $BTD_{i,t}$ have significantly negative coefficients. The results are consistent with our hypothesis (H4.1). In addition, $ETR_{i,t-1}$ and $LETR_{i,t-1}$ have significant and negative coefficients, while $BTD_{i,t-1}$ has a significant and positive coefficient. Thus, corporate tax management is positively correlated with future crash risk, thereby supporting our hypothesis (H4.2). Moreover, the coefficients of the four interaction terms, $Central*TAX_{i,t-1}$ ($Central*ETR_{i,t-1}$, $Central*LERT_{i,t-1}$, $Central*DTAX_{i,t-1}$, and $Central*BTD_{i,t-1}$), are not statistically significant leading to the rejection of the influence of government hypothesis (H4.3a).

Panel B of Table 4.6 presents the results when crash risk is proxied by $DUVOL_{i,t}$. The coefficients of both main effect terms, that is, $TAX_{i,t}$ and $TAX_{i,t-1}$, are highly significant with the expected signs, but $DTAX_{i,t-1}$ is insignificant. In addition, the coefficients of the four interaction terms in Panel B of Table 4.7, $Central*ETR_{i,t-1}$, $Central*LERT_{i,t-1}$, $Central*DTAX_{i,t-1}$, $Central*BTD_{i,t-1}$ are also not statistically significant. Hence, the results reported in Panel A and Panel B of Table 4.6

suggest that central government control has no impact on future stock price crash risk, and with that the rejection of the related hypothesis (H4.3a).

Table 4.7 presents the results of the moderating effect of provincial government ownership on the relationship between tax management and future crash risk. Panels A and B show the results with $NCSKEW_{i,t}$ and $DUVOL_{i,t}$ as the dependent variables, respectively. The independent variable of tax management is proxied by ETR, $LETR$, $DTAX$, and BTD, respectively. The moderator is $Provincial_{i,t-1}$, and the four interaction terms deployed are $Provincial*ETR_{i,t-1}$, $Provincial*LETR_{i,t-1}$, $Provincial*BTD_{i,t-1}$, and $Provincial*DTAX_{i,t-1}$. The regressions include the following control variables: $NCSKEW_{i,t-1}$, $DTURN_{i,t-1}$, $RET_{i,t-1}$, $SIGMA_{i,t-1}$, $SIZE_{i,t-1}$, $MB_{i,t-1}$, $LEV_{i,t-1}$, $ROA_{i,t-1}$, $Discacc_{i,t-1}$, with industry fixed effects and year fixed effects. Standard errors in parentheses are heteroskedasticity-robust and clustered at both firm and year levels.

The results show that corporate tax management has a significantly negative relationship with contemporaneous crash risk, and positive relationship with future crash risk, which support our hypotheses (H4.1 and H4.2) again. In addition, the coefficients of the four interaction terms of $Provincial*ETR_{i,t-1}$, $Provincial*LETR_{i,t-1}$, $Provincial*DTAX_{i,t-1}$, and $Provincial*BTD_{i,t-1}$) in Panels A and B of Table 4.7 are not statistically significant, but $Province*LETR_{i,t-1}$ is significant and positive at 10% in Panel B. Therefore, the results suggest that provincial government control does not show a significant influence on the relationship between tax management and future stock price crash risk, which allows the rejection of hypothesis H4.3b.

Table 4.8 presents the results of the moderating impact of municipal government ownership on the relationship between tax management and stock price crash risk. Once again, the dependent variable of stock price crash risk was measured by $NCSKEW$ and $DUVOL$, respectively in Panels A and B. The independent variable of tax management is measured separately by ETR, $LETR$, $DTAX$, and BTD. The moderator is $Muni_{i,t-1}$, while the four interaction terms were: $Muni*ETR_{i,t-1}$, $Muni*LETR_{i,t-1}$, $Muni*BTD_{i,t-1}$, and $Muni*DTAX_{i,t-1}$. Control variables include $NCSKEW_{i,t-1}$, $DTURN_{i,t-1}$, $RET_{i,t-1}$, $SIGMA_{i,t-1}$, $SIZE_{i,t-1}$, $MB_{i,t-1}$, $LEV_{i,t-1}$, $ROA_{i,t-1}$, $Discacc_{i,t-1}$, with industry fixed effects and year fixed effects. Standard errors in parentheses are heteroskedasticity-robust and clustered at the firm and time level.

Table 4.7 Impact of provincial government ownership on relationship between tax management and future stock price crash risk

	(1) ETR	(2) LETR	(3) DTAX	(4) BTD
Panel A: Dependent variable: NCSKEW$_{i,t}$				
ETR$_{i,t}$	0.318***			
	(3.289)			
ETR$_{i,t-1}$	−0.376***			
	(−4.022)			
Provincial*ETR$_{i,t-1}$	0.221			
	(1.643)			
LETR$_{i,t}$		0.062		
		(0.572)		
LETR$_{i,t-1}$		−0.290**		
		(−2.470)		
Provincial*LETR$_{i,t-1}$		0.269		
		(1.476)		
DTAX$_{i,t}$			−0.186***	
			(−18.585)	
DTAX$_{i,t-1}$			0.107*	
			(1.869)	
Provincial*DTAX$_{i,t-1}$			0.037	
			(0.232)	
BTD$_{i,t}$				−0.974***
				(−5.567)
BTD$_{i,t-1}$				0.623***
				(7.487)
Provincial*BTD$_{i,t-1}$				−0.087
				(−0.248)
Provincial$_{i,t-1}$	−0.098**	−0.109**	−0.048*	−0.042
	(−2.143)	(−2.308)	(−1.684)	(−1.458)
NCSKEW$_{i,t-1}$	0.054*	0.053*	0.054*	0.055*
	(1.825)	(1.785)	(1.875)	(1.763)
DTURN$_{i,t-1}$	−0.169	−0.157	−0.179	−0.226*
	(−1.374)	(−1.323)	(−1.399)	(−1.859)
RET$_{i,t-1}$	16.597***	16.488***	17.356***	18.417***
	(2.811)	(2.757)	(2.968)	(3.139)
SIGMA$_{i,t-1}$	1.383	1.402	1.427	1.414
	(0.803)	(0.829)	(0.835)	(0.787)
SIZE$_{i,t-1}$	0.113**	0.118**	0.109**	0.089*
	(2.148)	(2.265)	(1.982)	(1.749)
MB$_{i,t-1}$	−0.018	−0.019	−0.036	−0.049
	(−0.392)	(−0.442)	(−0.869)	(−1.006)
LEV$_{i,t-1}$	−0.048	−0.038	−0.042	−0.036
	(−0.596)	(−0.499)	(−0.473)	(−0.382)
ROA$_{i,t-1}$	1.606***	1.612***	1.538***	1.686***

(continued)

Table 4.7 (continued)

	(1) ETR	(2) LETR	(3) DTAX	(4) BTD
	(5.229)	(5.180)	(5.037)	(4.056)
$Discacc_{i,t-1}$	0.066	0.069	0.040	−0.020
	(0.869)	(0.890)	(0.516)	(−0.299)
Industry effect	Yes	Yes	Yes	Yes
Year effect	Yes	Yes	Yes	Yes
Constant	−2.059***	−2.109***	−2.022***	−1.7735***
	(−3.276)	(−3.368)	(−3.074)	(−2.755)
N	4464	4464	4464	4464
Adjusted R^2	0.223	0.221	0.222	0.227

Panel B: Dependent variable: $DUVOL_{i,t}$

	(1) ETR	(2) LETR	(3) DTAX	(4) BTD
$ETR_{i,t}$	0.167***			
	(4.591)			
$ETR_{i,t-1}$	−0.151***			
	(−4.309)			
$Provincial*ETR_{i,t-1}$	0.057			
	(1.135)			
$LETR_{i,t}$		0.095*		
		(1.895)		
$LETR_{i,t-1}$		−0.139***		
		(−3.284)		
$Provincial*LETR_{i,t-1}$		0.128*		
		(1.879)		
$DTAX_{i,t}$			−0.066***	
			(−3.447)	
$DTAX_{i,t-1}$			0.046**	
			(2.041)	
$Provincial*DTAX_{i,t-1}$			0.025	
			(0.436)	
$BTD_{i,t}$				−0.533***
				(−8.294)
$BTD_{i,t-1}$				0.250***
				(4.537)
$Provincial*BTD_{i,t-1}$				−0.049
				(−0.465)
$Provincial_{i,t-1}$	−0.029**	−0.046**	−0.017**	−0.013**
	(−2.054)	(−2.434)	(−2.333)	(−2.106)
$NCSKEW_{i,t-1}$	0.014	0.014	0.014	0.015
	(1.384)	(1.340)	(1.478)	(1.377)
$DTURN_{i,t-1}$	−0.062	−0.056	−0.064	−0.092
	(−1.006)	(−0.937)	(−1.005)	(−1.489)
$RET_{i,t-1}$	5.647***	5.570**	5.892***	6.714***
	(2.602)	(2.528)	(2.722)	(3.086)
$SIGMA_{i,t-1}$	0.741	0.749	0.760	0.766

	(1) ETR	(2) LETR	(3) DTAX	(4) BTD
	(1.504)	(1.546)	(1.537)	(1.449)
$SIZE_{i,t-1}$	0.056**	0.058**	0.055**	0.044*
	(2.124)	(2.229)	(1.990)	(1.717)
$MB_{i,t-1}$	−0.017	−0.018	−0.024	−0.030*
	(−1.116)	(−1.202)	(−1.556)	(−1.758)
$LEV_{i,t-1}$	−0.044	−0.042	−0.041	−0.037
	(−1.567)	(−1.540)	(−1.393)	(−1.119)
$ROA_{i,t-1}$	0.326***	0.331***	0.283**	0.515**
	(2.817)	(2.994)	(2.344)	(2.470)
$Discacc_{i,t-1}$	−0.031	−0.029	−0.042	−0.060**
	(−1.113)	(−1.029)	(−1.396)	(−2.064)
Industry effect	Yes	Yes	Yes	Yes
Year effect	Yes	Yes	Yes	Yes
Constant	−1.011***	−1.031***	−1.002***	−0.872***
	(−3.595)	(−3.655)	(−3.380)	(−2.885)
N	4464	4464	4464	4464
Adjusted R^2	0.341	0.338	0.339	0.351

Note ***, **, and * are significance at 1, 5, and 10% levels, respectively
Source Computed by authors

As reported in Panel A of Table 4.8, when $NCSKEW_{i,t}$ is used as the dependent variable, the results of the relationship between tax management and stock price crashes again support our hypotheses (H4.1 and H4.2). Furthermore, the coefficients of the interaction terms of $Muni*ETR_{i,t-1}$, $Muni*BTD_{i,t-1}$, and $Muni*DTAX_{i,t-1}$ are statistically significant with the expected signs, except for the coefficient of the interaction term of $Muni*LETR_{i,t-1}$, which is insignificant. Hence, the results indicate that municipal listed SOEs would have a higher probability of future stock price crashes than central and provincial SOEs, which supports Hypothesis H4.3c.

Panel B of Table 4.8 shows the regression results when the dependent variable of stock price crashes is $DUVOL_{i,t}$. The results show that all the coefficients of the interaction terms are statistically significant with their expected signs, except for $Muni*ETR_{i,t-1}$ in column (1), which is insignificant. The results presented in Panel B of Table 4.9 also lend support to hypothesis H4.3c, which means that the role of municipal governments would strengthen the positive relationship between corporate tax management and future stock price crash risk. Thus, the listed enterprises controlled by municipal government would show a higher likelihood of future crash risk because of corporate tax management.

Table 4.8 Impact of municipal government ownership on relationship between tax management and future stock price crash risk

	(1) ETR	(2) LETR	(3) DTAX	(4) BTD
Panel A: Dependent variable: NCSKEW$_{i,t}$				
ETR$_{i,t}$	0.328***			
	(3.293)			
ETR$_{i,t-1}$	−0.279**			
	(−2.329)			
Muni*ETR$_{i,t-1}$	−0.229*			
	(−1.771)			
LETR$_{i,t}$		0.077		
		(0.661)		
LETR$_{i,t-1}$		−0.196*		
		(−1.746)		
Muni*LETR$_{i,t-1}$		−0.179		
		(−0.919)		
DTAX$_{i,t}$			−0.193***	
			(−19.713)	
DTAX$_{i,t-1}$			0.069	
			(1.266)	
Muni*DTAX$_{i,t-1}$			0.297*	
			(1.849)	
BTD$_{i,t}$				−0.995***
				(−5.836)
BTD$_{i,t-1}$				0.480***
				(3.813)
Muni*BTD$_{i,t-1}$				0.772**
				(2.087)
Muni$_{i,t-1}$	0.030	0.021	−0.021	−0.090*
	(0.870)	(0.740)	(−1.064)	(−1.799)
NCSKEW$_{i,t-1}$	0.056*	0.055*	0.056*	0.057*
	(1.832)	(1.807)	(1.915)	(1.775)
DTURN$_{i,t-1}$	−0.169	−0.158	−0.175	−0.221*
	(−1.379)	(−1.308)	(−1.403)	(−1.835)
RET$_{i,t-1}$	16.896***	16.779***	17.564***	18.759***
	(2.832)	(2.776)	(2.957)	(3.097)
SIGMA$_{i,t-1}$	1.306	1.347	1.363	1.382
	(0.769)	(0.808)	(0.832)	(0.799)
SIZE$_{i,t-1}$	0.103*	0.108**	0.101*	0.079
	(1.926)	(2.075)	(1.807)	(1.507)
MB$_{i,t-1}$	−0.022	−0.023	−0.042	−0.053
	(−0.495)	(−0.522)	(−1.001)	(−1.070)
LEV$_{i,t-1}$	−0.034	−0.024	−0.033	−0.026
	(−0.410)	(−0.303)	(−0.363)	(−0.272)
ROA$_{i,t-1}$	1.642***	1.645***	1.555***	1.691***

4 ECONOMIC REFORMS AND MARKET OUTCOMES OVER TIME 99

	(1) ETR	(2) LETR	(3) DTAX	(4) BTD
	(5.021)	(4.994)	(4.855)	(3.546)
$Discacc_{i,t-1}$	0.064	0.064	0.044	−0.014
	(0.843)	(0.844)	(0.606)	(−0.217)
Industry effect	Yes	Yes	Yes	Yes
Year effect	Yes	Yes	Yes	Yes
Constant	−1.990***	−2.041***	−1.961***	−1.667**
	(−2.777)	(−2.886)	(−2.631)	(−2.356)
N	4464	4464	4464	4464
Adjusted R^2	0.223	0.221	0.223	0.228

Panel B: Dependent variable: $DUVOL_{i,t}$

	(1) ETR	(2) LETR	(3) DTAX	(4) BTD
$ETR_{i,t}$	0.170***			
	(4.622)			
$ETR_{i,t-1}$	−0.136***			
	(−3.175)			
$Muni{*}ETR_{i,t-1}$	−0.017			
	(−0.526)			
$LETR_{i,t}$		0.101**		
		(2.034)		
$LETR_{i,t-1}$		−0.107**		
		(−2.484)		
$Muni{*}LETR_{i,t-1}$		−0.034*		
		(−1.688)		
$DTAX_{i,t}$			−0.068***	
			(−3.615)	
$DTAX_{i,t-1}$			0.034	
			(1.398)	
$Muni{*}DTAX_{i,t-1}$			0.111*	
			(1.819)	
$BTD_{i,t}$				−0.541***
				(−8.786)
$BTD_{i,t-1}$				0.191***
				(3.465)
$Muni{*}BTD_{i,t-1}$				0.296**
				(2.097)
$Muni_{i,t-1}$	−0.002	0.003	−0.005	−0.031**
	(−0.110)	(0.455)	(−0.471)	(−2.020)
$NCSKEW_{i,t-1}$	0.015	0.014	0.015	0.016
	(1.416)	(1.412)	(1.527)	(1.407)
$DTURN_{i,t-1}$	−0.061	−0.057	−0.063	−0.091
	(−1.016)	(−0.955)	(−1.023)	(−1.494)
$RET_{i,t-1}$	5.734***	5.671**	5.954***	6.834***
	(2.628)	(2.569)	(2.712)	(3.046)
$SIGMA_{i,t-1}$	0.721	0.747	0.748	0.763

(continued)

Table 4.8 (continued)

	(1) ETR	(2) LETR	(3) DTAX	(4) BTD
	(1.486)	(1.553)	(1.610)	(1.484)
$SIZE_{i,t-1}$	0.052**	0.054**	0.052*	0.041
	(2.009)	(2.078)	(1.892)	(1.577)
$MB_{i,t-1}$	−0.018	−0.019	−0.025	−0.031*
	(−1.141)	(−1.186)	(−1.583)	(−1.721)
$LEV_{i,t-1}$	−0.041	−0.037	−0.038	−0.034
	(−1.466)	(−1.437)	(−1.307)	(−1.049)
$ROA_{i,t-1}$	0.335***	0.342***	0.289**	0.519**
	(2.870)	(3.099)	(2.386)	(2.387)
$Discacc_{i,t-1}$	−0.032	−0.031	−0.040	−0.057*
	(−1.164)	(−1.134)	(−1.392)	(−1.898)
Industry effect	Yes	Yes	Yes	Yes
Year effect	Yes	Yes	Yes	Yes
Constant	−0.989***	−1.010***	−0.982***	−0.834**
	(−3.104)	(−3.174)	(−2.939)	(−2.567)
N	4464	4464	4464	4464
Adjusted R^2	0.341	0.338	0.339	0.352

Note ***, **, and * are significance at 1, 5, and 10% levels, respectively
Source Computed by authors

Robustness Check for Endogeneity Problems

Although the analysis has controlled for firm characteristics and accounting properties of variables in the regressions, the results may still be biased if the explanatory variables are not strictly exogenous and the panel's time dimension is small (Wintoki, Linck, & Netter, 2012). Hence, the endogeneity issue would lead to the regression results to have spurious correlation between corporate tax management and crash risk. To obtain reliable and unbiased results, a dynamic system Generalized Method of Moments (system GMM) estimator is used to reexamine the relationships (Eq. 4.4).

Table 4.9 reports the system-GMM results when the dependent variable used was $NCSKEW_{i,t}$, which is estimated using the Windmeijer (2005) corrected-robust standard errors. The table also reports the p-values for the four additional specification tests, that is, the AR (1) and AR (2) tests for first order and second order serial correlation in the first-differenced residuals under the null hypothesis of no serial correlation. The results of the AR tests suggest that the underlying conditional

4 ECONOMIC REFORMS AND MARKET OUTCOMES OVER TIME

Table 4.9 Impact of tax management on stock price crash risk using system GMM

	(1) ETR	(2) LETR	(3) DTAX	(4) BTD
Panel A: Dependent variable: $NCSKEW_{i,t}$				
$ETR_{i,t}$	0.244**			
	(2.106)			
$ETR_{i,t-1}$	−0.404***			
	(−3.207)			
$LETR_{i,t}$		−0.050		
		(−0.217)		
$LETR_{i,t-1}$		−0.316*		
		(−1.657)		
$DTAX_{i,t}$			−0.205***	
			(−2.701)	
$DTAX_{i,t-1}$			0.264***	
			(2.823)	
$BTD_{i,t}$				−0.498**
				(−2.274)
$BTD_{i,t-1}$				2.252***
				(4.204)
$NCSKEW_{i,t-1}$	0.118***	0.120***	0.121***	0.107***
	(3.986)	(4.020)	(4.082)	(3.630)
$DTURN_{i,t-1}$	−0.227**	−0.209*	−0.263**	−0.232**
	(−1.999)	(−1.847)	(−2.281)	(−2.065)
$RET_{i,t-1}$	29.211***	29.269***	30.400***	27.943***
	(9.172)	(9.182)	(9.387)	(8.731)
$SIGMA_{i,t-1}$	6.705***	6.644***	6.843***	6.462***
	(4.465)	(4.422)	(4.557)	(4.235)
$SIZE_{i,t-1}$	0.219***	0.225***	0.207***	0.170***
	(6.811)	(7.076)	(6.440)	(5.443)
$MB_{i,t-1}$	−0.183	−0.175	−0.189	−0.271*
	(−1.295)	(−1.251)	(−1.356)	(−1.820)
$LEV_{i,t-1}$	−0.390***	−0.364***	−0.411***	−0.382***
	(−3.402)	(−3.216)	(−3.525)	(−3.465)
$ROA_{i,t-1}$	−1.537*	−1.401*	−1.956**	−4.590***
	(−1.833)	(−1.723)	(−2.222)	(−3.012)
$Discacc_{i,t-1}$	−0.039	−0.039	−0.123	−0.515***
	(−0.307)	(−0.307)	(−0.914)	(−3.291)
Industry effect	Yes	Yes	Yes	Yes
Year effect	Yes	Yes	Yes	Yes
Constant	−2.985***	−3.316***	−3.095***	−2.648***
	(−9.316)	(−9.838)	(−8.973)	(−7.444)
N	4464	4464	4464	4464
AR (1) test	0.000	0.000	0.000	0.000
AR (2) test	0.165	0.142	0.131	0.275

(continued)

Table 4.9 (continued)

	(1) ETR	(2) LETR	(3) DTAX	(4) BTD
Sargan test	0.173	0.158	0.148	0.128
Hansen test	0.226	0.222	0.225	0.190
Difference in Hansen	0.197	0.172	0.162	0.179

Note ***, **, and * are significance at 1, 5, and 10% levels, respectively
Source Computed by authors

errors are not autocorrelated, where the *AR (1)* tests are shown to be significant, and the *AR (2)* tests are shown to be non-significant with p-value between 0.131 and 0.275. The Sargan and Hansen *J* tests of over-identification supports the null hypothesis that the instruments as a group is exogenous. The difference in Hansen test of exogeneity also supports the null hypothesis that the levels of instruments in the GMM and the IV are exogenous. The results of the Hansen *J* test of over-identifying restrictions are non-significant with the p-values of the Hansen test falling between 0.190 and 0.226, which does not allow the rejection of the null hypothesis that these instruments are exogenous. Thus, endogeneity is not an important concern in the regression results produced.

The system-GMM results shown in Table 4.9 are in sync with the results of Table 4.5, suggesting that manipulative tax management can be used undesirably as a tool to conceal adverse information and manipulate performance for an extended period as it shows a negative relationship between tax management and contemporaneous stock price crash risks but one that would hasten future crash risks.

In short, the results support all our hypotheses that corporate tax management is unlikely to cause stock price crashes immediately, but is likely to cause such crashes in the future once the concealed information breaks out. While both the central and provincial governments show no moderating effect, municipal governments show a statistically significant impact on this relationship.

Chapter Summary

Using data from China's A-share listed companies over the period 2008 to 2013, this chapter examined the economic consequences of corporate tax management through investors' current perceptions of corporate tax management and future market outcomes. Given the China-specific characteristics of state-owned/controlled shareholding, it further explored the role of the central, provincial, and municipal government on the relationship between corporate tax management and future stock price crash risk.

The first finding is that there is a negative relationship between corporate tax management and stock price crash risk, which supports the contention that corporate tax management can be used to conceal adverse operating outcomes and manipulate management performance, but one that avoids immediate crash risk. However, these opportunists short-term conduct would ultimately increase the likelihood of corporate stock price crashes in future, so that the relationship is reversed with the passage of time. This result is consistent with the findings of Kim, Li, and Zhang (2011), who found that the accumulation of bad news concealed through tax management would increase the likelihood of future crash risk. In doing so, the chapter found that central and provincial listed state-owned/controlled enterprises do not statistically mitigate the positive relationship between tax management and future crash risk. It is only the municipal listed SOEs that show a higher probability of future stock price crash.

Two caveats need to be noted in this conclusion. First, the sample consists primarily of A-share listed SOEs, of which government is the ultimate controller. Accordingly, the results may not be generalizable beyond wholly state-owned enterprises. Second, even if SOEs are found to have a high probability of stock price crash, the reality is that the government, with its substantial financial resources, is unlikely to let its enterprises fail, especially the central or provincial SOEs. However, keeping under-performing firms afloat implies the wasteful use of public resources.

Thus, the results of this chapter point to the need for action at two levels. At the level of the firms, they should strengthen their internal supervision and management ability for optimal decision-making in tax planning activities. Having said that, it must be stated that tax management is not synonymous with concealment. There are legitimate reasons for tax management that include identifying actual costs borne by firms and the incentive structure defined by the government so that filing will be cognizant of them. However, to the extent that it affords opportunities for managers to pursue short-term unproductive rent-seeking, it is important to check its unproductive aspects so that it does not harm the future interests of the enterprises. The current tax system in China is complicated and opaque, which gives managers opportunities to undertake manipulative tax management that can harm government tax revenues and raise the cost of ensuring compliance. The State Administration of Taxation Department should therefore strengthen its external supervision and inspection ability to reduce the possibility of illegal tax activities to protect national interests. In addition, policymakers should enact effective tax laws to create fair competition.

References

Abdul Wahab, N. S., & Holland, K. (2012). Tax planning, corporate governance and equity value. *The British Accounting Review, 44*(2), 111–124.
Acemoglu, D., & Robinson, J. (2012). *Why nations fail: The origins of power, prosperity, and poverty*. New York: Crown Business.
Amsden, A. H. (1989). *Asia's next giant: South Korea and late industrialization*. New York: Oxford University Press.
Badertscher, B. A., Katz, S. P., & Rego, S. O. (2013). The separation of ownership and control and corporate tax avoidance. *Journal of Accounting and Economics, 56*(2–3), 228–250. https://doi.org/10.1016/j.jacceco.2013.08.005.
Bradshaw, M., Liao, G., & Ma, M. S. (2012). *State ownership, tax and political promotion: Evidence from China* (SSRN Working Paper).
Chen, J., Hong, H., & Stein, J. C. (2001). Forecasting crashes: Trading volume, past returns, and conditional skewness in stock prices. *Journal of Financial Economics, 61*(3), 345–381.
Chen, S., Chen, X., Cheng, Q., & Shevlin, T. (2010). Are family firms more tax aggressive than non-family firms? *Journal of Financial Economics, 95*(1), 41–61. https://doi.org/10.1016/j.jfineco.2009.02.003.
Chen, X., Lee, C.-W. J., & Li, J. (2008). Government assisted earnings management in China. *Journal of Accounting and Public Policy, 27*(3), 262–274. https://doi.org/10.1016/j.jaccpubpol.2008.02.005.
Claessens, S., & Fan, J. P. H. (2002). Corporate governance in Asia: A survey. *International Review of Finance, 3*(2), 71–103. https://doi.org/10.1111/1468-2443.00034.
Dechow, P. M., Sloan, R. G., & Sweeney, A. P. (1995). Detecting earnings management. *The Accounting Review, 70*(2), 193–225.
Desai, M. A., & Dharmapala, D. (2006). Corporate tax avoidance and high-powered incentives. *Journal of Financial Economics, 79*(1), 145–179.
Desai, M. A., & Dharmapala, D. (2009a). Corporate tax avoidance and firm value. *The Review of Economics and Statistics, 91*(3), 537–546.
Desai, M. A., & Dharmapala, D. (2009b). Earnings management, corporate tax shelters, and book-tax alignment. *National Tax Journal, 62*(1), 169–186.

Dyreng, S. D., Hanlon, M., & Maydew, E. L. (2008). Long-run corporate tax avoidance. *Accounting Review, 83*(1), 61–82. https://doi.org/10.2308/accr.2008.83.1.61.

Fan, J. P., Wong, T. J., & Zhang, T. (2007). *Organizational structure as a decentralization device: Evidence from corporate pyramids* (Working Paper). http://dx.doi.org/10.2139/ssrn.963430.

Garnaut, R., Song, L., Tenev, S., & Yao, Y. (2005). *China's ownership transformation: Process, outcomes, prospects.* Washington, DC: International Finance Corporation.

Hanlon, M., & Heitzman, S. (2010). A review of tax research. *Journal of Accounting and Economics, 50*(2), 127–178. https://doi.org/10.1016/j.jacceco.2010.09.002.

Hua, J., Miesing, P., & Li, M. (2006). An empirical taxonomy of SOE governance in transitional China. *Journal of Management & Governance, 10*(4), 401–433. https://doi.org/10.1007/s10997-006-9008-z.

Hutton, A. P., Marcus, A. J., & Tehranian, H. (2009). Opaque financial reports, R^2, and crash risk. *Journal of Financial Economics, 94*(1), 67–86. https://doi.org/10.1016/j.jfineco.2008.10.003.

Jensen, M. C., & Meckling, W. H. (1976). Theory of the firm: Managerial behavior, agency costs and ownership structure. *Journal of Financial Economics, 3*(4), 305–360. https://doi.org/10.1016/0304-405X(76)90026-X.

Jin, L., & Myers, S. C. (2006). R^2 around the world: New theory and new tests. *Journal of Financial Economics, 79*(2), 257–292. https://doi.org/10.1016/j.jfineco.2004.11.003.

Kang, Y.-S., & Kim, B.-Y. (2012). Ownership structure and firm performance: Evidence from the Chinese corporate reform. *China Economic Review, 23*(2), 471–481. https://doi.org/10.1016/j.chieco.2012.03.006.

Kim, H.-D., Kim, Y., Mantecon, T., & Song, K. R. (2019). Short-term institutional investors and agency costs of debt. *Journal of Business Research, 95*, 195–210. https://doi.org/10.1016/j.jbusres.2018.10.019.

Kim, J.-B., Li, Y., & Zhang, L. (2011). Corporate tax avoidance and stock price crash risk: Firm-level analysis. *Journal of Financial Economics, 100*(3), 639–662. https://doi.org/10.1016/j.jfineco.2010.07.007.

Kim, Y., Li, H., & Li, S. (2014). Corporate social responsibility and stock price crash risk. *Journal of Banking & Finance, 43*, 1–13. https://doi.org/10.1016/j.jbankfin.2014.02.013.

Krugman, P. (2009). *The return of depression economics and the crisis of 2008.* New York and London: W. W. Norton.

Leung, N. W., & Cheng, M.-A. (2013). Corporate governance and firm value: Evidence from Chinese state-controlled listed firms. *China Journal of Accounting Research, 6*(2), 89–112. https://doi.org/10.1016/j.cjar.2013.03.002.

Leutert, W. (2016). Challenges ahead in China's reform of state-owned enterprises. *Asia Policy, 21*(1), 83–99. https://doi.org/10.1353/asp.2016.0013.
Li, R., & Cheong, K. C. (2019). State enterprises, economic growth, and distribution (Chapter 3). In *China's state enterprises: Changing role in a rapidly transforming economy*. Singapore: Palgrave Macmillan.
Liu, G. S., Sun, P., & Woo, W. T. (2006). The political economy of Chinese-style privatization: Motives and constraints. *World Development, 34*(12), 2016–2033. https://doi.org/10.1016/j.worlddev.2006.06.001.
Mi, Z., & Wang, X. (2000). Agency cost and the crisis of China's SOE. *China Economic Review, 11*(3), 297–317. https://doi.org/10.1016/S1043-951X(00)00023-7.
Piotroski, J. D., & Wong, T. J. (2012). Institutions and information environment of Chinese listed firms. In J. P. H. Fan & R. Morck (Eds.), *Capitalizing China* (pp. 201–242). Chicago and London: University of Chicago Press.
Piotroski, J. D., Wong, T. J., & Zhang, T. (2011). *Political incentives to suppress negative information: Evidence from Chinese listed firms* (Working Paper). Stanford University.
Piotroski, J. D., Wong, T. J., & Zhang, T. (2015). Political incentives to suppress negative information: Evidence from Chinese listed firms. *Journal of Accounting Research, 53*(2), 405–459. https://doi.org/10.1111/1475-679X.12071.
Pogach, J. (2018). Short-termism of executive compensation. *Journal of Economic Behavior & Organization, 148*, 150–170. https://doi.org/10.1016/j.jebo.2018.02.014.
Ross, S. A. (1973). The economic theory of agency: The principal's problem. *The American Economic Review, 63*(2), 134–139.
Shleifer, A. (1998). State versus private ownership. *Journal of Economic Perspectives, 12*(4), 133–150. https://doi.org/10.1257/jep.12.4.133.
Stiglitz, J. E. (2010). *Freefall: America, free markets, and the sinking of the world economy*. New York·and London: W. W. Norton.
Tenev, S., Zhang, C., & Brefort, L. (2002). *Corporate governance and enterprise reform in China: Building the institutions of modern markets*. Washington, DC: World Bank and International Finance Corporation.
Tu, G., Lin, B., & Liu, F. (2013). Political connections and privatization: Evidence from China. *Journal of Accounting and Public Policy, 32*(2), 114–135. https://doi.org/10.1016/j.jaccpubpol.2012.10.002.
Wade, R. (1990). *Governing the market: Economic theory and the role of government in East Asian industrialization*. Princeton, NJ: Princeton University Press.
Wang, Q., Wong, T. J., & Xia, L. (2008). State ownership, the institutional environment, and auditor choice: Evidence from China. *Journal of Accounting and Economics, 46*(1), 112–134. https://doi.org/10.1016/j.jacceco.2008.04.001.

Windmeijer, F. (2005). A finite sample correction for the variance of linear efficient two-step GMM estimators. *Journal of Econometrics, 126*(1), 25–51. https://doi.org/10.1016/j.jeconom.2004.02.005.

Wintoki, M. B., Linck, J. S., & Netter, J. M. (2012). Endogeneity and the dynamics of internal corporate governance. *Journal of Financial Economics, 105*(3), 581–606. https://doi.org/10.1016/j.jfineco.2012.03.005.

Wu, L., Wang, Y., Luo, W., & Gillis, P. (2012). State ownership, tax status and size effect of effective tax rate in China. *Accounting and Business Research, 42*(2), 97–114. https://doi.org/10.1080/00014788.2012.628208.

Xu, L. C., Zhu, T., & Lin, Y.-M. (2005). Politician control, agency problems and ownership reform. *Economics of Transition, 13*(1), 1–24. https://doi.org/10.1111/j.1468-0351.2005.00205.x.

Xu, N., Jiang, X., Chan, K. C., & Yi, Z. (2013). Analyst coverage, optimism, and stock price crash risk: Evidence from China. *Pacific-Basin Finance Journal, 25*, 217–239. https://doi.org/10.1016/j.pacfin.2013.09.001.

Xu, N., Li, X., Yuan, Q., & Chan, K. C. (2014). Excess perks and stock price crash risk: Evidence from China. *Journal of Corporate Finance, 25*, 419–434. https://doi.org/10.1016/j.jcorpfin.2014.01.006.

Yang, Z. (2016). Tax reform, fiscal decentralization, and regional economic growth: New evidence from China. *Economic Modelling, 59*, 520–528. https://doi.org/10.1016/j.econmod.2016.07.020.

Zhang, M., & Rasiah, R. (2015). *Institutionalization of state policy: Evolving urban housing reforms in China*. Singapore: Springer. https://doi.org/10.1007/978-981-287-570-9.

CHAPTER 5

Corruption, Institutions, and Markets

INTRODUCTION

Although it is extremely difficult to define its scope as its boundaries are fuzzy, and to measure corruption since only those convicted are figured in statistics, which may or may not be reflected in perceptions that are themselves subjective, the Corruption Perceptions Index (CPI) constructed by Transparency International ranked China as the 79th most corrupt nation among 175 countries in 2016.[1] Regardless of its veracity, corruption is a major social problem in contemporary China. Following the large-scale crackdown on corruption in the past few years, especially since the accession of Xi Jinping to the chairmanship of the Communist Party, this topic has moved to the forefront among topics of concern and has attracted considerable attention among researchers (Jiang & Nie, 2014; Liu, 2016; Wang & You, 2012; Xu & Yano, 2016).

A commonly held perception is that corruption is inimical to the proper functioning of economic activities, and hence, ultimately hurts both growth and distribution. Unlike productive rent-seeking that deals with the creation of rents to correct market failures and to initiate economic activity when markets are missing, corruption is part of outright unproductive rent-seeking activity (Rasiah, 2018). However, the question of how corruption influences economic activities is still being

---

[1] Source from http://www.transparency.org/news/feature/corruption_perceptions_index_2016.

contested, with opinions supporting and opposing the above view. On the one hand, some researchers support the conventional view that corruption of government acts as a "grabbing hand" that creates unnecessary costs that distort resource allocation, thereby negatively affecting long-run economic activities. On the other hand, other researchers argue that if a country suffers poor governance and heavy regulation, a bribing mechanism actually facilitates the successful completion of economic transactions, and hence, can be viewed as a "helping hand" (see Jiang and Nie [2014]). These contrasting conjectures suggest that the relationship between corruption and economic activities may vary even in theory, which raises the intriguing question as to whether the extent of corruption, however defined, can affect economic activity differently with different conditions, and the consequences not necessarily the worst always.

How does corruption affect business? It does so through its impact on determinants of firm performance. One such determinant is tax management. This relationship can take two forms. Firstly, corruption may encourage the use of tax management, both legal and illegal. For instance, corrupt officials could be bribed to allow less stringent audits so as to allow enterprise managers greater freedom for rent extraction. Secondly, tax management may become part of the practice of corruption. For instance, bribes may be offered to enterprise managers through resource diversion under tax management.

There is evidence of the above occurring. Using cross-country survey data, Alm, Martinez-Vazquez, and McClellan (2016) found corruption by tax officials to affect firms' tax reporting decisions resulting in an understatement of sales reported to tax authorities. Under-reporting of tax liability is part and parcel of tax management, which is defined to include efforts to minimize a firm's tax burden at any time. Still, although a large body of theoretical and empirical research on corruption and tax management has emerged, the relationship between the two issues has remained a largely under-explored area.

With the increased focus on corruption, researchers have also started to consider the role of the institutional environment in moderating the impact of corruption. For instance, using cross-country data, Heckelman and Powell (2010) found that improvements in the institutional environment changed the impact of corruption on growth.

In China, neither the corruption-tax management link nor the role of institutional environment has attracted much research. While both issues are particularly salient in China, despite the tax system having undergone considerable reforms, especially since the 1990s, a well-developed legal framework to stem corruption is not yet in place, thereby allowing enterprises to pursue manipulative tax avoidance. The situation has offered managers the room to bribe to obtain tax preferences and to evade legal restrictions. To make matters worse, China's implementation in 1994 of a tax shared system offers opportunities for local officials to pursue new rent-seeking opportunities, which has added to the complexity of corruption in the country's tax management.

In spite of the digressions, China has undergone dramatic economic transformation from a centrally planned to a market-oriented economy that is driven from central command since 1978. In contrast to neoclassical arguments that marketization should reduce corruption (Krueger, 1974), many commentators believe that corruption is still rife in China (Dong & Torgler, 2013; Foo, Wu, & Chin, 2014; You & Nie, 2017). A relationship-based culture that pervades the institutional environment not only allows but also abets the resort to corrupt practices. Ironically, in this environment, whether an act represents corruption or is relationship-based depends entirely on perception. What is corruption to some may be considered entirely legal by others, especially for those involved in the act.

The above paradoxes provide the rationale for this Chapter, which seeks to complement Chapters 3 and 4, to offer further insight into the opaque world of tax management. Thus, this chapter will answer the third question posed in this book, **namely what the impact of corruption and marketization on tax management and firm performance is.** The following sub-questions are addressed. First, what are the effects of corruption on corporate tax management? Second, how does marketization moderate the relationship between corruption and tax management? Finally, how does corruption affect the relationship between tax management and firm performance? In other words, how does corruption's impact on tax management translate into firm performance? The rest of the chapter is organized as follows: Section two reviews past research to develop the hypotheses. Section three discusses the data and methodology. Section four analyzes the empirical results. Section five finishes with the summary.

LITERATURE REVIEW AND HYPOTHESES DEVELOPMENT

Businessmen typically understand becorruption as a phenomenon in which government bureaucrats abuse their public power to sell government property, or influence or circumvent government regulations for private gain (Jiang & Nie, 2014; Ngo, 2008; Petrou & Thanos, 2014).

From a theoretical perspective, rational choice theory characterizes corruption as an activity in which rational and self-interested individuals engage in rentier activities (Scott, 2000). Hence, as a group of rational individuals, firms bribe government officials when they deem their benefits reaped from such conduct to be higher than their costs. To this one can be added the low risks of getting caught (Becker, 1968). The costs of bribes have at least two parts, viz., bribe-related payments and potential risks of detection and punishment once caught. Consequently, the impact of corruption on tax management may not only be nonlinear, but may also support two opposite theoretical views, the "helping hand" and the "grabbing hand". With "helping hand", firms can make more profits by paying a bribe premium (Jiang & Nie, 2014; Petrou & Thanos, 2014; You & Nie, 2017), whereas the "grabbing hand" saddles firms with higher costs.

In the China context, several developments have raised the likelihood of corruption. First, under fiscal decentralization, the central government granted more autonomy and authority to local governments to give local officials more discretionary powers. Since the tax-sharing reform in 1994, China has started to adopt a dual system of tax collection and administration, and the revenue from corporate taxation is shared by central and local governments, with the central government's share being 60%.[2] Under such taxation system, local governments, especially local tax bureaus, have been granted more taxing authority, thereby giving local officials increased opportunities to seek bribes (Ngo, 2008).

Second, with extensive government intervention in the Chinese economy, markets have become more relationship-based (*guanxi*) rather than rule-based (Martinsons, 2005), resulting in corruption being accepted as normal behavior (Jain, 2001). Thus, under the "helping hand" view firms are apt to bribe local government officials to obtain extra economic advantages. such as direct subsidies in tax benefits, tax breaks or tax reduction, and grants (Ngo, 2008).

However, in the "grabbing hand" view, firms operating in an environment with widespread and rampant corruption have to expend more financial and human resources to insulate themselves with bribes. Bribes

---

[2] The State Administration of Taxation (SAT) is responsible for the collection of corporate tax of central-SOEs. Local governments are responsible for collecting the corporate tax from local SOEs and all other non-SOEs, and then transfer the 60% revenue collected to the central government.

not only result in unnecessary costs, they also expose them to risks of getting caught, which can then attract severe penalties (Jain, 2001). In this case, covert bribing systems act as "grabbing hands", whereby firms' net losses/costs via bribing are higher than their net profits. Consequently, it may affect negatively the enthusiasm of firms for avoiding tax or obtaining tax-related benefits via bribes. In light of the above arguments about the impact of corruption on tax management, we hypothesize that *the impact of corruption on corporate tax management is inverted U-shaped so that tax management rises when corruption increases from low to moderate level, but falls when corruption increases from moderate to high levels* (H5.1).

Scholars have also begun to consider the impact of the institutional environment on corruption (Ali & Isse, 2003). When the government plays an intrusive role that hurts competition, corruption tends to become rampant (Ades & Di Tella, 1999; Giavazzi & Tabellini, 2005). However, driven by the superiority of markets logic, this literature has attempted to show that improving marketization leads to decreased corruption via the mechanisms of governmental deregulation, simplification of regulations, and reduction of bureaucratic discretionary power (Dong & Torgler, 2013; Svensson, 2005). Heckelman and Powell (2010) found that in an environment with limited economic freedom, corruption plays a beneficial role in promoting growth via avoiding inefficient policies and regulations. Also, when unbridled markets dominate in locations gripped by lawlessness, bribes often act as an essential transaction cost to support business activity. Under such circumstances, Khan (1989) had argued over the positive impact of bribes as an essential transactions cost to sustain economic activity. Therefore, a strong correlation between decreased corruption and market development can be expected in environments with poor institutions (Goel & Nelson, 2005; Heckelman & Powell, 2010).

However, recent empirical studies provide evidence of paradoxical co-development of marketization and corruption in China. Using data from a Chinese mid-size city, Gong and Zhou (2015) found that the essence of market competition has often been circumvented, modified, or simply replaced by conditions conductive to corruption. Hence, along with the promotion of market-oriented economic reforms, local officials have been given discretionary powers to influence the setting and implementation of local regulations that may increase officials' rent-seeking activities. Ko and Weng (2012) report that in the rapidly growing private sector, bribery has become the leading form of corruption in China. Dong and Torgler (2013) further found that in the process of transition to a market-oriented economy, economic development has increased corruption. As a result, the transition from communism can lead to new forms and characteristics of corruption (Karklins, 2005). Hence, we hypothesize that *the relationship between corruption and tax management is moderated by development of institutions that support markets* (H5.2).

Few empirical studies have examined the impact of corruption on economic outcomes at the firm-level, and whatever studies that exist have failed to give an unambiguous answer as to how corruption impacts firm performance. On the one hand, the broad consensus on corruption is that it is a pervasive obstacle to economic activities, negatively impacting on firm performance. For example, Gaviria (2002) examined the impact of corruption on firm performance indicators of Latin American private firms, and their results showed that corruption has a negative correlation with firms' sales growth and reduced firms' competitiveness. Using survey data from Indian enterprises, Sharma and Mitra (2015) find a negative impact of corruption on firms' profitability and efficiency. Thus, according to these studies, firm performance is hindered by corruption.

On the other hand, some recent research supports the argument that corruption has a positive effect on firm performance, supporting the view of effective or necessary corruption. Using survey data from Armenian businesses, Sahakyan and Stiegert (2012) found that large firms facing less competition are more likely to perceive corruption as favorable to firm performance. In the context of the Chinese market, Wang and You (2012) found that corruption can benefit firms' growth. Furthermore, the results of Jiang and Nie (2014) show a positive relationship between regional corruption and profitability of Chinese private firms, arguing that these firms can avoid legal restrictions through bribes to enhance profits.

While the above studies support two alternative views of firm-level consequences of corruption, they overlooked how corruption impacts firm performance through firms' specific practices, such as corporate tax management. Thus, an attempt is made here to examine the direct impact of corruption on corporate tax management (H5.1), and on how corruption interacts with corporate tax management to impact firm performance. Thus, we hypothesize that *the relationship between tax management and firm performance is moderated by corruption* (H5.3).

DATA AND METHODOLOGY

This section presents the methodology, sampled data, and statistical measures of the main, moderator, and control variables. The empirical models used to examine the three hypotheses are also specified.

Sample and Data

This chapter uses the period from 2008 to 2013, and firm-level and province-level data with a focus on Chinese A-share (domestic market) companies listed on the Shanghai and Shenzhen Stock Exchanges. The firm-level data, corporate tax management, and other financial control variables (e.g., size, leverage, firm age) data are drawn from the China Stock Market and Accounting Research (CSMAR) database.[3]

Following Dong and Torgler (2013), Jiang and Nie (2014), and Xu, Li, Liu, and Gan (2017), this chapter uses number of registered cases of corruption per 10,000 officials in each province in a given year to measure corruption at the provincial level. Thus, the provincial-level panel data for corruption are from the Procuratorial Yearbooks of China (published by the Supreme People's Procuratorate of China and listed in the Provincial People's Procuratorate websites). The indexes of provincial institutions coordinating marketization are used to measure marketization. The data for provincial institutions for marketization indexes were collected from the Marketization Index of China's Provinces contained in the NERI Report 2016 prepared by Wang, Fan, and Yu (2017).

Following Wu, Wu, Zhou, and Wu (2012), Xu and Yano (2016), and Zhang, M, Zhang, and Yi (2016), firms in the financial industry were excluded because their financial reporting and corporate tax practices differ from firms in other industries. Also excluded were firm-year observations that are labeled as Special Treatment (ST) shares, covering firms with financial problems and/or other abnormal challenges. In addition, the sample is confined to firm-year observations with both measures of corporate effective tax rates (*ETRs*) between zero and one, which will be discussed in next section. Finally, firm-year observations with missing information were deleted. To reduce the effect of extreme outliers, the chapter trims the continuous variables at the 1st and 99th percentiles, which leaves 9033 firm-year observations for use in this chapter.

---

[3]The CSMAR database is developed by Shenzhen GTA Information Technology Corporation Limited. Co., Ltd., and designed by the China Accounting and Finance Research Centre of the Hong Kong Polytechnic University.

Variables

We proceed to identify and establish the measurement formulas of the variables that will be used in the chapter. To capture the overall level of corporate tax management, two categories of corporate effective tax rates were used since effective corporate tax rates can reflect several kinds of tax management transactions, including manipulative tax avoidance through permanent book-tax differences (Chen, Chen, Cheng, & Shevlin, 2010). The first category, which is the current effective tax rate (*ETR*), is calculated as income tax expenses minus deferred tax expenses over pre-tax profits, which denotes the firms' overall tax burden (see also Chapter 3). To adjust for *ETRs* in different industries, a second category, that is, industry-adjusted effective tax rate (*ETR_adj*), were estimated as *ETR* minus average industry *ETR*. China enacted a new corporate income tax law, which set a unified corporate income tax rate of 25% for both domestic and foreign-funded companies in 2008. To support the development of special industry, tax preference and incentives are granted to income from these industries, such as new high tech, agriculture, forestry, livestock farming and fishery companies.

Following Dong and Torgler (2013), Jiang and Nie (2014), and Xu, Li, Liu, and Gan (2017), this chapter uses as the *measure of corruption* number of registered cases of corruption per 10,000 public officials in a given province and in a given year. Although the measure will understate the magnitude of corruption as those not caught will not be included, it is the most commonly used proxy to measure Chinese bureaucratic corruption at the provincial level (Jiang & Nie, 2014). Importantly, this conviction-rate-based[4] proxy provides a relatively less subjective measure to study Chinese provincial corruption, and avoids problems of sampling error and survey non-response (Glaeser & Saks, 2006).

The *provincial-level marketization index* prepared by Wang, Fan, and Yu (2017), is used as the measure of institutional coordination of

---

[4]Theoretically, the conviction rate and the number of registered cases of corruption are different. But in China, they tend to be highly correlated, even not identical. Generally, in most cases in China, suspect officials are first investigated by the discipline inspection commission of the Chinese Communist Party and its local branches. Only after they have obtained enough evidence, the discipline inspection commission and its local branches will refer corrupt cases to the procuratorates, then the procuratorates will register the cases. Moreover, in China, the courts and the procuratorates are both controlled by the government. Thus, except in a few very limited circumstances, the courts will not reject public prosecutions against corrupt cases.

marketization, which denotes the provincial market environment in the registered place of listed enterprises, and reflects the extent of provincial institutional transition from a government-based to a market-based economic environment. The index has five dimensions, viz., relationship between government and market, the extent of development of the non-state sector, development of product markets, development of factor markets, and development of market intermediaries and the legal environment, which together offer a comprehensive assessment of the level of evolution of institutions coordinating regional marketization. A higher index means the provincial environment is more equipped with institutional support for market-orientation and vice versa.

In addition to the above variables, several other firm-level variables were included as *control variables,* viz., firm size (*Size*), ROA *(ROA)*, firm age (*Age*), market/book ratio (*MB*), firm leverage (*Leverage*), firm sales growth (*Growth*), largest and top 10 shareholders' shareholdings (*Largest* and *Top10*), and discretionary accruals (*Discacc*).

Past studies show that *firm size* and growth may impact corporate tax management practice because large firms possess superior resources and political power to lobby for tax preferences compared to small firms (Dyreng, Hanlon, & Maydew, 2008; Minnick & Noga, 2010; Siegfried, 1973). *Size* was calculated by taking the natural logarithm of firms' total assets, while *Growth* was measured estimating firms' sales growth. *Leverage* is the ratio of total liabilities to total assets, which denotes the overall level of firms' debts. Because of tax-deductible interest payments, higher leverage may cause lower *ETRs* that may influence corporate tax management (Gupta & Newberry, 1997; Richardson, Taylor, & Lanis, 2013).

ROA is the return on total assets, which is deployed as a control variable to test H5.1 and H5.2. The results will be important as past research has shown inconsistent results in the relationship between *ROA* and *ETRs*. On the one hand, firms with more taxable income can mean that they are more profitable leading to a positive relationship between *ROA* and *ETRs* (Dyreng, Hanlon, & Maydew, 2008). On the other hand, firms with higher *ROA* may mean that they are more efficient, and hence, have the ability to pay less taxes (Zhang, M, Zhang, & Yi, 2016).

MB was estimated as the market value of equity over the book value of the equity to test H5.1 and H5.2. The firm that has a higher *MB* has more investment opportunities to impact on corporate decisions (Zhang, M, Zhang, & Yi, 2016).

Table 5.1 Variables and descriptions

Variable	Description
Panel A: Tax management	
ETR	Corporate effective tax rate, corporate tax expenses minus deferred tax expenses to the pre-tax profit
ETR_adj	Corporate industry-adjusted effective tax rate, calculated by corporate ETR minus average-industry ETR
Panel B: Corruption, institutional support for marketization, and firm performance	
Corruption	Number of registered cases of corruption per 10,000 public officials in a province in each year, data stems from Procuratorial Yearbook of China and China Statistical Yearbook
Institutional support for marketization	The overall marketization index in China's 31 provinces. The higher index suggests higher marketization. The indexes are obtained from National Economic Research Institute (NERI) Index of Marketization of China's provinces in 2016 to measure the quality of market-supporting institutions at the provincial level. The NERI Index project was sponsored by the National Economic Research Institute and the China Reform Foundation and conducted by Wang, Fan, and Yu (2017). The NERI indices capture the progress of the institutional transition in China's 31 provinces. Appraisals of the regional institutions are made along several dimensions, namely, the relationship between the government and the market, the extent of development of the non-state sector, the development of the factor markets, the development of the product markets, and the development of market intermediaries and the legal environment
ROA	Return on total assets, net income/total assets
ROE	Return on equity, net income/shareholder equity
Panel C: Other Control Variables	
Size	Firm size, the natural logarithm of total assets
Age	Firm age, the natural logarithm of current year minus the year when the firm went public
Leverage	Firm's overall debt levels, total debts/total assets in book value
Growth	Firm sales growths, the changes in sales scaled by lag sales
MB	Market-to-book ratio, the market value of equity over book value of equity
Discacc	The absolute value of abnormal accruals, measured as the absolute value of discretionary accruals estimated by the modified Jones model. See Appendix A
Largest	Percentage of shareholding by the largest shareholder
Top10	Percentage of shareholding by the top 10 largest shareholders

Source Prepared by authors

Firm age (*Age*) was measured as the natural logarithm of the number of years since the firm went public. The longer the firms existence, the more complex and mature are likely their corporate management and governance (Chen, 2015).

Discacc is the absolute value of discretionary accruals, computed using the modified Jones model. Past research shows that there is a relationship between tax management and earnings management (Frank, Lynch, & Rego, 2009; Kubick & Masli, 2016). This chapter also includes the percentage of shareholding by the largest and top 10 shareholders to represent ownership concentration of listed firms, for which previous studies have produced inconclusive results on its impact on corporate tax management (Badertscher, Katz, & Rego, 2013; Richardson, Wang, & Zhang, 2016).

To address the potential problem of endogeneity, provincial fixed effects have been included in the regressions to avoid unobserved regional characteristics, which may affect provincial corruption and tax management estimates. Following Zhang, M, Zhang, and Yi (2016) and Richardson, Wang, and Zhang (2016), industry and year dummies were added to control for industry and year fixed effects. Table 5.1 shows the variables and related details used in the chapter.

Model Specification

To examine the relationship between corruption and corporate tax management (Hypothesis 5.1), the following regression models, Eqs. (5.1 and 5.2), were deployed:

$$TAX_{i,t} = \alpha_0 + \beta_1 Corruption_{i,t} + \beta_2 SIZE_{i,t} + \beta_3 ROA_{i,t} + \beta_4 Age_{i,t} + \beta_5 MB_{i,t}$$
$$+ \beta_6 Leverage_{i,t} + \beta_7 Top10_{i,t} + \beta_8 Largest_{i,t} + \beta_9 Growth_{i,t}$$
$$+ \beta_{10} Discacc_{i,t} + Industry\,Dummies + Province\,Dummies$$
$$+ Year\,Dummies + \varepsilon_{i,t} \qquad (5.1)$$

$$TAX_{i,t} = \alpha_0 + \beta_1 Corruption_{i,t} + \beta_2 Corruption_{i,t}^2 + \beta_3 SIZE_{i,t} + \beta_4 ROA_{i,t}$$
$$+ \beta_5 Age_{i,t} + \beta_6 MB_{i,t} + \beta_7 Leverage_{i,t} + \beta_8 Top10_{i,t} + \beta_9 Largest_{i,t}$$
$$+ \beta_{10} Growth_{i,t} + \beta_{11} Discacc_{i,t} + Industry\,Dummies$$
$$+ Province\,Dummies + Year\,Dummies + \varepsilon_{i,t} \qquad (5.2)$$

Equation (5.1) is used to test the linear relationship between corruption and corporate tax management, while Eq. (5.2) is used to examine the nonlinear relationship between them. In the model, $TAX_{i,t}$ represents corporate tax management for firm i in year t, which is the dependent variable proxied by $ETR_{i,t}$ and $ETR\_adj_{i,t}$. The independent variable, $Corruption_{i,t}$, denotes provincial corruption. A set of control variables were used in the model. Which firm size ($SIZE_{i,t}$), return on assets ($ROA_{i,t}$), firm age ($Age_{i,t}$), market-to-book ratio ($MB_{i,t}$), firm leverage ($Leverage_{i,t}$), shareholding by the top 10 shareholders ($TOP10_{i,t}$), shareholding by the largest shareholders ($Largest_{i,t}$), firm growth rate ($Growth_{i,t}$), absolute value of discretionary accruals ($Discacc_{i,t}$). In addition, the three dummy variables of *Province, Industry,* and *Year* were included to control for regional, industry, and time fixed effects.

To test the moderating role of increased institutional support for marketization on the relationship between corruption and tax management (Hypothesis 5.2), the following regression models, Eqs. (5.3a and 5.3b), were used:

$$TAX_{i,t} = \alpha_0 + \beta_1 Corruption_{i,t} + \beta_2 Marketization * Corruption_{i,t}$$
$$+ \beta_3 Marketization_{i,t} + \beta_4 SIZE_{i,t} + \beta_5 ROA_{i,t} + \beta_6 Age_{i,t} + \beta_7 MB_{i,t}$$
$$+ \beta_8 Leverage_{i,t} + \beta_9 Top10_{i,t} + \beta_{10} Largest_{i,t} + \beta_{11} Growth_{i,t}$$
$$+ \beta_{12} Discacc_{i,t} + Industry\ Dummies + Province\ Dummies$$
$$+ Year\ Dummies + \varepsilon_{i,t} \quad (5.3a)$$

$$TAX_{i,t} = \alpha_0 + \beta_1 Corruption_{i,t} + \beta_2 Corruption_{i,t}^2$$
$$+ \beta_3 Marketization * Corruption_{i,t} + \beta_4 Marketization * Corruption_{i,t}^2$$
$$+ \beta_5 Marketization_{i,t} + \beta_6 SIZE_{i,t} + \beta_7 ROA_{i,t}$$
$$+ \beta_8 Age_{i,t} + \beta_9 MB_{i,t} + \beta_{10} Leverage_{i,t} + \beta_{11} Top10_{i,t}$$
$$+ \beta_{12} Largest_{i,t} + \beta_{13} Growth_{i,t} + \beta_{14} Discacc_{i,t}$$
$$+ Industry\ Dummies + Province\ Dummies + Year\ Dummies + \varepsilon_{i,t} \quad (5.3b)$$

If the results of Eq. (5.1) are supported, then Eq. (5.3a) will be used to test the moderating role of institutional support for marketization, but if the results of Eq. (5.2) are significant, then Eq. (5.3b) will be used to examine the impact of institutional support for marketization. In the models of Eqs. (5.3a and 5.3b), the dependent variable is corporate tax management, represented by $TAX_{i,t}$, and proxied by $ETR_{i,t}$ and $ETR\_adj_{i,t}$. $Marketization_{i,t}$ which is the moderator variable, denotes Chinese provincial marketization level. *Marketization*Corruption*$_{i,t}$ is an interaction term to capture provincial marketization and provincial corruption status. The set of control variables used are firm size ($SIZE_{i,t}$), return on assets ($ROA_{i,t}$), firm age ($Age_{i,t}$), market-to-book ratio ($MB_{i,t}$), firm leverage ($Leverage_{i,t}$), shareholding by the top 10 shareholders ($TOP10_{i,t}$), shareholding by the largest shareholders ($Largest_{i,t}$), firm growth rate ($Growth_{i,t}$), absolute value of discretionary accruals ($Discacc_{i,t}$). In addition, three dummy variables of *Province*, *Industry*, and *Year* are included to control for regional, industry, and time fixed effects.

To test the moderating role of corruption on the relationship between tax management and firm performance (Hypothesis 5.3), Eqs. (5.4 and 5.5) were specified as follows:

$$Performance_{i,t} = \alpha_0 + \beta_1 TAX_{i,t} + \beta_2 Corruption_{i,t} + \beta_3 SIZE_{i,t} + \beta_4 Age_{i,t}$$
$$+ \beta_5 Leverage_{i,t} + \beta_6 Top10_{i,t} + \beta_7 Largest_{i,t} + \beta_8 Growth_{i,t}$$
$$+ \beta_9 Discacc_{i,t} + Industry\ Dummies + Province\ Dummies$$
$$+ Year\ Dummies + \varepsilon_{i,t} \tag{5.4}$$

$$Performance_{i,t} = \alpha_0 + \beta_1 TAX_{i,t} + \beta_2 TAX * Corruption_{i,t} + \beta_3 Corruption_{i,t}$$
$$+ \beta_4 SIZE_{i,t} + \beta_5 Age_{i,t} + \beta_6 Leverage_{i,t} + \beta_7 Top10_{i,t} + \beta_8 Largest_{i,t}$$
$$+ \beta_9 Growth_{i,t} + \beta_{10} Discacc_{i,t} + Industry\ Dummies$$
$$+ Province\ Dummies + Year\ Dummies + \varepsilon_{i,t} \tag{5.5}$$

Equation (5.4) is used to test the relationship between corporate tax management and firm performance, while Eq. (5.5) is used to examine the moderating influence of corruption on the relationship between tax management and firm performance. The dependent variable is firm performance, which is represented by *Performance*$_{i,t}$, proxied by $ROA_{i,t}$ and $ROE_{i,t}$. The independent variable is corporate tax management, which is represented by $TAX_{i,t}$, proxied by $ETR_{i,t}$ and $ETR\_adj_{i,t}$. *Corruption*$_{i,t}$ is the moderator variable, and *TAX*Corruption*$_{i,t}$ is the interaction term of tax management and provincial corruption. The set of control variables used are firm size ($SIZE_{i,t}$), firm age ($Age_{i,t}$), firm leverage ($Leverage_{i,t}$), shareholding by the top 10 shareholders ($TOP10_{i,t}$), shareholding by the largest shareholders ($Largest_{i,t}$), firm growth rate ($Growth_{i,t}$), absolute value of discretionary accruals ($Discacc_{i,t}$). In addition, of *Province*, *Industry*, and *Year* as three dummy variables are included to control for regional, industry, and time fixed effects.

Results and Analysis

In this section we analyze the results of the statistical exercise. The first part presents the descriptive statistics, while the statistical analysis is carried out in the second part.

Descriptive Statistics

Table 5.2 displays the distribution of *ETRs* by industry in the sample. The industrial classification is based on specifications used by the China Securities Regulatory Commission (CSRC). The sample is highly skewed toward manufacturing, which comprises approximately 61% of the total sample (5524 out of 9033 firm-years). In addition, Table 5.2 also shows that the different industries have different levels of *ETRs* because of the preferential tax policy to support specific industries, such as agriculture, forestry, livestock farming and fisheries, and high-tech industries. Thus, the chapter controls for industry effects by including industry dummies.

Table 5.3 shows the summary statistics for all the corporate financial variables. The mean and median *ETR* are 21.6% and 18.8%,

Table 5.2 Distribution of *ETR* by industry

Industry	ETR	N
Agriculture, forestry, livestock farming and fishery	0.097	125
Mining	0.264	272
Manufacturing	0.201	5524
Electric power, heat, gas, and water production	0.228	355
Construction	0.272	247
Wholesale and retail	0.277	694
Transportation, storage, and post	0.209	368
Accommodation and catering services	0.248	46
Information technology and software	0.141	378
Real estate	0.303	619
Leasing and commercial service	0.244	90
Scientific research and technological service	0.190	31
Water conservancy, environment and public establishment	0.226	101
Education	0.488	4
Health and social work	0.293	12
Communication and culture	0.149	72
Miscellaneous	0.242	95
Total	0.216	9033

Source Computed by authors

respectively, and the 75th percentile of *ETR* is 26.7%. Thus, more than half of the sample firms have a lower corporate *ETR* than the 25% statutory rate, and only about one-fourth of the sample firms have *ETR* more than 25%. Therefore, corporate tax management appears to have become a common and significant strategy of corporate management in Chinese listed enterprises. In addition, the median of *ETR_adj* is −2.5%, which means that more than half of the

Table 5.3 Summary statistics of all corporate financial variables

Variables	N	Mean	Sd.	p25	p50	p75
ETR	9033	0.216	0.140	0.140	0.188	0.267
ETR_adj	9033	0.000	0.133	−0.069	−0.025	0.041
Size	9033	9.514	0.533	9.120	9.439	9.819
ROA	9033	0.051	0.040	0.021	0.041	0.070
Age	9033	1.853	0.931	1.099	2.197	2.639
MB	9033	0.277	0.271	0.004	0.219	0.517
Leverage	9033	0.447	0.207	0.287	0.456	0.612
Top10	9033	57.740	15.930	46.450	59.040	70.210
Largest	9033	37.060	15.440	24.430	35.580	48.560
Growth	9033	0.174	0.358	0.006	0.091	0.235
Discacc	9033	0.146	0.130	0.053	0.113	0.203

Source Computed by authors

Table 5.4 Descriptive statistics of corruption and marketization

	2008	2009	2010	2011	2012	2013
Panel A: Corruption across seven districts						
Northern	23.359	24.047	25.892	25.834	27.792	27.679
Northeast	41.615	43.018	45.797	46.173	49.948	56.965
East	31.647	30.097	30.930	30.506	33.253	32.614
Central	33.798	32.312	32.375	32.841	30.297	33.893
Southern	32.203	29.464	30.704	28.664	31.898	32.502
Southwest	32.366	27.998	28.483	25.447	28.100	25.142
Northwest	25.508	28.585	30.347	28.230	28.017	27.665
Total	30.606	29.942	31.185	30.133	32.076	32.284
Panel B: Marketization across seven districts						
Northern	5.700	5.732	5.774	5.960	6.598	6.836
Northeast	5.717	5.810	5.563	5.700	6.270	6.377
East	6.967	7.143	7.270	7.521	7.819	7.959
Central	5.613	5.697	5.757	5.970	6.177	6.417
Southern	5.830	5.830	5.810	5.973	6.667	6.900

(continued)

Table 5.4 (continued)

	2008	2009	2010	2011	2012	2013
Southwest	4.436	4.388	4.188	4.202	4.368	4.444
Northwest	3.802	3.758	3.340	3.466	3.702	3.932
Total	5.482	5.529	5.445	5.604	5.981	6.156

Note Seven district classification
1. **Eastern**: Shandong province, Jiangsu province, Anhui province, Shanghai, Zhejiang province, Jiangxi province, Fujian province;
2. **Southern**: Guangdong province, Guangxi province, Hainan province;
3. **Central**: Hubei province, Hunan province, Henan province;
4. **Northern**: Beijing province, Tianjin province, Hebei province, Shanxi province, Inner Mongolia autonomous region;
5. **Northwest**: Ningxia Hui Autonomous Region, Xinjiang Autonomous Region, Qinghai province, Gansu province, Shaanxi Province;
6. **Southwest**: Sichuan province, Yunnan province, Guizhou province, Tibet Autonomous Region, Chongqing;
7. **Northeast**: Liaoning province, Jilin province, Heilongjiang province.
Source Computed by authors

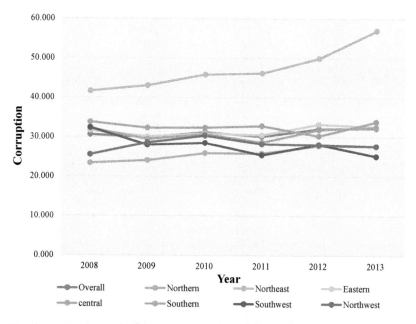

Fig. 5.1 Degree of regional corruption by regions, China, 2008–2013 (*Note* The seven-region classification is shown in Table 5.4. *Source* Plotted by authors)

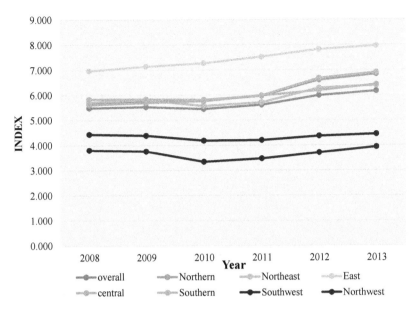

Fig. 5.2 NERI index of overall marketization (*Note* The seven-district classification is shown in Table 5.4. *Source* Plotted by authors)

sample firms are below their industry average level, which is consonant with the reported *ETR*.

Panels A and B of Table 5.4 display the descriptive statistics of corruption and institutional support for marketization across seven districts in the period between 2008 and 2013, respectively. The results show that the degree of corruption and the institutional support for marketization are heterogenous across different locations. Specifically, Fig. 5.1 shows the degree of provincial corruption in China's seven different regions. The northeast provinces in China are shown to have the highest corruption with an upward trend over the period from 2008 to 2013. Figure 5.2 shows the NERI index of overall marketization in China's 31 provinces and seven different districts from 2008 to 2013, published by Wang, Fan, and Yu (2017). The figures show that regional institutional quality is unequal. Also, we can see that the overall marketization index shows an upward trend from 2008 to 2013 (Fig. 5.2), which means that institutional quality has been improving. In addition, the degree of marketization in the southwestern and northwestern provinces is below the

Table 5.5 Correlations between variables

	ETR	ETR_adj	Marketization	Corruption	Size	ROA	Age
ETR_adj	0.951***						
Marketization	−0.003	−0.026**					
Corruption	0.021*	0.029***	−0.193***				
Size	0.111***	0.044***	−0.034***	−0.066***			
ROA	−0.285***	−0.258***	0.044***	−0.068***	−0.062***		
Age	0.156***	0.086***	−0.159***	0.051***	0.307***	−0.157***	
MB	−0.088***	−0.059***	0.056***	−0.033***	−0.159***	0.137***	−0.582***
Leverage	0.244***	0.158***	−0.127***	0.059***	0.515***	−0.407***	0.448***
Top10	−0.068***	−0.057***	0.123***	−0.073***	0.147***	0.220***	−0.454***
Largest	0.009	−0.011	0.029***	−0.076***	0.258***	0.066***	−0.075***
Growth	−0.029***	−0.031***	−0.029***	−0.0160	0.080***	0.208***	−0.083***
Discacc	0.021*	0.0140	−0.122***	0.040***	0.146***	−0.044***	0.0100

	MB	Leverage	Top10	Largest	Growth
Leverage	−0.276***				
Top10	0.519***	−0.137***			
Largest	0.230***	0.075***	0.645***		
Growth	0.165***	0.106***	0.164***	0.078***	
Discacc	0.110***	0.181***	0.108***	0.090***	0.245***

Note *Significant at the 10% level; **Significant at the 5% level; ***Significant at the 1% level
The independent and control variables are shown in bold
Source Computed by authors

overall average, while the eastern part of China is the most developed district. Therefore, China's local market development shows obvious imbalances.

Table 5.5 reports the correlation coefficients between all variables. The results show that most variables are correlated with the dependent variables, proxied by *ETR* and *ETR_adj*. Since the correlations between all independent and control variables are less than 0.7, multicollinearity is not a problem in the following regression analysis (Jr., Black, Babin, & Anderson, 2009). Furthermore, the variance inflation factor (VIF) statistics show that VIF values of all variables are less than 5, which confirms that multicollinearity is not an issue with the results.

Corruption and Corporate Tax Management

Tables 5.6 and 5.7 present the empirical results of the relationship between corruption and tax management (H5.1) using ordinary least squares (OLS) and fixed-effect (FE) models with the two dependent variables, *ETR* and *ETR_adj*, respectively. Standard errors in parentheses are heteroskedasticity-robust and clustered at the firm level. A Hausman test was run to identify whether the fixed or random effects model fits best the data. In this case, it is the fixed effects model that came out best.

Through columns (1) to (4) in Table 5.6, the results show that there is no statistically significant linear relationship between corruption and corporate tax management, which suggest that the effect of corruption on firm activities cannot be simply ascribed to a monotonic detrimental or beneficial effect. However, by including a linear term ($Corruption_{i,t}$) and a quadratic term ($Corruption\ squared_{i,t}$) of corruption with two measures of tax management (*ETR* and *ETR_adj*) in both the OLS and fixed-effect (FE) regressions, the coefficients of the linear terms are significantly negative indicating that corruption leads to a reduction in corporate *ETRs* (Table 5.7, columns (2) to (4)). The low corporate *ETRs* denote low corporate tax burden, demonstrating that firms are engaged in tax management. In other words, corruption is positively correlated with corporate tax management at low to moderate levels of corruption. In addition, the quadratic coefficients shown in columns (2) to (4) of Table 5.7 are significantly positive, indicating that corruption leads to increasing *ETRs*. Thus, when corruption is over the moderate level, there is a negative correlation between corruption and corporate tax management.

Table 5.6 Linear relationship between corruption and corporate tax management

	(1) OLS	(2) FE	(3) OLS	(4) FE
Dependent variable:	ETR	ETR	ETR_adj	ETR_adj
$Corruption_{i,t}$	0.000	0.000	0.000	0.000
	(0.43)	(0.81)	(0.34)	(0.73)
$Size_{i,t}$	−0.003	0.013	−0.003	0.013
	(−0.66)	(0.65)	(−0.60)	(0.63)
$Age_{i,t}$	0.009***	−0.005	0.009***	−0.005
	(3.14)	(−0.74)	(3.06)	(−0.80)
$ROA_{i,t}$	−0.836***	−1.334***	−0.825***	−1.307***
	(−14.41)	(−16.24)	(−14.28)	(−15.98)
$Leverage_{i,t}$	0.050***	0.036	0.048***	0.029
	(3.39)	(1.33)	(3.29)	(1.09)
$MB_{i,t}$	−0.000	0.004	0.000	0.005
	(−0.03)	(0.38)	(0.06)	(0.57)
$Growth_{i,t}$	0.005	0.008*	0.005	0.008*
	(1.06)	(1.65)	(1.17)	(1.69)
$Top10_{i,t}$	0.000	−0.000	0.000	−0.000
	(1.30)	(−0.48)	(1.16)	(−0.49)
$Largest_{i,t}$	−0.000	−0.000	−0.000	−0.000
	(−0.47)	(−0.13)	(−0.36)	(−0.15)
$Discacc_{i,t}$	−0.013	−0.002	−0.008	0.006
	(−1.00)	(−0.13)	(−0.65)	(0.41)
Province effects	Yes	Yes	Yes	Yes
Industry effects	Yes	Yes	Yes	Yes
Year effects	Yes	Yes	Yes	Yes
Constant	0.118**	0.174	0.013	−0.058
	(2.53)	(0.95)	(0.28)	(−0.32)
N	9033	9033	9033	9033
Adjusted R^2	0.164	0.094	0.082	0.079

Note ***, **, and * are significance at 1%, 5%, and 10% levels, respectively
Source Computed by authors

These results provide evidence of a U-shaped relationship between corruption and corporate *ETRs*, which indicates that *ETRs* fall as corruption rises from low to middle levels but the reverse takes place thereafter as *ETRs* increase from medium and high levels as corruption rises. Hence, Hypothesis 5.1 is supported. Figures 5.3 and 5.4 show a quadratic U-shape curve between corruption and corporate effective tax rates. Probability values in Figs. 5.3 and 5.4 were computed from the estimated models reported in columns (2) and (4) in Table 5.7.

Table 5.7 Relationship between corruption and corporate tax management

	(1) OLS	(2) FE	(3) OLS	(4) FE
Dependent variable:	ETR	ETR	ETR_adj	ETR_adj
$Corruption_{i,t}$	−0.003	−0.004*	−0.004*	−0.004*
	(−1.47)	(−1.76)	(−1.73)	(−1.96)
$Corruption\ squared_{i,t}$	0.000	0.000**	0.000*	0.000**
	(1.60)	(1.98)	(1.84)	(2.16)
$Size_{i,t}$	−0.003	0.013	−0.003	0.012
	(−0.66)	(0.63)	(−0.61)	(0.60)
$Age_{i,t}$	0.009***	−0.004	0.009***	−0.004
	(3.14)	(−0.63)	(3.05)	(−0.67)
$ROA_{i,t}$	−0.836***	−1.331***	−0.826***	−1.304***
	(−14.41)	(−16.25)	(−14.29)	(−15.99)
$Leverage_{i,t}$	0.049***	0.035	0.048***	0.029
	(3.38)	(1.33)	(3.28)	(1.08)
$MB_{i,t}$	−0.000	0.003	0.000	0.005
	(−0.04)	(0.36)	(0.05)	(0.55)
$Growth_{i,t}$	0.005	0.008*	0.005	0.009*
	(1.08)	(1.69)	(1.19)	(1.73)
$Top10_{i,t}$	0.000	−0.000	0.000	−0.000
	(1.30)	(−0.47)	(1.16)	(−0.47)
$Largest_{i,t}$	−0.000	−0.000	−0.000	−0.000
	(−0.47)	(−0.11)	(−0.35)	(−0.14)
$Discacc_{i,t}$	−0.013	−0.002	−0.009	0.005
	(−1.01)	(−0.14)	(−0.67)	(0.39)
Province effects	Yes	Yes	Yes	Yes
Industry effects	Yes	Yes	Yes	Yes
Year effects	Yes	Yes	Yes	Yes
Constant	0.147***	0.217	0.046	−0.011
	(2.98)	(1.19)	(0.95)	(−0.06)
N	9033	9033	9033	9033
Adjusted R^2	0.164	0.095	0.082	0.080

Note ***, **, and * are significance at 1%, 5%, and 10% levels, respectively
Source Computed by authors

These results also show that when regional corruption is below a certain threshold, corruption plays a positive role to facilitate enterprises engaged in tax management activities to reduce firms' tax burden, indicating that the benefits of firms doing such activities outweigh the costs, and thus, supports the "helping hand" view. However, when corruption exceeds the moderate level, corruption shows a negative effect on

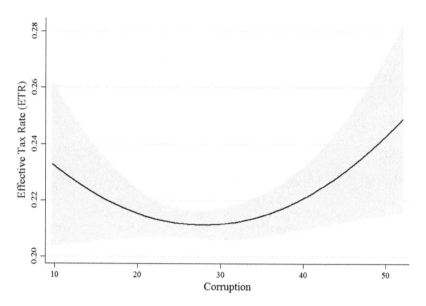

Fig. 5.3 The u-shaped effect of corruption on corporate effective tax rate (*Source* Plotted by authors)

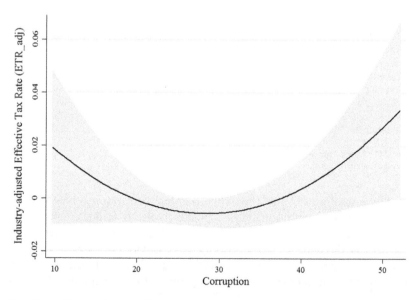

Fig. 5.4 The u-shaped effect of corruption on industry-adjusted corporate effective tax rate (*Source* Plotted by authors)

tax management, indicating that when firms operate in a highly corrupt environment, the costs and/or risks of doing tax management would be greater than the benefits, which support the "grabbing hand" view of government.

Moderating Effect of Institutional Support

Table 5.8 presents results of the moderating effect of institutional support for marketization on the U-shaped relationship between corruption and tax management using OLS and fixed-effect models (FE) using the two dependent variables of ETR and ETR_adj [columns (1) to (4)]. All the regressions control for province, industry, and year effects. Standard errors in parentheses are heteroskedasticity-robust and clustered at the firm level. The interaction terms between marketization and the linear term of corruption (*Corruption*Marketization$_{i,t}$*) and quadratic term of corruption (*Corruption squared*Marketization$_{i,t}$*) are the key explanatory variables in this section. A Hausman test was run to identify whether the fixed or random effects model fits the data. In this case, the fixed effect was better suited. And hence, was deployed.

In columns (1) to (4) of Table 5.8, the coefficients of the interaction terms between corruption and the linear term of corruption (*Corruption*Marketization$_{i,t}$*) are highly significant and positive, while the interaction terms of marketization and quadratic term of corruption (*Corruption squared*Marketization$_{i,t}$*) are highly significant and negative. Thus, these results support H5.2, which indicates that institutional support for marketization moderates the curvilinear relationship between corruption and tax management. Specifically, institutional support for marketization diminishes the impact of corruption on corporate tax management in both low to moderate levels and in moderate to high levels of corruption.

We now analyze the NERI Marketization index results, which used the five dimensions of provincial institutional environment, that is, (1) the relationship between government and market, (2) development of non-state sectors, (3) development of product markets, (4) development of production factor markets, and (5) development of market intermediaries and legal environment. The three dimensions of government-market relationship, non-state sectors development, and market intermediaries and legal environment development were examined to obtain more specific and robust results of the moderating effects of

Table 5.8 Impact of marketization on the relationship between tax management and corruption

	OLS	OLS	FE	FE
Dependent variable:	(1) ETR	(2) ETR_adj	(3) ETR	(4) ETR_adj
$Corruption_{i,t}$	−0.018***	−0.019***	−0.019***	−0.019***
	(−2.87)	(−2.93)	(−2.91)	(−2.89)
$Corruption\ squared_{i,t}$	0.000***	0.000***	0.000***	0.000***
	(2.78)	(2.79)	(2.81)	(2.75)
$Corruption*Marketization_{i,t}$	0.002***	0.002***	0.002***	0.002**
	(2.64)	(2.63)	(2.63)	(2.55)
$Corruption\ squared*Marketization_{i,t}$	−0.000**	−0.000**	−0.000**	−0.000**
	(−2.48)	(−2.44)	(−2.44)	(−2.34)
$Marketization_{i,t}$	−0.034***	−0.036***	−0.035***	−0.036***
	(−2.65)	(−2.81)	(−2.76)	(−2.87)
$Size_{i,t}$	−0.003	−0.003	0.011	0.010
	(−0.67)	(−0.62)	(0.53)	(0.49)
$Age_{i,t}$	0.009***	0.008***	−0.004	−0.004
	(3.09)	(3.00)	(−0.56)	(−0.58)
$ROA_{i,t}$	−0.835***	−0.824***	−1.329***	−1.302***
	(−14.38)	(−14.26)	(−16.16)	(−15.90)
$Leverage_{i,t}$	0.050***	0.048***	0.036	0.030
	(3.40)	(3.30)	(1.36)	(1.12)
$MB_{i,t}$	−0.001	0.000	0.003	0.004
	(−0.08)	(0.01)	(0.27)	(0.46)
$Growth_{i,t}$	0.005	0.005	0.008	0.008*
	(1.05)	(1.16)	(1.65)	(1.70)
$Top10_{i,t}$	0.000	0.000	−0.000	−0.000
	(1.30)	(1.16)	(−0.45)	(−0.44)
$Largest_{i,t}$	−0.000	−0.000	−0.000	−0.000
	(−0.46)	(−0.35)	(−0.05)	(−0.07)
$Discacc_{i,t}$	−0.013	−0.009	−0.003	0.005
	(−1.03)	(−0.68)	(−0.18)	(0.35)
Province	Yes	Yes	Yes	Yes
Industry	Yes	Yes	Yes	Yes
Year	Yes	Yes	Yes	Yes
Constant	0.378***	0.292***	0.472**	0.256
	(3.71)	(2.87)	(2.27)	(1.24)
N	9033	9033	9033	9033
Adjusted R^2	0.164	0.083	0.096	0.081

Note ***, **, and * are significance at 1%, 5%, and 10% levels, respectively
Source Computed by authors

institutional support for marketization. The results show that strengthening the role of the non-state sectors in the economy and improving the market intermediaries and legal environment can mitigate the effect of corruption on corporate tax management at both low to moderate levels of corruption and moderate to high levels of corruption. In short, the government should synchronously improve its market and legal systems to curb corruption. Appendix B shows detailed results of the effects of the three specific dimensions of marketization on the relationship between corruption and tax management.

Corporate Tax Management, Corruption, and Firm Performance

No less important is the question of how corruption affects the relationship between tax management and firm performance. To answer this question requires a two-step process, the first to examine the relationship between tax management and firm performance, and the second, to analyze the moderating effect of corruption on the relationship between tax management and firm performance.

We estimated first the relationship between tax management and firm performance using fixed-effect models, where standard errors in parentheses refer to heteroskedasticity-robust and clustered at the firm level. The choice of the fixed effects model over the random effects model was made using the Hausman test. The dependent variable of firm performance used the measures of *ROA* and *ROE*. The independent variable of tax management used the two measures of *ETR* and *ETR_adj*. The results are shown in column (1) to (4) of Table 5.9, which shows that the coefficients of *ETR* and *ETR_adj* are highly significant with a negative sign (-0.050, -0.049, -0.109, and -0.109, respectively). Since the lower *ETRs* denote a lower tax burden and more tax management, the results show that corporate tax management is positively correlated with firm performance.

Next, the moderating effect of corruption on the relationship between tax management and firm performance is tested using fixed-effect models (columns (1) to (4) of Table 5.10). The dependent variable of firm performance and independent variable of tax management are as indicated in Table 5.9. In addition, the interaction terms between tax management and corruption are $ETR*corruption_{i,t}$ and $ETR\_adj*corruption_{i,t}$.

Table 5.9 Impact of corporate tax management on firm performance

Dependent variable:	(1) ROA	(2) ROA	(3) ROE	(4) ROE
$ETR_{i,t}$	−0.050***		−0.109***	
	(−18.44)		(−18.40)	
$ETR\_adj_{i,t}$		−0.049***		−0.109***
		(−18.22)		(−18.30)
$Corruption_{i,t}$	0.000	0.000	0.000	0.000
	(0.73)	(0.71)	(1.42)	(1.40)
$Size_{i,t}$	−0.005	−0.005	−0.005	−0.005
	(−1.47)	(−1.47)	(−0.68)	(−0.69)
$Age_{i,t}$	0.000	0.000	0.007***	0.007***
	(0.15)	(0.13)	(2.79)	(2.76)
$Leverage_{i,t}$	−0.074***	−0.075***	0.027**	0.026**
	(−12.22)	(−12.31)	(2.31)	(2.21)
$Growth_{i,t}$	0.018***	0.018***	0.038***	0.038***
	(14.87)	(14.88)	(15.19)	(15.19)
$Top10_{i,t}$	0.000***	0.000***	0.001***	0.001***
	(4.94)	(4.96)	(5.30)	(5.32)
$Largest_{i,t}$	0.000*	0.000*	0.001***	0.001***
	(1.90)	(1.90)	(3.42)	(3.42)
$Discacc_{i,t}$	−0.014***	−0.013***	−0.020***	−0.020***
	(−3.91)	(−3.81)	(−3.12)	(−3.00)
Province	Yes	Yes	Yes	Yes
Industry	Yes	Yes	Yes	Yes
Year	Yes	Yes	Yes	Yes
Constant	0.081**	0.070**	0.018	−0.007
	(2.37)	(2.03)	(0.27)	(−0.11)
N	9033	9033	9030	9030
Adjusted R^2	0.239	0.237	0.212	0.211

Note ***, **, and * are significance at 1%, 5%, and 10% levels, respectively
Source Computed by authors

The coefficients of the equations explaining $ETR_{i,t}$ and $ETR\_adj_{i,t}$ in columns (1) to (4) are highly significant (1%) and negative, which is consistent with the results in Table 5.9. Furthermore, the coefficients of the interaction terms between tax management and corruption, $ETR*corruption_{i,t}$ and $ETR\_adj*corruption_{i,t}$, are significant and negative, while the coefficient of the interaction term of $ETR\_adj*corruption_{i,t}$ in column (2) is insignificant. In short, the results suggest that the positive correlation between tax management and firm performance can be strengthened by corruption, corroborating the argument that the corrupt use of tax management could improve firm performance.

Table 5.10 Moderating effect of corruption on relationship between tax management and firm performance

Dependent variable:	(1) ROA	(2) ROA	(3) ROE	(4) ROE
$ETR_{i,t}$	−0.035***		−0.072***	
	(−3.92)		(−3.86)	
$ETR*corruption_{i,t}$	−0.001*		−0.001**	
	(−1.75)		(−2.09)	
$ETR\_adj_{i,t}$		−0.036***		−0.065***
		(-4.04)		(-3.42)
$ETR\_adj*corruption_{i,t}$		−0.000		−0.002**
		(−1.46)		(−2.34)
$Corruption_{i,t}$	0.000	0.000	0.001**	0.000
	(1.51)	(0.72)	(2.30)	(1.41)
$Size_{i,t}$	−0.005	−0.006	−0.005	−0.005
	(−1.45)	(−1.47)	(−0.66)	(−0.69)
$Age_{i,t}$	0.000	0.000	0.007***	0.007***
	(0.11)	(0.11)	(2.73)	(2.72)
$Leverage_{i,t}$	−0.074***	−0.074***	0.027**	0.026**
	(−12.23)	(−12.33)	(2.34)	(2.26)
$Growth_{i,t}$	0.018***	0.019***	0.038***	0.038***
	(14.90)	(14.90)	(15.23)	(15.24)
$Top10_{i,t}$	0.000***	0.000***	0.001***	0.001***
	(4.97)	(4.98)	(5.35)	(5.36)
$Largest_{i,t}$	0.000*	0.000*	0.001***	0.001***
	(1.89)	(1.90)	(3.40)	(3.41)
$Discacc_{i,t}$	−0.014***	−0.013***	−0.021***	−0.020***
	(−3.94)	(−3.83)	(−3.16)	(−3.04)
Province	Yes	Yes	Yes	Yes
Industry	Yes	Yes	Yes	Yes
Year	Yes	Yes	Yes	Yes
Constant	0.076**	0.069**	0.005	−0.010
	(2.21)	(2.00)	(0.07)	(−0.16)
N	9033	9033	9030	9030
Adjusted R^2	0.239	0.238	0.213	0.212

Note ***, **, and * are significance at 1%, 5%, and 10% levels, respectively
Source Computed by authors

Taken together, the evidence from China's listed firms show that ETRs fall as corruption rises in the low to medium phase of corruption first declines but the reverse takes place after that with ETRs rising with rising corruption in the middle to high phase of corruption. Nevertheless, the negative role of corruption on tax management declines as the institutions that govern markets effectively evolve.

Chapter Summary

Corruption is a subject that has been much debated in China, with the conventional wisdom being that it is uniformly bad for firm performance and ultimately the whole society. In investigating corruption's role in the application of corporate tax management, this chapter finds this view to be an oversimplification. There exists an inverted U-shaped relationship between corruption and corporate tax management. The relationship is positive at low to moderate levels of corruption but negative as corruption escalates. This means that low to moderate levels of corruption can be helpful to tax management, but this role is reversed as corruption continues to intensify. Nevertheless, this relationship is mitigated by increased institutional support for marketization, so that as institutions that are critical for market economies to function evolve effectively, corruption's impact is reduced.

Furthermore, the positive relationship between tax management and firm performance with corruption strengthening this relationship suggests that the corruption level that exists in China is still at the downward-sloping part of the corruption-ETR curve, which is why it has not negatively impacted on firm performance. That, despite the mitigating impact of institutional support for marketization, corruption's moderating role remains positive may at least partially explain why corruption continues to thrive as China liberalizes. However, the positive impact of corruption may pose undue challenges to China's governance and regulatory instruments as it presents the wrong signals to firms.

Finally, the results of this chapter provide several important implications. From a policy perspective, the results suggest that further liberalization will have salutary effects in terms of reducing the incentive to engage in corruption. At the same time, efforts to curb corruption without the corresponding strengthening of institutions and clarification of rules and regulations can have adverse short-term consequences for firm performance without garnering long-term benefits.

References

Ades, A., & Di Tella, R. (1999). Rents, competition, and corruption. *The American Economic Review, 89*(4), 982–993.

Ali, A. M., & Isse, H. S. (2003). Determinants of economic corruption: A cross-country comparison. *Cato Journal, 22*(3), 449–466.

Alm, J., Martinez-Vazquez, J., & McClellan, C. (2016). Corruption and firm tax evasion. *Journal of Economic Behavior & Organization, 124,* 146–163. https://doi.org/10.1016/j.jebo.2015.10.006.

Badertscher, B. A., Katz, S. P., & Rego, S. O. (2013). The separation of ownership and control and corporate tax avoidance. *Journal of Accounting and Economics, 56*(2–3), 228–250. https://doi.org/10.1016/j.jacceco.2013.08.005.

Becker, G. S. (1968). Crime and punishment: An economic approach. *Journal of Political Economy, 76*(2), 169–217. https://doi.org/10.1086/259394.

Chen, S., Chen, X., Cheng, Q., & Shevlin, T. (2010). Are family firms more tax aggressive than non-family firms? *Journal of Financial Economics, 95*(1), 41–61. https://doi.org/10.1016/j.jfineco.2009.02.003.

Chen, T. (2015). Institutions, board structure, and corporate performance: Evidence from Chinese firms. *Journal of Corporate Finance, 32,* 217–237. https://doi.org/10.1016/j.jcorpfin.2014.10.009.

Dong, B., & Torgler, B. (2013). Causes of corruption: Evidence from China. *China Economic Review, 26,* 152–169. https://doi.org/10.1016/j.chieco.2012.09.005.

Dyreng, S. D., Hanlon, M., & Maydew, E. L. (2008). Long-run corporate tax avoidance. *Accounting Review, 83*(1), 61–82. https://doi.org/10.2308/accr.2008.83.1.61.

Foo, C.-T., Wu, W., & Chin, T. (2014). Governance for China: A multi-method research in corruption studies. *Chinese Management Studies, 8*(3), 288–312. https://doi.org/10.1108/CMS-08-2014-0160.

Frank, M. M., Lynch, L. J., & Rego, S. O. (2009). Tax reporting aggressiveness and its relation to aggressive financial reporting. *The Accounting Review, 84*(2), 467–496. https://doi.org/10.2308/accr.2009.84.2.467.

Gaviria, A. (2002). Assessing the effects of corruption and crime on firm performance: Evidence from Latin America. *Emerging Markets Review, 3*(3), 245–268. https://doi.org/10.1016/S1566-0141(02)00024-9.

Giavazzi, F., & Tabellini, G. (2005). Economic and political liberalizations. *Journal of Monetary Economics, 52*(7), 1297–1330. https://doi.org/10.1016/j.jmoneco.2005.05.002.

Glaeser, E. L., & Saks, R. E. (2006). Corruption in America. *Journal of Public Economics, 90*(6–7), 1053–1072. https://doi.org/10.1016/j.jpubeco.2005.08.007.

Goel, R. K., & Nelson, M. A. (2005). Economic freedom versus political freedom: Cross-country influences on corruption. *Australian Economic Papers, 44*(2), 121–133. https://doi.org/10.1111/j.1467-8454.2005.00253.x.

Gong, T., & Zhou, N. (2015). Corruption and marketization: Formal and informal rules in Chinese public procurement. *Regulation & Governance, 9*(1), 63–76. https://doi.org/10.1111/rego.12054.

Gupta, S., & Newberry, K. (1997). Determinants of the variability in corporate effective tax rates: Evidence from longitudinal data. *Journal of Accounting and Public Policy, 16*(1), 1–34. https://doi.org/10.1016/S0278-4254(96)00055-5.

Hair, J. F., Jr., Black, W. C., Babin, B. J., & Anderson, R. E. (2009). *Multivariate data analysis* (7th ed.). London: Pearson.

Heckelman, J. C., & Powell, B. (2010). Corruption and the institutional environment for growth. *Comparative Economic Studies, 52*(3), 351–378. https://doi.org/10.1057/ces.2010.14.

Jain, A. K. (2001). Corruption: A review. *Journal of Economic Surveys, 15*(1), 71–121. https://doi.org/10.1111/1467-6419.00133.

Jiang, T., & Nie, H. (2014). The stained China miracle: Corruption, regulation, and firm performance. *Economics Letters, 123*(3), 366–369. https://doi.org/10.1016/j.econlet.2014.03.026.

Karklins, R. (2005). *The system made me do it: Corruption in post-communist societies*. Armonk: M.E. Sharpe.

Khan, M. H. (1989). *Clientelism, corruption and capitalist development: An analysis of state intervention with special reference to Bangladesh* (PhD thesis). Cambridge University, Cambridge.

Ko, K., & Weng, C. (2012). Structural changes in Chinese corruption. *The China Quarterly, 211*, 718–740. https://doi.org/10.1017/S0305741012000793.

Krueger, A. O. (1974). The political economy of the rent-seeking society. *American Economic Review, 64*(3), 291.

Kubick, T. R., & Masli, A. N. S. (2016). Firm-level tournament incentives and corporate tax aggressiveness. *Journal of Accounting and Public Policy, 35*(1), 66–83. https://doi.org/10.1016/j.jaccpubpol.2015.08.002.

Liu, X. (2016). Corruption culture and corporate misconduct. *Journal of Financial Economics, 122*(2), 307–327. https://doi.org/10.1016/j.jfineco.2016.06.005.

Martinsons, M. G. (2005). Online success in a relationship-based economy—Profiles of e-commerce in China. In R. M. Davison, R. W. Harris, S. Qureshi, D. R. Vogel, & G.-J. de Vreede (Eds.), *Information systems in developing countries: Theory and practice* (pp. 173–191). Hong Kong: City University of Hong Kong Press.

Minnick, K., & Noga, T. (2010). Do corporate governance characteristics influence tax management? *Journal of Corporate Finance, 16*(5), 703–718. https://doi.org/10.1016/j.jcorpfin.2010.08.005.

Ngo, T.-W. (2008). Rent-seeking and economic governance in the structural nexus of corruption in China. *Crime, Law and Social Change, 49*(1), 27–44. https://doi.org/10.1007/s10611-007-9089-x.

Petrou, A. P., & Thanos, I. C. (2014). The "grabbing hand" or the "helping hand" view of corruption: Evidence from bank foreign market entries. *Journal of World Business, 49*(3), 444–454. https://doi.org/10.1016/j.jwb.2013.10.004.
Rasiah, R. (2018). *Developmental states: Land schemes, parastatals and poverty alleviation in Malaysia*. Bangi: Universiti Kebangsaan Malaysia Press.
Richardson, G., Taylor, G., & Lanis, R. (2013). The impact of board of director oversight characteristics on corporate tax aggressiveness: An empirical analysis. *Journal of Accounting and Public Policy, 32*(3), 68–88. https://doi.org/10.1016/j.jaccpubpol.2013.02.004.
Richardson, G., Wang, B., & Zhang, X. (2016). Ownership structure and corporate tax avoidance: Evidence from publicly listed private firms in China. *Journal of Contemporary Accounting & Economics, 12*(2), 141–158. https://doi.org/10.1016/j.jcae.2016.06.003.
Sahakyan, N., & Stiegert, K. W. (2012). Corruption and firm performance. *Eastern European Economics, 50*(6), 5–27. https://doi.org/10.2753/EEE0012-8775500601.
Scott, J. (2000). Rational choice theory. In G. Browning, A. Halcli, & F. Webster (Eds.), *Understanding contemporary society: Theories of the present*. Thousand Oaks, CA: Sage.
Sharma, C., & Mitra, A. (2015). Corruption, governance and firm performance: Evidence from Indian enterprises. *Journal of Policy Modeling, 37*(5), 835–851. https://doi.org/10.1016/j.jpolmod.2015.05.001.
Siegfried, J. J. (1973). *The relationship between economic structure and the effect of political influence: Empirical evidence from the Federal Corporation Income Tax program*. Madison: University of Wisconsin.
Svensson, J. (2005). Eight questions about corruption. *The Journal of Economic Perspectives, 19*(3), 19–42. https://doi.org/10.1257/089533005774357860.
Wang, X., Fan, G., & Yu, J. (2017). *Marketization index of China's provinces* (NERI Report 2016). Beijing, China: Social Science Academic Press.
Wang, Y., & You, J. (2012). Corruption and firm growth: Evidence from China. *China Economic Review, 23*(2), 415–433. https://doi.org/10.1016/j.chieco.2012.03.003.
Wu, W., Wu, C., Zhou, C., & Wu, J. (2012). Political connections, tax benefits and firm performance: Evidence from China. *Journal of Accounting and Public Policy, 31*(3), 277–300. https://doi.org/10.1016/j.jaccpubpol.2011.10.005.
Xu, G., & Yano, G. (2016). How does anti-corruption affect corporate innovation? Evidence from recent anti-corruption efforts in China. *Journal of Comparative Economics*. http://dx.doi.org/10.1016/j.jce.2016.10.001.

Xu, X., Li, Y., Liu, X., & Gan, W. (2017). Does religion matter to corruption? Evidence from China. *China Economic Review, 42,* 34–49. https://doi.org/10.1016/j.chieco.2016.11.005.

You, J., & Nie, H. (2017). Who determines Chinese firms' engagement in corruption: Themselves or neighbors? *China Economic Review, 43,* 29–46. https://doi.org/10.1016/j.chieco.2017.01.002.

Zhang, M., M, L., Zhang, B., & Yi, Z. (2016). Pyramidal structure, political intervention and firms' tax burden: Evidence from China's local SOEs. *Journal of Corporate Finance, 36,* 15–25. doi:https://doi.org/10.1016/j.jcorpfin.2015.10.004.

CHAPTER 6

Conclusions

INTRODUCTION

As an important area of governance, corporate tax management has been researched a great deal in western countries. But the corporate environment in these countries differs, often significantly, from that in transition or only partially marketized economies. This book deals with the latter, focusing on China as a special case. Even if the country is unique in that it has undergone market reforms within a socialist structure; it is an important case not only because it has the world's largest population, but also for such a large country it has recorded rapid economic growth since the 1980s, and for both these reasons, is home to enterprises that are global in scale.

The earlier chapters presented a systematic analysis of firm-level and market-level outcomes of corporate tax management among China's listed enterprises using quantitative analysis to answer three specific questions. We draw important implications from this study with a view toward elucidating corporate tax management practices. These questions are addressed again below. Following a synthesis of the findings in the next section, subsequent sections discuss implications for theory, policy, and firms, respectively. The last section proposes the recommendations for future research.

Synthesis of Findings

The results not only show the consequences of corporate tax management in the Chinese context, but also addresses the question of whether the economic transition and reforms have moved China's enterprise environment closer to the norm of the developed countries so that the outcomes of tax management in China converges with what is found in the latter countries. And more important, this book should also serve as reference for other emerging countries, especially those undergoing transition from socialism to market economics, such as Vietnam, Peoples Republic of Lao, and Myanmar.

We investigated in this book two consequences of firm-level and market-level outcomes of corporate tax management in China by examining three major questions. In the first question, we analyzed the relationship between corporate tax management and firm performance in China's A-share listed enterprises over the period 2004 till 2012, and how does the after-tax cash arise from tax management benefit firms' market value in Chapter 3. The results revealed a significant and positive overall relationship between tax management and firm value, which is made up of significant negative direct and positive indirect impacts. Specifically, the significant and negative direct relationship between tax management and firm value supports the agency theory, whereby tax management surfaces as a hidden managerial rent. The significant and positive indirect relationship between tax management and market value is achieved through the mediating role of increasing firm profitability and growth performance. Therefore, the results suggest that tax management as an important firm strategy could be continued but requires bolstering through legal regulations to reduce the possible negative consequences from managerial rent-seeking. Thus, Chapter 3 provides direct evidence on how tax avoidance can help maximize firm value.

In the second question, we examined the extreme market outcomes, viz., the likelihood of stock price crashes arising from increased corporate tax management conduct in Chinese A-share listed enterprises over the period 2008 till 2013, and how does government ownership influence these extreme outcomes in Chapter 4. Unlike studies by Kim, Li, and Zhang (2011) and Li, Luo, Wang, and Foo (2016), which focused on future extreme outcomes, Chapter 4 investigated the extreme market outcomes of tax management in current and future periods. The results show that there is a negative relationship between tax management and contemporaneous stock price crash risk, which means that tax management activities will reduce the immediate possibility of stock price crash. However, the results also show that tax management will increase firms' future stock price crash, which supports bad news hoarding theory. In other words, corporate tax management activities can be used undesirably as a tool to conceal bad news, such as adverse operating outcomes, and to manipulate management performance, but that can only be done up to a point. Once this threshold point is reached in future, a stock price crash will occur. This opportunistic short-term conduct can only postpone the pain from the concealment of bad news but would ultimately increase future enterprise risk as the positive initial outcome reverses with the passage of time.

Given the specific characteristics of Chinese government controlled shareholdings by the level of government, Chapter 4 also examined whether listed state-owned/controlled enterprises (LSOEs) carry less risks than other enterprises. The empirical results show no evidence of central- and provincial-LSOEs being able to mitigate the probability of future stock price crashes. Municipal-LSOEs show a higher probability of future stock price crashes because of corporate tax management.

These findings raise questions and pose challenges for the state. Firstly, could it be that the autonomy granted to state enterprises has left them inadequately monitored as to permit them to undertake rent-seeking activities. Second, being furthest from central government oversight and with the system of decentralization in place, municipal LSOEs pose a danger for stock market stability. The fact that their objectives may also differ from those of central and provincial level LSOEs only compounds the problem. Further research in this area is urgently needed.

The third and final question we investigated in this book in Chapter 5 is, how does corruption and marketization impact corporate tax management in China's A-share listed enterprises over the period 2008 till 2013, and how does corruption impact the consequences of corporate tax management. The evidence shows an inverted U-shaped relationship existing between corruption and corporate tax management. There is a positive relationship between corruption and tax management at low to moderate levels of corruption, but it becomes negative beyond these levels of corruption. Hence, when regional corruption is below a certain level, corruption can induce firms to engage in tax management. However, when the firms operate in an environment of high levels of corruption over the critical point, it will inhibit tax management.

In addition, Chapter 5 also finds that regional market enhancement through the strengthening of institutions can mitigate the impact of corruption on corporate tax management regardless of the level of corruption. However, the results also show that corruption strengthens the positive correlation between tax management and firm performance, which could be viewed as evidence corroborating the transactions cost argument that however undesirable corruption can be, it can be beneficial in certain circumstances.

Taken together, the findings suggest that tax management will likely increase given the net positive performance impact it provides. However, while this will confer benefits both to listed firms and their managements, it will generate immediate revenue losses to the state. However, balanced against these benefits is the vulnerability to future crashes as bad news masked through manipulative tax management finally break out. If the firm is large, this impact can extend beyond the firm to destroy the entire financial market. State ownership or control cannot mitigate this vulnerability. Indeed, municipal listed SOEs, being far removed from central government control, are actually likely to raise the possibility of future crash risk.

Corruption, which is emerging as a serious topic in China, can influence tax management unproductively, but this impact varies with the severity of corruption. At low levels of corruption, tax management can be appropriated productively, but this relationship reverses when the level of corruption exceeds a certain threshold. In other words, at high levels of corruption it is possible to bypass the productive instruments of tax management altogether by blatant bribery, thereby rendering tax management ineffective. Also, in environments facing weak institutions, bribes can act as a transactions cost to remove impasses.

Regardless of the relationship between corruption and tax management, the former is found to affect the relationship between tax management and firm performance positively. The overall assessment of tax management then is that it confers gains to firms, which can be enhanced by the existence of corruption. At the same time, it is likely that these magnified benefits come with heightened risks of future stock price crashes, so that corruption at low to moderate levels of the kind prevalent in China is not all a bed of roses. Importantly, even when corruption acts positively as transactions cost is borne to solve coordination problems, its unproductive nature means that the introduction and strengthening of institutions to support the increased role of markets must be the eventual focus of governments.

IMPLICATIONS FOR THEORY

Existing studies on tax management in emerging markets in general, and in China in particular, are still at an embryonic stage. Under China's evolving environment of market reforms, the analyses undertaken here contribute to enrich the extant research on this literature by providing a robust and systematic analysis of the consequences of corporate tax management. Based the size of China, the findings of these analyses provide several implications for theory.

Firstly, the negative direct relationship between tax management and market value, which was examined in Chapter 3, supports the agency theory on corporate tax management. The separation of ownership and control inherent in modern corporations can raise managerial opportunism resulting in negative consequences for tax management (Chen, Chen, Cheng, & Shevlin, 2010; Desai & Dharmapala, 2009; Kim, Li, & Zhang, 2011). Pushing China toward greater marketization has the unintended consequence of magnifying agency costs. Fortunately, the indirect impact of tax management is that it improves firm value through increasing profitability and growth, which sheds light into how governance can increase shareholder wealth.

Secondly, the results from the second question in Chapter 4 supports the "bad news hoarding" theory developed by Jin and Myers (2006), and Bleck and Liu (2007). Most past studies examining the bad news hoarding theory of stock price crash risk of economic activities have only focused on the future (Kim, Li, & Zhang, 2011; Li, Luo, Wang, & Foo, 2016; Xu, Jiang, Chan, & Yi, 2013), and in doing so, overlook how current outcomes impact on future outcomes. The empirical results of lower contemporaneous stock price crash risk of tax management provide empirical evidence of how corporate tax management can be deployed to conceal adverse operating outcomes through the manipulation of firm performance so as to reduce immediate crash risks. Our results help validate the "bad news hoarding" theory with a more robust methodology than that used by past studies. However, when concealed short-term opportunist behavior is eventually uncovered, it will result ultimately in future stock price crash. Thus, the relationship between tax management and stock price crash risk will change with the passage of time. Overall, the support the view tax management can offer managers to engage in managerial opportunism, but the risks of "bad news hoarding" will increase over time.

Thirdly, the government-level results in Chapter 4 demonstrate that municipal listed SOEs face a higher probability of future stock price crash than the central and provincial listed SOEs (examined in Chapter 4), which is contrary to conventional wisdom of SOEs as stabilizing factors. Thus, the results are not only consistent with simple conflict of interests between shareholders and managers' arguments, they also reveal more complicated and deeper problems that exist between governments and listed SOEs' managers at lower echelons of government. As transition economy, China's state-owned/controlled enterprises account for a considerable portion of China's economy and play an important role in national development. While listed state-owned/controlled enterprises have experienced several reforms, they are characterized by complicated special principal–agent relationships. Thus, the results from this study extend the agency theory by considering modern listed SOEs as a feature specific to China.

Finally, the inverted U-shaped relationship between corruption and tax management established in Chapter 5 provides empirical evidence to support the assumption that corruption in government can play a dual role of both a helping hand and a grabbing hand in impacting corporate performance. In contrast to Krueger (1974) neoclassical argument, corruption cannot be simply ascribed to having a monotonic detrimental or beneficial effect. As a large transition and heterogenous economy, the development of institutions is critical in China to ensure that the regulatory framework is strengthened to check the unproductive opportunism that comes with market liberalization (Aguilera, 2005; Khan, 1989). Also, China's heterogeneity that has resulted in uneven market development across regions (Zhang & Rasiah, 2015), calls with a diverse range of regulatory instruments to both enable markets and to check corruption.

IMPLICATIONS FOR POLICY

Taxation, as the main source of national revenue, is an important tool in macroeconomic regulation, the performance of markets, and decision-making of enterprises and investors' activities. Therefore, the findings of this study provide several implications for policy.

Firstly, it is clear that economic liberalization brings with it the benefits of the market economy, but also its vulnerabilities. It is for these reasons, Sen (1983) and Stiglitz (2010) have called for the strengthening of the regulatory function of the state, though it in itself does not guarantee that these problems will be resolved. In the context of this study, increased liberalization raised firms' participation in tax management activities, which is made worse by China's less than transparent markets and reliance on relationship-based transactions.

Secondly, the findings allow us to conclude that since focused enterprise reforms were intensified from the 1990s, the Chinese corporate environment has moved closer to that of the market economies. However, it has also opened the floodgate of corporate governance problems, such as conflicting interests of shareholders and managers, and the resort to corruption. Indeed, while listing state enterprises on stock exchanges brings with its market discipline, it also abets tax management to the detriment of government finances, which requires careful monitoring. Thus, the government should not only improve market transparency by reducing government intervention, but also strengthen the institutions for the development of a healthy market mechanism to prevent manipulative managerial rent-seeking. Taxation has an important role in helping to deepen economic and social development.

Thirdly, China's privatization exercise, though is essential to open it to the market mechanism, has also brought with its problems. Instead of going for full privatization of state enterprises, China introduced partial privatization to reform SOEs. Thus, profit-oriented listed state-owned/controlled enterprises (LSOEs) have become a confusing phenomenon in China's stock market. Compared to the wholly state-owned enterprises that have to bear social responsibilities, LSOEs have profit-seeking as a major objective (Kang & Kim, 2012). Because of partial privatization, LSOEs are still ultimately controlled by the different levels of governments, which has exposed them to institutional and agency problems. Importantly, local governments are viewed as privatization-friendly with trigger-happy attitude toward privatizing troubled state-controlled enterprises (Liu, 2014). This leaves the space for collusion between local officials and managers of state enterprises to utilize the transition process to pursue their individual interests and even acquire national assets. Thus, the findings suggest that policymakers should pay heed to the processes of state enterprise privatization and assess prudently privatization of local state enterprises. Central government also needs to strengthen its assets' supervision and administration.

Fourthly, fiscal decentralization has given local governments more autonomy, an example being the tax-sharing system giving local governments more financial power and discretionary funds, which allows local administrators to engage in rent-seeking and other self-interests activities, which may sap the firms and country resources and raise the probability of potential stock price crash. The findings imply that the prior tax distribution system (1994–2018) bestowed major benefits to both central and local governments, which opened the door for rent-seeking behavior by local administrators. The reform of the tax system in 2018 integrated national and local tax collection, while removing local tax bureaus, which helped reduce inefficiencies and rent-seeking conduct associated with the decentralized tax system before that.

Fifth, since China is still in the process of economic and social transformation, problems such as weak institutions, allowing officials to abuse their power eventually leading to their corruption and downfall are inevitable. Firms resort to corruption when they operate in a weak institutional environment, with corruption sought more as "speed money" to gain preferences to benefit corporate performance and/or circumvent cumbersome regulations. The positive role corruption plays on tax management and firm performance provides another important policy implication when institutions are weak. Under such circumstances, firms have no alternative when corruption is the only way of effecting decisions, which is the necessary transactions costs firms incur to function (see Khan, 1989). With continuous improvement of institutions, such as the strengthening of laws and their enforcement, the negative rents through corruption can be reduced. However, to succeed in the fight against corruption, the Chinese government must have deep and precise insights into the problem of corruption, making proper structural reforms, strengthening institutions, and setting up an effective anti-corruption supervision system.

The evidence also shows that marketization requires simultaneous development in institutions so that markets are disciplined to insulate it from managerial opportunism and corruption (see Williamson, 1985). Emerging economies experience more severe agency problems than developed economies due to the lack of forceful legal protection and related governance mechanisms (Li & Xia, 2008; Tu, Lin, & Liu, 2013). Hence, when governments make a decision on resource allocation, they should synchronously establish a sound monitoring mechanism combined with governance practices.

Yet, as convincingly argued by Ang (2016), the many facets of institutional weaknesses should not lead us to conclude that the strengthening of institutional capabilities will have salutary effects on firm performance and governance. Indeed, the evidence provides empirical vindication that institutions and markets "co-evolve" during the development process. Even "bad" institutions have their place at certain junctures of development while "good" institutions can be constrained by barriers to development.

IMPLICATIONS FOR FIRMS

This study can be beneficial to senior managers, board members, and shareholders to help them better understand corporate tax management issues. Because tax management brings both benefits to enterprises as well as can lead to potential risks, it may create uncertainty that can influence future corporate outcomes, which may damage the firm. Thus, enterprises making decisions on tax management should ensure after-tax returns maximization rather than to simply reduce corporate tax burden.

Besides, markets and governments also rely on investment bankers, security analysts, and auditors for the orderly and efficient functioning of enterprises. Hence, a profound understanding of how corporate tax management is managed by firms, taking account of the motivations of managers and the institutional environment they interact with, will help these government agencies and organizations to anticipate better the conduct of enterprises. On the one hand, firms can pursue legally right and economically productive management of taxes. On the other hand, it can help the evolution of institutions to reduce the potential for managerial opportunism. Governance mechanisms for regulating the market must take this into account in the monitoring of enterprises.

Last but not least, despite its socialist structure, market reforms in China present features and characteristics that can be adapted for introduction in other developing and transition economies. The results of this study can provide useful guidelines and lessons for managers in these countries to improve their tax system to promote institution-building and economic development.

Overall, while the China example investigated produced interesting results, it raised more questions rather than to offer concrete directions for how institutional change should be managed to check corruption and for firms to mobilize resources toward productive activities. The non-linear U-shaped relationship between corruption and corporate tax management was an interesting finding that resonates well with evolving institutions that are essential to coordinate the processes of market reforms. Further work will be necessary to investigate the impact of trade and non-trade instruments used to shield firms in particular industries, ownership structures, and localities across the world to refine further these findings.

References

Aguilera, R. V. (2005). Corporate governance and director accountability: An institutional comparative perspective. *British Journal of Management, 16*, S39–S53. https://doi.org/10.1111/j.1467-8551.2005.00446.x.

Ang, Y. Y. (2016). *How China escaped the poverty trap*. Ithaca: Cornell University Press.

Bleck, A., & Liu, X. (2007). Market transparency and the accounting regime. *Journal of Accounting Research, 45*(2), 229–256. https://doi.org/10.1111/j.1475-679X.2007.00231.x.

Chen, S., Chen, X., Cheng, Q., & Shevlin, T. (2010). Are family firms more tax aggressive than non-family firms? *Journal of Financial Economics, 95*(1), 41–61. https://doi.org/10.1016/j.jfineco.2009.02.003.

Desai, M. A., & Dharmapala, D. (2009). Corporate tax avoidance and firm value. *The Review of Economics and Statistics, 91*(3), 537–546.

Jin, L., & Myers, S. C. (2006). R^2 around the world: New theory and new tests. *Journal of Financial Economics, 79*(2), 257–292. https://doi.org/10.1016/j.jfineco.2004.11.003.

Kang, Y.-S., & Kim, B.-Y. (2012). Ownership structure and firm performance: Evidence from the Chinese corporate reform. *China Economic Review, 23*(2), 471–481. https://doi.org/10.1016/j.chieco.2012.03.006.

Khan, M.H. (1989). *Clientelism, corruption and capitalist development: An analysis of state intervention with special reference to Bangladesh* (PhD thesis). Cambridge University, Cambridge.

Kim, J.-B., Li, Y., & Zhang, L. (2011). Corporate tax avoidance and stock price crash risk: Firm-level analysis. *Journal of Financial Economics, 100*(3), 639–662. https://doi.org/10.1016/j.jfineco.2010.07.007.

Krueger, A. O. (1974). The political economy of the rent-seeking society. *American Economic Review, 64*(3), 291.

Li, S., & Xia, J. (2008). The roles and performance of state firms and non-state firms in China's economic transition. *World Development, 36*(1), 39–54. https://doi.org/10.1016/j.worlddev.2007.01.008.

Li, Y., Luo, Y., Wang, J., & Foo, C.-T. (2016). A theory of managerial tax aggression: Evidence from china, 2008–2013 (9702 observations). *Chinese Management Studies, 10*(1), 12–40. https://doi.org/10.1108/CMS-01-2016-0001.

Liu, Z. (2014). *Tax system of the People's Republic of China* (In Chinese and English Version) (L. Du, Trans., 8th ed.). Beijing, China: China Taxation Publishing House.

Sen, A. (1983). Carrots, sticks and economics: Perception problems in incentives. *Indian Economic Review, 18*(1), 1–16.

Stiglitz, J. E. (2010). *Freefall: America, free markets, and the sinking of the world economy*. New York and London: W.W. Norton.

Tu, G., Lin, B., & Liu, F. (2013). Political connections and privatization: Evidence from China. *Journal of Accounting and Public Policy, 32*(2), 114–135. https://doi.org/10.1016/j.jaccpubpol.2012.10.002.

Williamson, O. E. (1985). *The economic institutions of capitalism: Firms markets, relational contracting*. New York: The Free Press.

Xu, N., Jiang, X., Chan, K. C., & Yi, Z. (2013). Analyst coverage, optimism, and stock price crash risk: Evidence from China. *Pacific-Basin Finance Journal, 25*, 217–239. https://doi.org/10.1016/j.pacfin.2013.09.001.

Zhang, M., & Rasiah, R. (2015). *Institutionalization of state policy: Evolving urban housing reforms in China*. Singapore: Springer. https://doi.org/10.1007/978-981-287-570-9.

Appendix A: Measurement of Firm-Specific Earnings Management (Discacc)

Chapters 4 and 5 employed the modified Jones model (Patricia M Dechow, Richard G Sloan, & Amy P Sweeney, 1995) to estimate discretionary accruals, which is a common measure of earnings management.

$$\frac{TA_{i,t}}{Asset_{i,t-1}} = \alpha_0 \frac{1}{Asset_{i,t-1}} + \beta_1 \frac{\Delta Sales_{i,t}}{Asset_{i,t-1}} + \beta_2 \frac{PPE_{i,t}}{Asset_{i,t-1}} + \varepsilon_{i,t} \quad (A.1)$$

The estimated coefficients from Eq. A.1 are then used to compute discretionary accruals ($Discacc_{i,t}$) using the equation.

$$Discacc_{i,t} = \frac{TA_{i,t}}{Asset_{i,t-1}} - \left(\alpha_0 \frac{1}{Asset_{i,t-1}} + \beta_1 \frac{\Delta Sales_{i,t} - \Delta Rec_{i,t}}{Asset_{i,t-1}} + \beta_2 \frac{PPE_{i,t}}{Asset_{i,t-1}} \right) \quad (A.2)$$

where $TA_{i,t}$ is total accruals for firm i in year t, calculated as operating profits minus cash flow from operations; $Asset_{i,t-1}$ is the book value of total assets for firm i at the beginning of year t; $\Delta\text{Sales}_{i,t}$ is the change in total revenue of firm i in year t; $\Delta\text{Rec}_{i,t}$ is the change in accounts receivable for firm i in year t; and $\text{PPE}_{i,t}$ is the gross amount of fixed assets for firm i at the end of year t. The variable $\text{Discacc}_{i,t}$ is the absolute value of discretionary accruals for firm i at year t.

Appendix B: The Impacts of Three Specific Dimensions of Marketization on the Relationship Between Corruption and Tax Management

See Fig. B.1 and Table B.1.

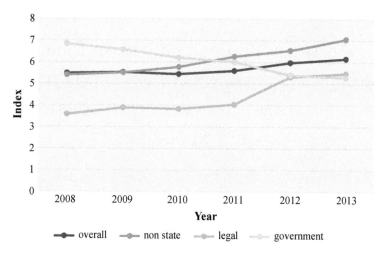

Fig. B.1 The three specific dimensions of marketization during 2008–2013 (*Note* **Blue line** of *overall* means the overall marketization index in China's 31 provinces; **Red line** of *non-state* means the index of the development of the non-state sector in China's 31 provinces. The index reflects the ownership structure of the economy and the transition from public ownership to private ownership; **Grey line** of *legal* means the index of market intermediaries and the legal environment development. The index captures the establishment of intermediate institutions such as law offices, accounting and auditing firms, and the institutional environment ensuring enforcement of contracts and protecting property rights; **Yellow line** of *government* means the index of Government and market relationship. The index refers to the size of government interventions in local markets. *Source* Marketization Index of China's Provinces: NERI Report 2016; Plotted by authors)

Table B.1 The impact of three specific dimensions of marketization on the relationship between corruption and tax management

	Government and market relationship		Market intermediaries and the legal environment development		Non-state sector development	
	ETR	ETR_adj	ETR	ETR_adj	ETR	ETR_adj
Corruption$_{i,t}$	−0.005*	−0.005*	−0.006**	−0.007**	−0.016***	−0.016***
	(−1.67)	(−1.68)	(−2.24)	(−2.49)	(−3.43)	(−3.53)
Corruption squared$_{i,t}$	0.000	0.000	0.000**	0.000**	0.000***	0.000***
	(1.39)	(1.44)	(2.32)	(2.54)	(3.44)	(3.51)
Corruption ^{a}Govmark$_{i,t}$	0.000	0.000				
	(0.81)	(0.64)				
Corruption squared ^{a}Govmark$_{i,t}$	−0.000	−0.000				
	(−0.41)	(−0.32)				
Govmark$_{i,t}$	−0.004	−0.004				
	(−0.60)	(−0.53)				
Corruption ^{a}Legal$_{i,t}$			0.001**	0.001**		
			(2.01)	(2.11)		
Corruption squared ^{a}Legal$_{i,t}$			−0.000*	−0.000*		
			(−1.84)	(−1.93)		
Legal$_{i,t}$			−0.010**	−0.010**		
			(−2.31)	(−2.46)		
Corruption ^{a}Non-state$_{i,t}$					0.002***	0.002***
					(3.21)	(3.19)
Corruption squared ^{a}Non-state$_{i,t}$					−0.000***	−0.000***
					(−3.22)	(−3.20)
Non-state$_{i,t}$					−0.023**	−0.023**
					(−2.35)	(−2.34)
Size$_{i,t}$	−0.003	−0.003	−0.003	−0.003	−0.003	−0.003
	(−0.64)	(−0.59)	(−0.67)	(−0.62)	(−0.67)	(−0.62)

(continued)

Table B.1 (continued)

	Government and market relationship		Market intermediaries and the legal environment development		Non-state sector development	
	ETR	ETR_adj	ETR	ETR_adj	ETR	ETR_adj
$Age_{i,t}$	0.009***	0.009***	0.009***	0.008***	0.009***	0.008***
	(3.14)	(3.06)	(3.12)	(3.03)	(3.11)	(3.02)
$ROA_{i,t}$	−0.836***	−0.826***	−0.836***	−0.825***	−0.835***	−0.824***
	(−14.41)	(−14.29)	(−14.40)	(−14.28)	(−14.39)	(−14.27)
$Leverage_{i,t}$	0.049***	0.048***	0.049***	0.048***	0.050***	0.048***
	(3.38)	(3.28)	(3.38)	(3.28)	(3.40)	(3.30)
$MB_{i,t}$	−0.000	0.001	−0.000	0.000	−0.000	0.000
	(−0.02)	(0.07)	(−0.05)	(0.04)	(−0.05)	(0.05)
$Growth_{i,t}$	0.005	0.005	0.005	0.005	0.004	0.005
	(1.05)	(1.17)	(1.11)	(1.23)	(0.99)	(1.10)
$Top10_{i,t}$	0.000	0.000	0.000	0.000	0.000	0.000
	(1.30)	(1.16)	(1.29)	(1.15)	(1.29)	(1.15)
$Largest_{i,t}$	−0.000	−0.000	−0.000	−0.000	−0.000	−0.000
	(−0.46)	(−0.35)	(−0.47)	(−0.35)	(−0.44)	(−0.33)
$Discacc_{i,t}$	−0.013	−0.009	−0.013	−0.009	−0.013	−0.008
	(−1.01)	(−0.67)	(−1.03)	(−0.68)	(−0.13)	(−0.008)
Province	0.009	0.015	0.001	0.004	0.014	0.018
Industry	0.123***	0.010	0.123***	0.010	0.123***	0.010
Year	0.002	−0.003	0.006	0.003	0.000	−0.004
Constant	0.174**	0.071	0.214***	0.118**	0.307***	0.206**
	(2.56)	(1.05)	(3.70)	(2.05)	(3.78)	(2.54)
N	9033	9033	9033	9033	9033	9033
Adjusted R^2	0.164	0.082	0.164	0.082	0.164	0.083

Note t statistics in parentheses; *$p < 0.1$, **$p < 0.05$, ***$p < 0.01$
[a]Govmark = government and market relationship; Legal = development of market intermediaries and the legal environment; Non-state = development of the non-state sector
Source Computed by the author

REFERENCES

Abdolmohammadi, M. J. (2005). Intellectual capital disclosure and market capitalization. *Journal of Intellectual Capital, 6*(3), 397–416. https://doi.org/10.1108/14691930510611139.

Acemoglu, D., & Robinson, J. (2012). *Why nations fail: The origins of power, prosperity, and poverty.* New York: Crown Business.

Ades, A., & Di Tella, R. (1999). Rents, competition, and corruption. *The American Economic Review, 89*(4), 982–993.

Adhikari, A., Derashid, C., & Zhang, H. (2006). Public policy, political connections, and effective tax rates: Longitudinal evidence from Malaysia. *Journal of Accounting and Public Policy, 25*(5), 574–595. https://doi.org/10.1016/j.jaccpubpol.2006.07.001.

Aguilera, R. V. (2005). Corporate governance and director accountability: An institutional comparative perspective. *British Journal of Management, 16,* S39–S53. https://doi.org/10.1111/j.1467-8551.2005.00446.x.

Ali, A. M., & Isse, H. S. (2003). Determinants of economic corruption: A cross-country comparison. *Cato Journal, 22*(3), 449–466.

Allen, F., Qian, J., & Qian, M. (2005). Law, finance, and economic growth in China. *Journal of Financial Economics, 77*(1), 57–116. https://doi.org/10.1016/j.jfineco.2004.06.010.

Allingham, M. G., & Sandmo, A. (1972). Income tax evasion: A theoretical analysis. *Journal of Public Economics, 1*(3–4), 323–338. https://doi.org/10.1016/0047-2727(72)90010-2.

Alm, J., Martinez-Vazquez, J., & McClellan, C. (2016). Corruption and firm tax evasion. *Journal of Economic Behavior & Organization, 124,* 146–163. https://doi.org/10.1016/j.jebo.2015.10.006.

© The Editor(s) (if applicable) and The Author(s),
under exclusive license to Springer Nature Singapore Pte Ltd. 2019
C. Zhang et al., *Governing Corporate Tax Management,*
https://doi.org/10.1007/978-981-13-9829-2

Amsden, A. H. (1989). *Asia's next giant: South Korea and late industrialization*. New York: Oxford University Press.

Anderson, J. C., & Gerbing, D. W. (1988). Structural equation modeling in practice: A review and recommended two-step approach. *Psychological Bulletin, 103*(3), 411–423. https://doi.org/10.1037/0033-2909.103.3.411.

Anderson, J. C., & Gerbing, D. W. (1992). Assumptions and comparative strengths of the two-step approach. *Sociological Methods and Research, 20*(3), 321–333.

Ang, Y. Y. (2016). *How China escaped the poverty trap*. Ithaca: Cornell University Press.

Anthony, J. H., & Ramesh, K. (1992). Association between accounting performance measures and stock prices. *Journal of Accounting and Economics, 15*(2), 203–227. https://doi.org/10.1016/0165-4101(92)90018-W.

Asker, J., Farre-Mensa, J., & Ljungqvist, A. (2014). Corporate investment and stock market listing: A puzzle? *The Review of Financial Studies, 28*(2), 342–390. https://doi.org/10.1093/rfs/hhu077.

Badertscher, B. A., Katz, S. P., & Rego, S. O. (2013). The separation of ownership and control and corporate tax avoidance. *Journal of Accounting and Economics, 56*(2–3), 228–250. https://doi.org/10.1016/j.jacceco.2013.08.005.

Ball, R. (2009). Market and political/regulatory perspectives on the recent accounting scandals. *Journal of Accounting Research, 47*(2), 277–323. https://doi.org/10.1111/j.1475-679X.2009.00325.x.

Barassi, M. R., & Zhou, Y. (2012). The effect of corruption on FDI: A parametric and non-parametric analysis. *European Journal of Political Economy, 28*(3), 302–312. https://doi.org/10.1016/j.ejpoleco.2012.01.001.

Baron, R. M., & Kenny, D. A. (1986). The moderator-mediator variable distinction in social psychological research: Conceptual, strategic, and statistical considerations. *Journal of Personality and Social Psychology, 51*(6), 1173–1182. https://doi.org/10.1037/0022-3514.51.6.1173.

Basu, S. (1997). The conservatism principle and the asymmetric timeliness of earnings. *Journal of Accounting and Economics, 24*(1), 3–37. https://doi.org/10.1016/S0165-4101(97)00014-1.

Becker, G. S. (1968). Crime and punishment: An economic approach. *Journal of Political Economy, 76*(2), 169–217. https://doi.org/10.1086/259394.

Berle, A., & Means, G. (1967). *The modern corporation and private property* (2nd ed.). New York: Harcourt.

Bleck, A., & Liu, X. (2007). Market transparency and the accounting regime. *Journal of Accounting Research, 45*(2), 229–256. https://doi.org/10.1111/j.1475-679X.2007.00231.x.

Bollen, K. A., & Stine, R. (1990). Direct and indirect effects: Classical and bootstrap estimates of variability. *Sociological Methodology, 20*, 115–140. https://doi.org/10.2307/271084.

Bradshaw, M., Liao, G., & Ma, M. S. (2012). *State ownership, tax and political promotion: Evidence from China* (SSRN Working Paper).
Bramall, C. (1995). The lessons of history: New economic policy in China and the USSR. In H.-J. Chang & P. Nolan (Eds.), *The transformation of the communist economies: Against the mainstream*. New York: St Martin's Press (Palgrave Macmillan).
Brealey, R. A., & Myers, S. C. (2000). *Principles of corporate finance* (6th ed.). Boston: McGraw-Hill.
Brush, T. H., Bromiley, P., & Hendrickx, M. (2000). The free cash flow hypothesis for sales growth and firm performance. *Strategic Management Journal, 21*(4), 455–472. https://doi.org/10.1002/(SICI)1097-0266(200004)21:4<455:AID-SMJ83>3.0.CO;2-P.
Byrne, B. M. (2009). *Structural equation modeling with AMOS: Basic concepts, applications, and programming* (2nd ed.). New York and London: Routledge.
Cable, J. R., & Mueller, D. C. (2008). Testing for persistence of profits' differences across firms. *International Journal of the Economics of Business, 15*(2), 201–228. https://doi.org/10.1080/13571510802134353.
Cabrera-Nguyen, P. (2010). Author guidelines for reporting scale development and validation results in the *Journal of the Society for Social Work and Research*. *Journal of the Society for Social Work and Research, 1*(2), 99–103.
Cao, X. J., Lemmon, M., Tian, G., & Pan, X. (2009). *Political promotion, CEO compensation, and their effect on firm performance*. Research Collection Lee Kong Chian School of Business.
Chang, H.-J., & Nolan, P. (1995). *The transformation of the communist economies: Against the mainstream*. New York: St Martin's Press (Palgrave Macmillan).
Chemmanur, T. J., & Ravid, S. A. (1999). Asymmetric information, corporate myopia, and capital gains tax rates: An analysis of policy prescriptions. *Journal of Financial Intermediation, 8*(3), 205–231. https://doi.org/10.1006/jfin.1999.0262.
Chen, J., Hong, H., & Stein, J. C. (2001). Forecasting crashes: Trading volume, past returns, and conditional skewness in stock prices. *Journal of Financial Economics, 61*(3), 345–381.
Chen, K.-P., & Chu, C. Y. C. (2005). Internal control versus external manipulation: A model of corporate income tax evasion. *The RAND Journal of Economics, 36*(1), 151–164.
Chen, S., Chen, X., Cheng, Q., & Shevlin, T. (2010). Are family firms more tax aggressive than non-family firms? *Journal of Financial Economics, 95*(1), 41–61. https://doi.org/10.1016/j.jfineco.2009.02.003.
Chen, T. (2015). Institutions, board structure, and corporate performance: Evidence from Chinese firms. *Journal of Corporate Finance, 32*, 217–237. https://doi.org/10.1016/j.jcorpfin.2014.10.009.

Chen, X., Hu, N., Wang, X., & Tang, X. (2014). Tax avoidance and firm value: Evidence from China. *Nankai Business Review International*, 5(1), 25–42. https://doi.org/10.1108/NBRI-10-2013-0037.

Chen, X., Lee, C.-W. J., & Li, J. (2008). Government assisted earnings management in China. *Journal of Accounting and Public Policy*, 27(3), 262–274. https://doi.org/10.1016/j.jaccpubpol.2008.02.005.

Chen, Y., Zhai, R.-R., Wang, C., & Zhong, C. (2015). Home institutions, internationalization and firm performance: Evidence from listed Chinese firms. *Management Decision*, 53(1), 160–178. https://doi.org/10.1108/MD-05-2014-0311.

Cheung, Y.-L., Rau, P. R., & Stouraitis, A. (2008, April). *The helping hand, the lazy hand, or the grabbing hand? Central vs. local government shareholders in publicly listed firms in China* (Center for Economic Institutions Working Paper Series).

Claessens, S., & Fan, J. P. H. (2002). Corporate governance in Asia: A survey. *International Review of Finance*, 3(2), 71–103. https://doi.org/10.1111/1468-2443.00034.

Coase, R. H. (1937). The nature of the firm. *Economica*, 4(16), 386–405. https://doi.org/10.2307/2626876.

Crocker, K. J., & Slemrod, J. (2005). Corporate tax evasion with agency costs. *Journal of Public Economics*, 89(9), 1593–1610. https://doi.org/10.1016/j.jpubeco.2004.08.003.

Dahya, J., Karbhari, Y., & Xiao, J. Z. (2002). The supervisory board in Chinese listed companies: Problems, causes, consequences and remedies. *Asia Pacific Business Review*, 9(2), 118–137. https://doi.org/10.1080/713999187.

Damodaran, A. (2007). *Return on Capital (ROC), return on Invested Capital (ROIC) and Return on Equity (ROE): Measurement and implications* (Working Paper). New York: University-Stern School of Business. http://ssrn.com/abstract=1105499.

Dechow, P. M., Sloan, R. G., & Sweeney, A. P. (1995). Detecting earnings management. *The Accounting Review*, 70(2), 193–225.

Delen, D., Kuzey, C., & Uyar, A. (2013). Measuring firm performance using financial ratios: A decision tree approach. *Expert Systems with Applications*, 40(10), 3970–3983. https://doi.org/10.1016/j.eswa.2013.01.012.

Desai, M. A., & Dharmapala, D. (2006). Corporate tax avoidance and high-powered incentives. *Journal of Financial Economics*, 79(1), 145–179.

Desai, M. A., & Dharmapala, D. (2009a). Corporate tax avoidance and firm value. *The Review of Economics and Statistics*, 91(3), 537–546.

Desai, M. A., & Dharmapala, D. (2009b). Earnings management, corporate tax shelters, and book-tax alignment. *National Tax Journal*, 62(1), 169–186.

Desai, M. A., Dyck, A., & Zingales, L. (2007). Theft and taxes. *Journal of Financial Economics*, 84(3), 591–623. https://doi.org/10.1016/j.jfineco.2006.05.005.

Desai, M. A., & Hines, J. R. J. (2002). Expectations and expatriations: Tracing the causes and consequences of corporate inversions. *National Tax Journal*, *55*(3), 409–440. https://doi.org/10.17310/ntj.2002.3.03.

Dong, B., & Torgler, B. (2013). Causes of corruption: Evidence from China. *China Economic Review*, *26*, 152–169. https://doi.org/10.1016/j.chieco.2012.09.005.

Durnev, A., & Kim, E. H. (2005). To steal or not to steal: Firm attributes, legal environment, and valuation. *The Journal of Finance*, *60*(3), 1461–1493. https://doi.org/10.1111/j.1540-6261.2005.00767.x.

Dyreng, S. D., Hanlon, M., & Maydew, E. L. (2008). Long-run corporate tax avoidance. *Accounting Review*, *83*(1), 61–82. https://doi.org/10.2308/accr.2008.83.1.61.

Edwards, A., Schwab, C. M., & Shevlin, T. J. (2013). *Financial constraints and the incentive for tax planning*. Paper presented at the 2013 American Taxation Association Midyear Meeting: New Faculty/Doctoral Student Session. https://ssrn.com/abstract=2216875.

Egger, P., & Winner, H. (2005). Evidence on corruption as an incentive for foreign direct investment. *European Journal of Political Economy*, *21*(4), 932–952. https://doi.org/10.1016/j.ejpoleco.2005.01.002.

Eisenhardt, K. M. (1989). Agency theory: An assessment and review. *Academy of Management Review*, *14*(1), 57–74. https://doi.org/10.5465/AMR.1989.4279003.

Ellman, M., & Kontorovich, V. (1998). *The destruction of the Soviet economic system: An insider's history*. Armonk, NY: M.E. Sharpe.

Erle, B. (2008). Tax risk management and board responsibility. In W. Schön (Ed.), *Tax and corporate governance* (pp. 205–220). Berlin and Heidelberg: Springer. https://doi.org/10.1007/978-3-540-77276-7_15.

Ette, E. I., & Onyiah, L. C. (2002). Estimating inestimable standard errors in population pharmacokinetic studies: The bootstrap with winsorization. *European Journal of Drug Metabolism and Pharmacokinetics*, *27*(3), 213–224. https://doi.org/10.1007/BF03190460.

Fama, E. F. (1980). Agency problems and the theory of the firm. *Journal of Political Economy*, *88*(2), 288–307.

Fama, E. F., & French, K. R. (1998). Taxes, financing decisions, and firm value. *The Journal of Finance*, *53*(3), 819–843. https://doi.org/10.1111/0022-1082.00036.

Fan, G., Wang, X., & Zhu, H. (2007). *NERI index of marketization of China's provinces: 2006 report*. Beijing: Economic Science Press (in Chinese).

Fan, J. P., Wong, T. J., & Zhang, T. (2007). *Organizational structure as a decentralization device: Evidence from corporate pyramids* (Working Paper). http://dx.doi.org/10.2139/ssrn.963430.

Faure, G. O., & Fang, T. (2008). Changing Chinese values: Keeping up with paradoxes. *International Business Review, 17*(2), 194–207. https://doi.org/10.1016/j.ibusrev.2008.02.011.

Firth, M., Gong, S. X., & Shan, L. (2013). Cost of government and firm value. *Journal of Corporate Finance, 21*, 136–152. https://doi.org/10.1016/j.jcorpfin.2013.01.008.

Foo, C.-T., Wu, W., & Chin, T. (2014). Governance for China: A multi-method research in corruption studies. *Chinese Management Studies, 8*(3), 288–312. https://doi.org/10.1108/CMS-08-2014-0160.

Fornell, C., & Larcker, D. F. (1981). Evaluating structural equation models with unobservable variables and measurement error. *Journal of Marketing Research, 18*(1), 39–50. https://doi.org/10.2307/3151312.

Frank, M. M., Lynch, L. J., & Rego, S. O. (2009). Tax reporting aggressiveness and its relation to aggressive financial reporting. *The Accounting Review, 84*(2), 467–496. https://doi.org/10.2308/accr.2009.84.2.467.

Frye, T., & Shleifer, A. (1997). The invisible hand and the grabbing hand. *The American Economic Review, 87*(2), 354–358.

Garnaut, R., Song, L., Tenev, S., & Yao, Y. (2005). *China's ownership transformation: Process, outcomes, prospects*. Washington, DC: International Finance Corporation.

Gaviria, A. (2002). Assessing the effects of corruption and crime on firm performance: Evidence from Latin America. *Emerging Markets Review, 3*(3), 245–268. https://doi.org/10.1016/S1566-0141(02)00024-9.

Giavazzi, F., & Tabellini, G. (2005). Economic and political liberalizations. *Journal of Monetary Economics, 52*(7), 1297–1330. https://doi.org/10.1016/j.jmoneco.2005.05.002.

Glaeser, E. L., & Saks, R. E. (2006). Corruption in America. *Journal of Public Economics, 90*(6–7), 1053–1072. https://doi.org/10.1016/j.jpubeco.2005.08.007.

Goel, R. K., & Nelson, M. A. (2005). Economic freedom versus political freedom: Cross-country influences on corruption. *Australian Economic Papers, 44*(2), 121–133. https://doi.org/10.1111/j.1467-8454.2005.00253.x.

Gong, T. (2002). Dangerous collusion: Corruption as a collective venture in contemporary China. *Communist and Post-communist Studies, 35*(1), 85–103. https://doi.org/10.1016/S0967-067X(01)00026-5.

Gong, T., & Zhou, N. (2015). Corruption and marketization: Formal and informal rules in Chinese public procurement. *Regulation & Governance, 9*(1), 63–76. https://doi.org/10.1111/rego.12054.

Grant, S., King, S., & Polak, B. (1996). Information externalities, share-price based incentives and managerial behaviour. *Journal of Economic Surveys, 10*(1), 1–21. https://doi.org/10.1111/j.1467-6419.1996.tb00001.x.

Graves, S. B., & Waddock, S. A. (1990). Institutional ownership and control: Implications for long-term corporate strategy. *The Executive*, *4*(1), 75–83. https://doi.org/10.5465/AME.1990.4274714.

Gunter, F. R. (2017). Corruption, costs, and family: Chinese capital flight, 1984–2014. *China Economic Review*, *43*, 105–117. https://doi.org/10.1016/j.chieco.2017.01.010.

Gupta, S., & Newberry, K. (1997). Determinants of the variability in corporate effective tax rates: Evidence from longitudinal data. *Journal of Accounting and Public Policy*, *16*(1), 1–34. https://doi.org/10.1016/S0278-4254(96)00055-5.

Hair, J. F., Jr., Black, W. C., Babin, B. J., & Anderson, R. E. (2009). *Multivariate data analysis* (7th ed.). London: Pearson.

Hanlon, M., & Heitzman, S. (2010). A review of tax research. *Journal of Accounting and Economics*, *50*(2), 127–178. https://doi.org/10.1016/j.jacceco.2010.09.002.

Hanlon, M., & Slemrod, J. (2009). What does tax aggressiveness signal? Evidence from stock price reactions to news about tax shelter involvement. *Journal of Public Economics*, *93*(1–2), 126–141. https://doi.org/10.1016/j.jpubeco.2008.09.004.

Harford, J., Mansi, S. A., & Maxwell, W. F. (2012). Corporate governance and firm cash holdings in the U.S. In S. Boubaker, B. D. Nguyen, & D. K. Nguyen (Eds.), *Corporate governance: Recent developments and new trends* (pp. 107–138). Berlin and Heidelberg: Springer. https://doi.org/10.1007/978-3-642-31579-4_5.

Hayes, A. F. (2009). Beyond Baron and Kenny: Statistical mediation analysis in the new millennium. *Communication Monographs*, *76*(4), 408–420. https://doi.org/10.1080/03637750903310360.

Healy, P. M., & Palepu, K. G. (2001). Information asymmetry, corporate disclosure, and the capital markets: A review of the empirical disclosure literature. *Journal of Accounting and Economics*, *31*(1–3), 405–440. https://doi.org/10.1016/S0165-4101(01)00018-0.

Heckelman, J. C., & Powell, B. (2010). Corruption and the institutional environment for growth. *Comparative Economic Studies*, *52*(3), 351–378. https://doi.org/10.1057/ces.2010.14.

Holden, C. W., & Lundstrum, L. L. (2009). Costly trade, managerial myopia, and long-term investment. *Journal of Empirical Finance*, *16*(1), 126–135. https://doi.org/10.1016/j.jempfin.2008.05.001.

Hong, J., Wang, C., & Kafouros, M. (2015). The role of the state in explaining the internationalization of emerging market enterprises. *British Journal of Management*, *26*(1), 45–62. https://doi.org/10.1111/1467-8551.12059.

Hu, L.-T., & Bentler, P. M. (1998). Fit indices in covariance structure modeling: Sensitivity to underparameterized model misspecification. *Psychological Methods, 3*(4), 424–453. https://doi.org/10.1037/1082-989X.3.4.424.

Hua, J., Miesing, P., & Li, M. (2006). An empirical taxonomy of SOE governance in transitional China. *Journal of Management & Governance, 10*(4), 401–433. https://doi.org/10.1007/s10997-006-9008-z.

Hussain, A., & Zhuang, J. (2013). Enterprise taxation and transition to a market economy. In D. J. S. Brean (Ed.), *Taxation in modern China* (pp. 43–68). New York, NY: Taylor & Francis.

Hutton, A. P., Marcus, A. J., & Tehranian, H. (2009). Opaque financial reports, R^2, and crash risk. *Journal of Financial Economics, 94*(1), 67–86. https://doi.org/10.1016/j.jfineco.2008.10.003.

Jain, A. K. (2001). Corruption: A review. *Journal of Economic Surveys, 15*(1), 71–121. https://doi.org/10.1111/1467-6419.00133.

Jang, S., & Park, K. (2011). Inter-relationship between firm growth and profitability. *International Journal of Hospitality Management, 30*(4), 1027–1035. https://doi.org/10.1016/j.ijhm.2011.03.009.

Jensen, M. C., & Meckling, W. H. (1976). Theory of the firm: Managerial behavior, agency costs and ownership structure. *Journal of Financial Economics, 3*(4), 305–360. https://doi.org/10.1016/0304-405X(76)90026-X.

Jian, M., Li, W., & Zhang, H. (2013). *How does state ownership affect tax avoidance? Evidence from China* (Working Paper). Nanyang Technological University and Fuzhou University.

Jiang, H., & Habib, A. (2012). Split-share reform and earnings management: Evidence from China. *Advances in Accounting, 28*(1), 120–127. https://doi.org/10.1016/j.adiac.2012.04.001.

Jiang, T., & Nie, H. (2014). The stained China miracle: Corruption, regulation, and firm performance. *Economics Letters, 123*(3), 366–369. https://doi.org/10.1016/j.econlet.2014.03.026.

Jianming, R., & Zhizhou, D. (2008). Institutionalized corruption: Power overconcentration of the first-in-command in China. *Crime, Law and Social Change, 49*(1), 45–59. https://doi.org/10.1007/s10611-007-9090-4.

Jiao, H., Dong, Y., Hou, W., & Lee, E. (2013). Independent directors and corporate performance in China. In *Developing China's capital market: Experiences and challenges* (pp. 176–189). London, UK: Palgrave Macmillan. https://doi.org/10.1057/9781137341570_8.

Jin, L., & Myers, S. C. (2006). R^2 around the world: New theory and new tests. *Journal of Financial Economics, 79*(2), 257–292. https://doi.org/10.1016/j.jfineco.2004.11.003.

Kang, Y.-S., & Kim, B.-Y. (2012). Ownership structure and firm performance: Evidence from the Chinese corporate reform. *China Economic Review, 23*(2), 471–481. https://doi.org/10.1016/j.chieco.2012.03.006.

Karklins, R. (2005). *The system made me do it: Corruption in post-communist societies*. Armonk: M.E. Sharpe.

Khan, M. H. (1989). *Clientelism, corruption and capitalist development: An analysis of state intervention with special reference to Bangladesh* (PhD thesis). Cambridge University, Cambridge.

Kim, H.-D., Kim, Y., Mantecon, T., & Song, K. R. (2019). Short-term institutional investors and agency costs of debt. *Journal of Business Research, 95*, 195–210. https://doi.org/10.1016/j.jbusres.2018.10.019.

Kim, J.-B., Li, Y., & Zhang, L. (2011). Corporate tax avoidance and stock price crash risk: Firm-level analysis. *Journal of Financial Economics, 100*(3), 639–662. https://doi.org/10.1016/j.jfineco.2010.07.007.

Kim, Y., Li, H., & Li, S. (2014). Corporate social responsibility and stock price crash risk. *Journal of Banking & Finance, 43*, 1–13. https://doi.org/10.1016/j.jbankfin.2014.02.013.

Ko, K., & Weng, C. (2012). Structural changes in Chinese corruption. *The China Quarterly, 211*, 718–740. https://doi.org/10.1017/S0305741012000793.

Koester, A., Shevlin, T., & Wangerin, D. (2016). The role of managerial ability in corporate tax avoidance. *Management Science*. https://doi.org/10.1287/mnsc.2016.2510.

Kothari, S. P., Shu, S., & Wysocki, P. D. (2009). Do managers withhold bad news? *Journal of Accounting Research, 47*(1), 241–276. https://doi.org/10.1111/j.1475-679X.2008.00318.x.

Krueger, A. O. (1974). The political economy of the rent-seeking society. *American Economic Review, 64*(3), 291.

Krugman, P. (2009). *The return of depression economics and the crisis of 2008*. New York and London: W. W. Norton.

Kubick, T. R., & Masli, A. N. S. (2016). Firm-level tournament incentives and corporate tax aggressiveness. *Journal of Accounting and Public Policy, 35*(1), 66–83. https://doi.org/10.1016/j.jaccpubpol.2015.08.002.

Lee, B. B., Dobiyanski, A., & Minton, S. (2015). Theories and empirical proxies for corporate tax avoidance. *The Journal of Applied Business and Economics, 17*(3), 21–34.

Leung, N. W., & Cheng, M.-A. (2013). Corporate governance and firm value: Evidence from Chinese state-controlled listed firms. *China Journal of Accounting Research, 6*(2), 89–112. https://doi.org/10.1016/j.cjar.2013.03.002.

Leutert, W. (2016). Challenges ahead in China's reform of state-owned enterprises. *Asia Policy, 21*(1), 83–99. https://doi.org/10.1353/asp.2016.0013.

Li, C., Wang, Y., Wu, L., & Xiao, J. Z. (2016). Political connections and tax-induced earnings management: Evidence from China. *The European Journal of Finance, 22*(4–6), 413–431. https://doi.org/10.1080/1351847X.2012.753465.

Li, R., & Cheong, K. C. (2019). State enterprises, economic growth, and distribution (Chapter 3). In *China's state enterprises: Changing role in a rapidly transforming economy*. Singapore: Palgrave Macmillan.

Li, S., & Xia, J. (2008). The roles and performance of state firms and non-state firms in China's economic transition. *World Development, 36*(1), 39–54. https://doi.org/10.1016/j.worlddev.2007.01.008.

Li, Y., Luo, Y., Wang, J., & Foo, C.-T. (2016). A theory of managerial tax aggression: Evidence from China, 2008–2013 (9702 observations). *Chinese Management Studies, 10*(1), 12–40. https://doi.org/10.1108/CMS-01-2016-0001.

Lin, B., Lu, R., & Zhang, T. (2012). Tax-induced earnings management in emerging markets: Evidence from China. *The Journal of the American Taxation Association, 34*(2), 19–44. https://doi.org/10.2308/atax-10236.

Liu, G. S., Sun, P., & Woo, W. T. (2006). The political economy of Chinese-style privatization: Motives and constraints. *World Development, 34*(12), 2016–2033. https://doi.org/10.1016/j.worlddev.2006.06.001.

Liu, X. (2016). Corruption culture and corporate misconduct. *Journal of Financial Economics, 122*(2), 307–327. https://doi.org/10.1016/j.jfineco.2016.06.005.

Liu, Z. (2014). *Tax system of the People's Republic of China* (In Chinese and English Version) (L. Du, Trans., 8th ed.). Beijing, China: China Taxation Publishing House.

Lundstrum, L. L. (2002). Corporate investment myopia: A horserace of the theories. *Journal of Corporate Finance, 8*(4), 353–371. https://doi.org/10.1016/S0929-1199(01)00050-5.

Ma, X., Tong, T. W., & Fitza, M. (2013). How much does subnational region matter to foreign subsidiary performance? Evidence from Fortune Global 500 corporations' investment in China. *Journal of International Business Studies, 44*(1), 66–87. https://doi.org/10.1057/jibs.2012.32.

MacCallum, R. C., & Austin, J. T. (2000). Applications of structural equation modeling in psychological research. *Annual Review of Psychology, 51*(1), 201–226.

MacKinnon, D. P., Fritz, M. S., Williams, J., & Lockwood, C. M. (2007). Distribution of the product confidence limits for the indirect effect: Program PRODCLIN. *Behavior Research Methods, 39*(3), 384–389. https://doi.org/10.3758/bf03193007.

Manion, M. (1996). Corruption by design: Bribery in Chinese enterprise licensing. *The Journal of Law, Economics, and Organization, 12*(1), 167–195. https://doi.org/10.1093/oxfordjournals.jleo.a023356.

Marsh, H. W., & Grayson, D. (1995). Latent variable models of multitrait-multimethod data. In R. H. Hoyle (Ed.), *Structural equation modeling: Concepts, issues, and applications* (pp. 177–198). Thousand Oaks, CA: Sage.

Martinsons, M. G. (2005). Online success in a relationship-based economy—Profiles of e-commerce in China. In R. M. Davison, R. W. Harris, S. Qureshi, D. R. Vogel, & G.-J. de Vreede (Eds.), *Information systems in developing countries: Theory and practice* (pp. 173–191). Hong Kong: City University of Hong Kong Press.

Mauro, P. (1995). Corruption and growth. *The Quarterly Journal of Economics, 110*(3), 681–712. https://doi.org/10.2307/2946696.

Mi, Z., & Wang, X. (2000). Agency cost and the crisis of China's SOE. *China Economic Review, 11*(3), 297–317. https://doi.org/10.1016/S1043-951X(00)00023-7.

Miller, C. C., Washburn, N. T., & Glick, W. H. (2013). Perspective—The myth of firm performance. *Organization Science, 24*(3), 948–964. https://doi.org/10.1287/orsc.1120.0762.

Minnick, K., & Noga, T. (2010). Do corporate governance characteristics influence tax management? *Journal of Corporate Finance, 16*(5), 703–718. https://doi.org/10.1016/j.jcorpfin.2010.08.005.

Mironov, M. (2013). Taxes, theft, and firm performance. *The Journal of Finance, 68*(4), 1441–1472. https://doi.org/10.1111/jofi.12026.

Montgomery, C. A., Thomas, A. R., & Kamath, R. (1984). Divestiture, market valuation, and strategy. *Academy of Management Journal, 27*(4), 830–840. https://doi.org/10.2307/255881.

Naceur, S. B., & Goaied, M. (2002). The relationship between dividend policy, financial structure, profitability and firm value. *Applied Financial Economics, 12*(12), 843–849. https://doi.org/10.1080/09603100110049457.

Ngo, T.-W. (2008). Rent-seeking and economic governance in the structural nexus of corruption in China. *Crime, Law and Social Change, 49*(1), 27–44. https://doi.org/10.1007/s10611-007-9089-x.

North, D. C. (2005). *Understanding the process of economic change*. Princeton: Princeton University Press.

Nusair, K., & Hua, N. (2010). Comparative assessment of structural equation modeling and multiple regression research methodologies: E-commerce context. *Tourism Management, 31*(3), 314–324. https://doi.org/10.1016/j.tourman.2009.03.010.

Nyman, I. (2005). Stock market speculation and managerial myopia. *Review of Financial Economics, 14*(1), 61–79. https://doi.org/10.1016/j.rfe.2004.06.002.

Oi, J. C. (1989). *State and peasant in contemporary China: The political economy of village government*. Berkeley: University of California Press.

O'Rourke, N., & Hatcher, L. (2013). *A step-by-step approach to using SAS for factor analysis and structural equation modeling* (2nd ed.). Cary, NC: SAS Institute.

Peng, M. W., & Luo, Y. (2000). Managerial ties and firm performance in a transition economy: The nature of a micro-macro link. *Academy of Management Journal, 43*(3), 486–501. https://doi.org/10.2307/1556406.

Peni, E., & Vähämaa, S. (2012). Did good corporate governance improve bank performance during the financial crisis? *Journal of Financial Services Research, 41*(1), 19–35. https://doi.org/10.1007/s10693-011-0108-9.

Penrose, E. (1959). *The theory of the growth of the firm.* Oxford: Oxford University Press.

Petrou, A. P., & Thanos, I. C. (2014). The "grabbing hand" or the "helping hand" view of corruption: Evidence from bank foreign market entries. *Journal of World Business, 49*(3), 444–454. https://doi.org/10.1016/j.jwb.2013.10.004.

Phillips, J. D. (2003). Corporate tax-planning effectiveness: The role of compensation-based incentives. *The Accounting Review, 78*(3), 847–874. https://doi.org/10.2308/accr.2003.78.3.847.

Piotroski, J. D., & Wong, T. J. (2012). Institutions and information environment of Chinese listed firms. In J. P. H. Fan & R. Morck (Eds.), *Capitalizing China* (pp. 201–242). Chicago and London: University of Chicago Press.

Piotroski, J. D., Wong, T. J., & Zhang, T. (2011). *Political incentives to suppress negative information: Evidence from Chinese listed firms* (Working Paper). Stanford University.

Piotroski, J. D., Wong, T. J., & Zhang, T. (2015). Political incentives to suppress negative information: Evidence from Chinese listed firms. *Journal of Accounting Research, 53*(2), 405–459. https://doi.org/10.1111/1475-679X.12071.

Pogach, J. (2018). Short-termism of executive compensation. *Journal of Economic Behavior & Organization, 148,* 150–170. https://doi.org/10.1016/j.jebo.2018.02.014.

Preacher, K. J., & Hayes, A. F. (2008). Asymptotic and resampling strategies for assessing and comparing indirect effects in multiple mediator models. *Behavior Research Methods, 40*(3), 879–891. https://doi.org/10.3758/brm.40.3.879.

Qian, Y., & Wu, J. (2003). China's transition to a market economy: How far across the river? In N. C. Hope, D. T. Yang, & M. Y. Li (Eds.), *How far across the river? Chinese policy reform at the millennium* (p. 31). Stanford, CA: Stanford University Press.

Rasiah, R. (2011). The role of institutions and linkages in learning and innovation. *Institutions and Economies, 3*(2), 165–172.

Rasiah, R. (2018). *Developmental states: Land schemes, parastatals and poverty alleviation in Malaysia.* Bangi: Universiti Kebangsaan Malaysia Press.

Rasiah, R., & Thangiah, G. (2017). Government policies, regional trading agreements and the economic performance of local electronics component

producing SMEs in Malaysia. *Journal of Southeast Asian Economies, 34*(2), 302–321.
Rego, S. O., & Wilson, R. (2012). Equity risk incentives and corporate tax aggressiveness. *Journal of Accounting Research, 50*(3), 775–810. https://doi.org/10.1111/j.1475-679X.2012.00438.x.
Richardson, G., Taylor, G., & Lanis, R. (2013). The impact of board of director oversight characteristics on corporate tax aggressiveness: An empirical analysis. *Journal of Accounting and Public Policy, 32*(3), 68–88. https://doi.org/10.1016/j.jaccpubpol.2013.02.004.
Richardson, G., Wang, B., & Zhang, X. (2016). Ownership structure and corporate tax avoidance: Evidence from publicly listed private firms in China. *Journal of Contemporary Accounting & Economics, 12*(2), 141–158. https://doi.org/10.1016/j.jcae.2016.06.003.
Robinson, J. R., Sikes, S. A., & Weaver, C. D. (2010). Performance measurement of corporate tax departments. *The Accounting Review, 85*(3), 1035–1064. https://doi.org/10.2308/accr.2010.85.3.1035.
Ross, S. A. (1973). The economic theory of agency: The principal's problem. *The American Economic Review, 63*(2), 134–139.
Rowe, W. G., & Morrow, J. L. (1999). A note on the dimensionality of the firm financial performance construct using accounting, market, and subjective measures. *Canadian Journal of Administrative Sciences, 16*(1), 58–71. https://doi.org/10.1111/j.1936-4490.1999.tb00188.x.
Saha, S., & Ben Ali, M. S. (2017). Corruption and economic development: New evidence from the Middle Eastern and North African countries. *Economic Analysis and Policy, 54*, 83–95. https://doi.org/10.1016/j.eap.2017.02.001.
Sahakyan, N., & Stiegert, K. W. (2012). Corruption and firm performance. *Eastern European Economics, 50*(6), 5–27. https://doi.org/10.2753/EEE0012-8775500601.
Santos, J. B., & Brito, L. A. L. (2012). Toward a subjective measurement model for firm performance. *BAR-Brazilian Administration Review, 9*(SPE), 95–117. http://dx.doi.org/10.1590/S1807-76922012000500007.
Scherer, F. M. (1988). Corporate takeovers: The efficiency arguments. *The Journal of Economic Perspectives, 2*(1), 69–82.
Scholes, M. S., Wolfson, M. A., Erickson, M., Hanlon, M., Maydew, E. L., & Shevlin, T. (2015). *Taxes and business strategy: A planning approach* (5th ed.). London, UK: Pearson Education.
Scott, J. (2000). Rational choice theory. In G. Browning, A. Halcli, & F. Webster (Eds.), *Understanding contemporary society: Theories of the present*. Thousand Oaks, CA: Sage.
Sen, A. (1983). Carrots, sticks and economics: Perception problems in incentives. *Indian Economic Review, 18*(1), 1–16.

Serrasqueiro, Z. (2009). Growth and profitability in Portuguese companies: A dynamic panel data approach. *Amfiteatru Economic, 11*(26), 565–573.

Sharma, C., & Mitra, A. (2015). Corruption, governance and firm performance: Evidence from Indian enterprises. *Journal of Policy Modeling, 37*(5), 835–851. https://doi.org/10.1016/j.jpolmod.2015.05.001.

Shleifer, A. (1998). State versus private ownership. *Journal of Economic Perspectives, 12*(4), 133–150. https://doi.org/10.1257/jep.12.4.133.

Shleifer, A., & Vishny, R. W. (1993). Corruption. *The Quarterly Journal of Economics, 108*(3), 599–617. https://doi.org/10.2307/2118402.

Siegfried, J. J. (1973). *The relationship between economic structure and the effect of political influence: Empirical evidence from the Federal Corporation Income Tax program*. Madison: University of Wisconsin.

Sikka, P. (2010). Smoke and mirrors: Corporate social responsibility and tax avoidance. *Accounting Forum, 34*(3–4), 153–168. https://doi.org/10.1016/j.accfor.2010.05.002.

Slemrod, J. (2004). The economics of corporate tax selfishness. *National Tax Journal, 57*(4), 877–899. https://doi.org/10.17310/ntj.2004.4.06.

Stiglitz, J. E. (2010). *Freefall: America, free markets, and the sinking of the world economy*. New York·and London: W. W. Norton.

Stone, C. A., & Sobel, M. E. (1990). The robustness of estimates of total indirect effects in covariance structure models estimated by maximum. *Psychometrika, 55*(2), 337–352. https://doi.org/10.1007/BF02295291.

Su, K., & Wan, R. (2014). State control, marketization, and firm value: Evidence from China. *Journal of Applied Business Research, 30*(6), 1577–1586. https://doi.org/10.19030/jabr.v30i6.8875.

Svensson, J. (2005). Eight questions about corruption. *The Journal of Economic Perspectives, 19*(3), 19–42. https://doi.org/10.1257/089533005774357860.

Swenson, C. (1999). Increasing stock market value by reducing effective tax rates. *Tax Notes, 83*, 1503–1505.

Tang, T., & Firth, M. (2011). Can book–tax differences capture earnings management and tax management? Empirical evidence from China. *The International Journal of Accounting, 46*(2), 175–204. https://doi.org/10.1016/j.intacc.2011.04.005.

Tenev, S., Zhang, C., & Brefort, L. (2002). *Corporate governance and enterprise reform in China: Building the institutions of modern markets*. Washington, DC: World Bank and International Finance Corporation.

Tu, G., Lin, B., & Liu, F. (2013). Political connections and privatization: Evidence from China. *Journal of Accounting and Public Policy, 32*(2), 114–135. https://doi.org/10.1016/j.jaccpubpol.2012.10.002.

Varaiya, N., Kerin, R. A., & Weeks, D. (1987). The relationship between growth, profitability, and firm value. *Strategic Management Journal, 8*(5), 487–497. https://doi.org/10.1002/smj.4250080507.

von Thadden, E.-L. (1995). Long-term contracts, short-term investment and monitoring. *The Review of Economic Studies, 62*(4), 557–575. https://doi.org/10.2307/2298077.

Wade, R. (1990). *Governing the market: Economic theory and the role of government in East Asian industrialization*. Princeton, NJ: Princeton University Press.

Wang, Q., Wong, T. J., & Xia, L. (2008). State ownership, the institutional environment, and auditor choice: Evidence from China. *Journal of Accounting and Economics, 46*(1), 112–134. https://doi.org/10.1016/j.jacceco.2008.04.001.

Wang, X., Fan, G., & Yu, J. (2017). *Marketization index of China's provinces* (NERI Report 2016). Beijing, China: Social Science Academic Press

Wang, Y., Wang, L., & Gong, C. (2009). Reform of enterprise income tax, earnings management and its economic consequences. *Journal of Economic Research Journal, 3*, 10.

Wang, Y., & You, J. (2012). Corruption and firm growth: Evidence from China. *China Economic Review, 23*(2), 415–433. https://doi.org/10.1016/j.chieco.2012.03.003.

Wedeman, A. (2012). *Double paradox: Rapid growth and rising corruption in China*. New York, NY: Cornell University Press.

Wederman, A. (2004). The intensification of corruption in China. *The China Quarterly, 180*, 895–921. https://doi.org/10.1017/S0305741004000670.

Wei, Z., Wu, S., Li, C., & Chen, W. (2011). Family control, institutional environment and cash dividend policy: Evidence from China. *China Journal of Accounting Research, 4*(1-2), 29–46. https://doi.org/10.1016/j.cjar.2011.04.001.

Whetten, D. A. (1987). Organizational growth and decline processes. *Annual Review of Sociology, 13*, 335–358. https://doi.org/10.1146/annurev.so.13.080187.002003.

Williamson, O. E. (1985). *The economic institutions of capitalism: Firms markets, relational contracting*. New York: The Free Press.

Wilson, R. J. (2009). An examination of corporate tax shelter participants. *The Accounting Review, 84*(3), 969–999. https://doi.org/10.2308/accr.2009.84.3.969.

Windmeijer, F. (2005). A finite sample correction for the variance of linear efficient two-step GMM estimators. *Journal of Econometrics, 126*(1), 25–51. https://doi.org/10.1016/j.jeconom.2004.02.005.

Wintoki, M. B., Linck, J. S., & Netter, J. M. (2012). Endogeneity and the dynamics of internal corporate governance. *Journal of Financial Economics,* *105*(3), 581–606. https://doi.org/10.1016/j.jfineco.2012.03.005.

Wu, L., Wang, Y., Luo, W., & Gillis, P. (2012). State ownership, tax status and size effect of effective tax rate in China. *Accounting and Business Research,* *42*(2), 97–114. https://doi.org/10.1080/00014788.2012.628208.

Wu, W., Wu, C., Zhou, C., & Wu, J. (2012). Political connections, tax benefits and firm performance: Evidence from China. *Journal of Accounting and Public Policy,* *31*(3), 277–300. https://doi.org/10.1016/j.jaccpubpol.2011.10.005.

Xu, G., & Yano, G. (2016). How does anti-corruption affect corporate innovation? Evidence from recent anti-corruption efforts in China. *Journal of Comparative Economics.* http://dx.doi.org/10.1016/j.jce.2016.10.001.

Xu, L. C., Zhu, T., & Lin, Y.-M. (2005). Politician control, agency problems and ownership reform. *Economics of Transition, 13*(1), 1–24. https://doi.org/10.1111/j.1468-0351.2005.00205.x.

Xu, N., Jiang, X., Chan, K. C., & Yi, Z. (2013). Analyst coverage, optimism, and stock price crash risk: Evidence from China. *Pacific-Basin Finance Journal, 25,* 217–239. https://doi.org/10.1016/j.pacfin.2013.09.001.

Xu, N., Li, X., Yuan, Q., & Chan, K. C. (2014). Excess perks and stock price crash risk: Evidence from China. *Journal of Corporate Finance, 25,* 419–434. https://doi.org/10.1016/j.jcorpfin.2014.01.006.

Xu, X., Li, Y., Liu, X., & Gan, W. (2017). Does religion matter to corruption? Evidence from China. *China Economic Review, 42,* 34–49. https://doi.org/10.1016/j.chieco.2016.11.005.

Yang, Z. (2016). Tax reform, fiscal decentralization, and regional economic growth: New evidence from China. *Economic Modelling, 59,* 520–528. https://doi.org/10.1016/j.econmod.2016.07.020.

Yen, S.-W. (2005). *Growth opportunities and governance structure choices.* Available at SSRN. http://dx.doi.org/10.2139/ssrn.687003.

You, J., & Nie, H. (2017). Who determines Chinese firms' engagement in corruption: Themselves or neighbors? *China Economic Review, 43,* 29–46. https://doi.org/10.1016/j.chieco.2017.01.002.

Yu, M. (2013). State ownership and firm performance: Empirical evidence from Chinese listed companies. *China Journal of Accounting Research, 6*(2), 75–87. https://doi.org/10.1016/j.cjar.2013.03.003.

Zhang, C., Cheong, K., & Rasiah, R. (2016). Corporate tax avoidance and performance: Evidence from China's listed companies. *Institutions and Economies, 8*(3), 61–63.

Zhang, M., M, L., Zhang, B., & Yi, Z. (2016). Pyramidal structure, political intervention and firms' tax burden: Evidence from China's local SOEs. *Journal of Corporate Finance, 36,* 15–25. https://doi.org/10.1016/j.jcorpfin.2015.10.004.

Zhang, M., & Rasiah, R. (2015). *Institutionalization of state policy: Evolving urban housing reforms in China.* Singapore: Springer. https://doi.org/10.1007/978-981-287-570-9.

Zhang, Y., Farrell, K. A., & Brown, T. A. (2008). Ex-dividend day price and volume: The case of 2003 dividend tax cut. *National Tax Journal, 61*(1), 105–127.

Index

A
absolute value of discretionary accruals, 119
Accounting Information Quality Inspection Announcement (No.21) of China's Ministry of Finance (2009), 74
agency theory, vi, 19, 20, 26, 27, 35, 46, 142, 145, 146
 agency conflict, 74
 agency costs, 11, 20, 21, 26, 35, 46, 61, 77
 agency problems, vi, 4, 76
 agent, 9, 19, 20, 35
 conflict of interest, 19, 20
 opportunistic managers, 27
 principal, 9, 19, 20, 35
 principal–agent relationships, 146
aggressiveness, 12
agricultural, 2
Amazon, 69
AMOS Version 21, 53
Analytic Framework, 46
annual report, 80
Apple, 26, 69

Armenian, 114
A-share, 142
Asian, 47, 76
asymmetric information, 24
autonomy, 2, 13, 30, 33, 73, 74, 112, 143, 147
 management autonomy, 3

B
bad news hoarding theory, vi, 19, 21, 35, 75, 143, 145
 career promotion, 22
 empire building, 22
 managerial compensation, 22
 self-benefits, 22
Beijing, 79
beneficial effect, 146
"big bang approach", 1
board structure, 48
 management-friendly, 48
book-tax difference (BTD), 81
bootstrap method, 53
bottom-line performance, 25
bribing mechanism, 110

bureaucratic discretion, 31
bureaucratic incentive effect, 29
bureaucrats, 23, 36, 73, 76, 111
　government property, 111
　government regulation, 111
　public power, 111
businessmen, 111

C
career concern, 13
cash compensation, 71
cash flow, 9, 10, 22, 24, 26
　after-tax, 26
　after-tax cash flows, 46
centrally planned economy, 9, 11
central objective, v
central-planned system, 32
Changling branch of Sinopec's, 74
China, vi, xi, 1, 2, 5, 6, 8–11, 11, 14, 15, 24, 27–35, 45–47, 53, 60, 61, 70–73, 76–79, 84, 103, 109–113, 115, 116, 118, 124, 136, 141, 142, 144–146, 148, 149
　economic growth, 32
China Securities Regulatory Commission (CSRC), 4, 122
China Securities Regulatory Commission Industry Classifications (CSRCIC), 53
China's State Council, 5
　Regulation on the Implementation of Enterprise Income Tax Law of China, 5
China Stock Market and Accounting Research (CSMAR) database, 53, 78, 115
Chinese economic system, 5
Chinese listed companies, v
Chinese-style privatization, 11
chi-square (x^2), 54

Chongqing, 79
Code of Corporate Governance for Listed Companies, 4
　in 2002, 4
coefficient, 97
co-evolve, 149
collinearity, 87
command economy, 9
Company Law
　in December 1993, 73
contract responsibility system, 3
contract termination, 70
control rights, 3, 8
control variables, 84, 93, 94
conventional view, 110
conventional wisdom, 136, 146
corporate accounting scandal, 69
corporate conduct, 69
corporate environment, 141
corporate governance, vi, 2, 3, 8, 10, 13, 21, 26, 46, 48, 52, 69, 76, 147
corporate governance mechanism, vi
corporate income tax, 5, 6, 27
Corporate Income Tax Law, 6
corporate myopia, 24, 25
corporate over-investment, 70
corporate performance, 12
corporate statutory tax rate, 5
corporate tax, v
corporate taxation, 8
corporate tax management, iv–vi, 1, 9–12, 14, 15, 19, 21, 22, 24–28, 31, 33–35, 45–50, 52, 54, 60–62, 69, 72, 74, 76, 78, 80, 81, 84, 87, 92–94, 97, 100, 102, 103, 111, 113–116, 119–121, 123, 127, 133, 136, 141–145, 149
corporate tax system, 62
corporate transparency, 47, 76
corporatization, 3, 8, 11, 73
correlation coefficients, 53, 84, 127

corruption, v, vi, 14, 15, 19, 23, 28, 30, 31, 34, 35, 76, 109–116, 119–121, 125, 127–129, 133, 135, 136, 143, 144, 147–149
  bribe premium, 112
  bribe-related payments, 112
  bribery, 30, 36, 114, 144
  bribe-taking, 30
  complexity, 30, 111
  costs of bribes, 112
  detection and punishment, 112
  economic growth, 30
  institutionalized, 30
  intensified, 30
  sophistication, 30
Corruption Perceptions Index (CPI), 109
  Transparency International, 109
crash risk, vi
  contemporaneous crash risk, 94
  future crash risk, vi, 94
critical point, 143
cross-country survey, 110

D
data, 22, 27, 49, 53, 54, 58, 61, 75, 76, 78, 80, 113, 115, 131
  firm-level, 115
  panel data, 80
  province-level, 115
decentralization, 143
decision-making, 20, 25, 28, 69, 103, 146
Deng Xiaoping, 1, 2
  "feeling the stones to cross the river", 1
  gradualist approach, 1
dependent variable, 84, 87, 92–94, 97, 100, 120, 121, 127, 133
descriptive statistics, 84, 122, 125
discretionary power, 30, 112

dominance, 3
down-to-up volatility (DUVOL), 81
dummy variable, 93
dynamic system Generalized Method of Moments, 14, 100
  first-differenced residuals, 100
  Sargan and Hansen J test, 102
  system GMM, 100

E
earnings management, 50, 119
earnings manipulation, 24, 46, 70, 71
economic consequences, v, 11, 14, 33, 102
economic liberalization, 146
economic reforms, 1, 2, 4–6, 30, 32, 35, 61, 73
economic transaction, 110
economic transition, 142
economy, v, 2, 30, 77
  centrally planned economy, 27
  emerging economies, 148
  market economics, 142
  market economy, 1, 146
  market-oriented economy, 1, 11, 27, 32, 111, 114
  strong institutions, 1
  transition economy, 11
effective or necessary corruption, 114
effective tax rate (ETR), xi, 21, 49, 81, 84, 115, 116
  Cash ETR, 50
  GAAP ETR, 50
embryonic stage, 145
emerging market, 145
employment contract, 70
Enron, 26, 46, 69
enterprise management, vi
enterprises, v, xi, xii, 2, 19, 29, 70, 73, 111
evasion, 12

explanatory variable, 84, 100
external markets, vi
external supervision, 104
extrinsic, 20
  risk aversion, 21

F
fangquan rangli, 9
  "decentralization of power and transfer of profits", 9
FDI, 34
fierce competition, 70
fifth Session of the tenth National People's Congress (NPC), 6
financial decision-making, v
financial market, 47
financial statement, 50
financial strategy, vi, 69
financial system, 28
Firm age, 119
firm performance, v, 14, 15, 26, 31, 33, 45, 46, 50, 54, 61, 62, 73, 76, 110, 111, 114, 121, 133, 136, 144, 145
firm size, 11, 117
firms' market value, vi
firms' profitability and growth, vi
firm value, v, 9, 12, 13, 26, 33, 46–48, 50, 58, 61, 62, 69, 74, 145
fiscal decentralization, 30, 35, 112, 147
fiscal decentralization reforms, 30
fiscal reform, 4, 8
fiscal revenue, 9, 28
fixed-effect (FE) model, 127, 131, 133
  fixed-effect, 14
fixed effects, 119
FLTRT, 5
  the policy of first levying and then rebating taxes, 5

foreign companies, 3
fubuji, 77
  vice-ministerial level, 77

G
GDP growth, 34
General Office of the Communist Party of China Central Committee, 6
General Office of the State Council, 6
German-Japanese model, 3
gongzuo danwei
  work units, 72
governance, 141
Governance Reform, 8
government, 2
  intrusive role, 113
government-based, 117
government intervention, 14, 23, 30, 32, 112, 147
government ownership, v, 13, 15, 19, 28, 33, 72, 77, 82, 93, 94, 142
  central, 93
  provincial, 94
government tax revenue, 6
government tiers, 71
  central, 71
  municipal, 71
  provincial, 71
"grabbing hand", vi, 20, 23, 31, 36, 110, 112, 131
grant, 112
grasping the large, letting go the small, 2, 8
"greasing the wheels", 31
growth, 15, 48, 52, 58, 60, 117, 142
  growth rate of net income (NIG), 52
  growth rate of sales income (SIG), 52

growth rates of sales revenue
(SALG), 52
guanxi, 28, 30, 112
  relationship-based, 27, 34, 111, 112, 147
  relationship-oriented, 30
gujing gongjiu, 71
  Gujing Distillery Company, 71

H
Hausman test, 127, 133
"helping hand", vi, 13, 20, 23, 29, 31, 36, 110, 112, 129
heterogeneity, 84, 146
heterogenous, 32
heterogenous economy, 146
heteroskedasticity-robust, 87, 93, 94, 127, 131, 133
homo economicus, 34

I
"ideal types", 23
Implications for Firms, 149
Implications for Policy, 146
Implications for Theory, 145
incentive, 2
income tax rate, 12, 80, 116
  of 25%, 116
incomplete market, 31
independent directors, 4
independent variable, 84, 87, 94, 120, 133
Indian, 114
inefficient and unpredictable, v
information asymmetry, 12, 21, 22, 25, 26, 32, 35, 70, 75, 77
information opaqueness, 22, 35
information transparency, 26, 47, 75, 76
insider transaction, 24, 46, 47

institution, 3, 136, 144, 147, 148
  'rules of the game', 3
  superior institution, 3
institutional development, vi
institutional environment, 110, 111, 113, 131, 148, 149
institutional homogeneity, 32
institutional ownership, 26, 47
institutional reform, 3
institutional strengthening, vi
institutional support, 131
institutional support for marketization, 131, 133, 136
interaction term, 93
internal corporate governance, vi
internal supervision, 103
intrinsic, 21
  civic virtue, 21
  duty, 21
inverted U-shaped, 113
  inverted U-shaped curve, vi
  inverted U-shaped relationship, 136, 143
investor protection, 11

J
juxtaposition, 1

K
Kingdom of Cambodia, 10
kurtosis, 58

L
labor contract system, 73
Lao People's Democratic Republic, 10
latent variables, 54
Latin American, 114
legal framework, 110
legal person, 2

legal protection, 28, 76, 148
legal regulation, 142
legal restriction, 111
legal system, 28
legislative protection, 10
leverage, 11, 80, 117, 120
liberalization, 2, 136
ligaishui, 5, 9
  "replacement of profit with tax", 9
  "substitution of tax payment for profit delivery", 5
literature, 19
local government collectives, 3
Local Taxation Bureau, 5
  dishuiju, 5
long-term, 70, 75

M

Mackinnon PRODCLIN2, 54
macroeconomic regulation, 146
macro-level characteristics, 37
managerial autonomy, 8
managerial diversion, 21, 26, 46
managerial myopia, 70
managerial opportunism, 9, 21, 24, 28, 35, 47, 75, 145, 148, 149
managerial rent, 142
managerial rent diversion, 26
managerial rent extraction, 12
manipulative tax management, 104
market, v, 81, 84, 117
  China's capital market, 4
  emerging markets, 45
market-based, 117
market capitalization, 52
market discipline, 147
marketization, v, vi, 1, 13–15, 19, 23, 31, 32, 34, 74, 111, 113, 115, 117, 125, 143, 145, 148
  mechanisms of governmental deregulation, 113

neoclassical arguments, 111
  reduction of bureaucratic discretionary power, 113
  simplification of regulations, 113
Marketization Index of China's Provinces, 115
NERI Report 2016, 115
market liberalization, 146
market outcomes, v, vi, 72, 142
market performance, 52
Market capitalization improvement (MCI), 52
  Price-to-book (PB) ratio, 52
  Tobin's Q (TobinQ), 52
market pricing, 2
market reforms, 145, 149
market-to-book (MB) ratio, 120
market transparency, 147
market value, vi, 14, 15, 48, 61
measurement model
  is shown to be valid and acceptable, 58
mediation, 60
mediation effects, 54
methodology, 14, 49, 78, 115, 145
mispricing, 70
model fit index, 54
  adjusted goodness of fit index (AGFI), 56
  comparative fit index (CFI), 56
  goodness of fit index (GFI), 56
  normed fit index (NFI), 56
  root mean square error of approximation (RMSEA), 56
  root mean square residual (RMR), 56
Model specification, 52, 82
moderating effect, 82, 94, 102, 131, 133
moderator, 93, 94, 115, 120, 121
modern enterprise system, 3
modified Jones model, 84

monotonic detrimental, 146
moral hazard, 9, 13, 77
motivation, 75
  career promotion, 75
  salary increment, 75
multicollinearity, 87, 127
municipal bond, 12
municipal listed state-controlled enterprises, vi
Myanmar, 142

N
National Audit Office, 74
National Taxation Bureau, 5
  guoshuiju, 5
negative conditional return skewness (NCSKEW), 81
negative direct impact, vi
noncompliance, 12
Nonlinear, 14
nonlinear relationship, 120
nonlinear way, vi
non-normal distribution, 54
non-state sector, 6

O
open-door policy, 32
opening-up, 4
  in 1978, 4
opportunist behavior, 10, 145
opportunistic, 143
Ordinary Least Square (OLS), 14, 87, 127
outliers, 53
oversimplification, 136
ownership reform, 2, 8
ownership structure, 11, 76
  concentrated, 76

P
paramount role, v
partially marketized economies, 141
People's Republic of China, 4
Peoples Republic of Lao, 142
The Performance Evaluation Guideline for State-Owned Enterprises in 2002 and 2006, 29
point estimate, 60
policymaker, 104
political advancement, 76
political career, 33
political career advancement, 71
political connection, 33, 72
political hierarchy, 28, 76
political rank, 72
preferential tax rates, 6
preferential tax treatment, 6
preferential treatment, 23, 29, 33, 71
privatization, 8, 11, 73, 77, 147
  partial privatization, 147
privatization-friendly, 147
Procuratorial Yearbooks of China, 115
  by the Supreme People's Procuratorate of China, 115
profitability, 15, 48, 50, 58, 60, 142
  return on assets (ROA), 50, 117
  return on invested capital (ROIC), 50
  return on sales (ROS), 50
profit maximization, 20
profit-oriented, 147
profit-seeking, 147
property rights, 21
provincial-level marketization index
  by Wang, Fan, and Yu (2017), 116
public goods, 22
public utilities, 22
purpose, 1
p-value, 100

Q

qianguize, 30
"hidden rules of the game", 30
quadratic U-shape curve, 128
quantitative, 14

R

rational choice theory, 112
rational and self-interested individuals, 112
reforms, v
regional economic development, 35
regulation, 136
relation-based, 76
remuneration, 13, 70
rent extraction, 10, 13, 24, 46, 61, 75, 110
rentier, 69
rent-seeking, 9, 36, 47, 61, 76, 103, 109, 111, 113, 142, 143, 147, 148
Republic of Kazakhstan, 10
research questions, v, 14
residual book-tax difference (DTAX), 81
resource allocation, 110
resource diversion, 21, 24, 71, 75, 110
Robustness Check for Endogeneity, 100
rule, 136
rule-based, 112
Russia, 1
  Russia's economic collapse, 1
  "you cannot cross a chasm in more than one leap", 1

S

salary increment, 75
sample, 14, 26, 53, 54, 59, 78, 84, 115
secondary data, 14
self-interests, 11, 22–24, 29, 33, 35, 71, 72, 75, 77, 148
self-serving, 29, 30, 35, 78
  political career advancement, 29
Shanghai, 79
Shanghai and Shenzhen Stock Exchanges, 78, 115
shareholders, 2
  individual, 2
  institutional, 2
  private shareholders, 4
  tradable, 2
shareholders' wealth effects, 25
shareholder value, 47
sheltering, 12
short-term, 13, 25, 51, 70, 75, 103, 136, 143, 145
short-termism, 25, 75
skewness, xi, 58, 76
social irresponsibility, 46
socialism, 142
Socialist Republic of Vietnam, 10
socialist structure, v, 11, 141, 149
social responsibilities, 147
social security, 28
South Korea, 71
Soviet Union, 5
  closed economic model, 5
Special Treatment (ST) shares, 115
Special Treatment (ST) stocks, 53
split-share reform, 2, 4, 8
standard error, 87, 133
State Administration of Taxation Department, 104
state assets, 11
state enterprises, 2, 4
state governance, 6
state-led growth, 71
State-owned Assets Supervision and Administration Commission of the State Council (SASAC) in June 2003, 73

state-owned/controlled shareholding, 103
state-owned enterprises (SOEs), 5, 9, 11, 13, 28, 29, 33, 71, 72, 74, 76, 77, 103, 147
  central SOEs *(yangqi)*, 71
  municipal SOEs, 72
  provincial SOEs, 71
state ownership, vi, 2, 8, 28, 62, 72, 80, 82, 92, 93
statutory corporate income tax rate, 84
statutory income, 6
statutory tax rate, 6
Stock exchanges, 2
  Shanghai, 2
  Shenzhen, 2
stock market, 2, 35, 71
stock price crash, vi, 13–15, 22, 27, 35, 72, 75, 76, 81, 82, 92–94, 97, 102, 103, 142–146, 148
Structural Equation Model (SEM), 14, 48, 54
  Confirmatory factor analysis (CFA), 54
  measurement model, 54, 56; average variance extracted (AVE), 56; composite reliability (CR), 56
  multiple-step multiple mediator model, 58
  structural model, 52, 54, 58
supervisory board, 3
systematic analysis, 145

T
Taiwan, 71
tax aggressiveness, 12
taxation, 5, 25, 69, 146
  national revenue national revenue, 146
taxation system, v, 5, 47, 112
tax audits, 29
tax avoidance, 4, 12, 15, 27, 46, 58, 60–62, 75, 81, 111, 116, 142
tax benefits, 30, 112
tax breaks, 30, 112
tax burden, 11, 21, 24, 49, 69, 74, 110, 116, 127, 129, 133, 149
tax collection, 8, 112, 148
tax distribution system, 148
tax evasion, 4, 29
tax holiday, 6
tax incentives, 5, 53
tax management, v, vi, 8–15, 19, 20, 26, 29, 60, 61, 69, 72, 82, 94, 97, 102, 103, 110, 119, 121, 133, 135
tax payment, 50, 74
tax planning, 12, 46, 103
tax preference, 111
tax rebate, 5
tax-reducing, 46
tax reduction, 30, 112
tax reform, 4–6, 8, 14, 61
  in 1994, 2008, and 2018, 5
tax revenue, 69
tax saving, 27, 70
tax shared system
  in 1994, 111
tax-sharing policy, 29
tax-sharing reform, 112
tax-sharing system, 8, 147
tax shelter, 26
tax sheltering, 12, 21, 26, 27
tax system, 4–6, 70, 110
Third Plenary Session of the Eleventh National Congress, 3
  in December 1978, 3
Third Plenum Session of the Fourteenth National Congress of the Communist Party of China (CPC), 3
  in November 1993, 3

threshold point, 143
Tianjin, 79
tiefanwan
 "iron rice bowl", 72
time horizon, 12
"tone at the top", 25, 70
tradable shares, 2, 3
transaction cost, 31, 113
transition, 141, 142
transitional provision, 6
transition economy, 20, 23, 31, 32, 35, 146

U
under-explored area, 110
unique transition, v
unproductive opportunism, 146
US, 45
U-shaped relationship, 128, 131

V
Vaclav Havel's caption, 1
value-oriented, 20

variance inflation factor (VIF), 87
 statistics, 127
Vietnam, 1, 142

W
wealth maximization, 26
wealth of shareholders, vi
winsorize, 53, 80
workers retrenched, 2

X
Xi Jinping, 109
 the chairmanship of the Communist Party, 109

Z
zhengtingji, 77
 departmental-level, 77
zhuadafangxiao
 "keeping the large and letting go the small approach", 73

CPSIA information can be obtained
at www.ICGtesting.com
Printed in the USA
LVHW081118011219
639058LV00009B/554/P